RELIGION AROUND MARY SHELLEY

RELIGION AROUND VOL. 5

PETER IVER KAUFMAN, *Founding Editor*

Books in the Religion Around series examine the religious forces surrounding cultural icons. By bringing religious background into the foreground, these studies give readers a greater understanding of and appreciation for individual figures, their work, and their lasting influence.

# RELIGION AROUND
# MARY SHELLEY

JENNIFER L. AIREY

THE PENNSYLVANIA STATE UNIVERSITY PRESS
UNIVERSITY PARK, PENNSYLVANIA

Frontispiece: Richard Rothwell, *Mary Shelley*, exhibited 1840, detail. National Portrait Gallery, London. NPG 1235. Image © National Portrait Gallery, London.

Library of Congress Cataloging-in-Publication Data

Names: Airey, Jennifer L., 1980– author.
Title: Religion around Mary Shelley / Jennifer L. Airey.
Other titles: Religion around.
Description: University Park, Pennsylvania : The Pennsylvania State University Press, [2019] | Series: Religion around | Includes bibliographical references and index.
Summary: "Explores Mary Shelley as an important religious thinker of the Romantic period. Analyzes her creative engagement with contemporary religious controversies and uncovers a belief system that was both influenced by and profoundly different from those of her male Romantic counterparts"— Provided by publisher.
Identifiers: LCCN 2019015079| ISBN 9780271083827 (pbk. : alk. paper) | ISBN 9780271082073 (cloth : alk. paper)
Subjects: LCSH: Shelley, Mary Wollstonecraft, 1797–1851—Religion. | Shelley, Mary Wollstonecraft, 1797–1851—Criticism and interpretation. | Romanticism—England—History—19th century.
Classification: LCC PR5398.A526 2019 | DDC 823/.7—dc23
LC record available at https://lccn.loc.gov/2019015079

The Pennsylvania State University Press is a member of the Association of University Presses.

It is the policy of The Pennsylvania State University Press to use acid-free paper. Publications on uncoated stock satisfy the minimum requirements of American National Standard for Information Sciences—Permanence of Paper for Printed Library Material, ANSI Z39.48–1992.

# CONTENTS

## ACKNOWLEDGMENTS

I want to begin by expressing my thanks to Kristin M. S. Bezio, who in 2014 invited me to speak about Mary Shelley at the Jepson School of Leadership Studies' "Leading Culture Forward" conference. At that conference, Kristin introduced me to Peter Iver Kaufman, the founding editor of the Religion Around series, and thus without her invitation, this monograph would never have come to be. I am grateful to Peter for immediately championing the project, and for seeing it through the initial stages of the publication process. I am also deeply grateful to Penn State University Press's Kathryn Yahner, who has been a tireless cheerleader of the book, offering encouragement and insightful feedback as she shepherded it through peer review. And I am grateful to James Winn, formerly my dissertation advisor at Boston University, who encouraged me to go for it when I was uncertain whether to make the leap from studying the late seventeenth century to studying the early nineteenth.

I was supported in my research for *Religion Around Mary Shelley* by a Chawton House Library Visiting Fellowship, which enabled me to spend focused time in the archives and where I first learned of the trial of Mary-Catherine Cadière. I want to express my deep thanks to Gillian Dow, Darren Bevin, and the rest of the staff at Chawton House Library and the University of Southampton for making my research possible; my month at Chawton was one of the best of my life. Thanks also to the staff at Harvard University's Widener and Houghton Libraries and the University of Tulsa's McFarlin Library, who were so helpful to me throughout the research process.

Writing a book is a solitary experience, and thus I am very lucky to be surrounded by supportive and generous friends and colleagues at the University of Tulsa, especially Dennis Denisoff, Lars Engle, Bob Jackson, and Laura Stevens, all of whom offered support throughout the project. I am especially grateful to Joli Jensen, Hazel Rogers Professor of Communication and director of TU's Heneke Faculty Writing Program, who held my hand through the entire composition process, and to Jennie Ikuta and Ben Peters, the members of my faculty writing group, for their assistance and advice. I wish every faculty member could experience such a supportive writing environment.

I am grateful to my current graduate students at the University of Tulsa, especially Lily Coleman, Blake Connelly, Megan Gibson, Linda Hudson, Dayne Riley, and Onyx Zhang, for allowing me to bounce around ideas about Shelley, and for inspiring me to think deeply about Romantic literature. I want to thank my friends near and far for listening to me when I needed to complain and cheering me when I wanted to celebrate, including Ashley Schoppe, Anu Narayan, Maureen Lubitz, Lisa Cromer, Karen Dutoi, Susan Green, Clara Hill, Chris Jacobs, Danielle Macdonald, Maria Mauer, Kirsten Olds, Liz Polcha, Mark Rideout, Lindi Smith, and Veronika Vaclavek. And as always, I am grateful to my parents, Barbara and Ron Airey, for their encouragement, and to my uncle, Stuart Millner, for his incisive critical feedback and keen understanding of the rules of punctuation. This book would not exist without them.

# INTRODUCTION

Mary Shelley (1797–1851) grew up surrounded by atheists and agnostics. Her father, William Godwin, trained as a Calvinist minister, only to abandon his faith in favor of his own brand of revolutionary optimism. Her husband, Percy, was expelled from Oxford and lost custody of his children for proclaiming atheist beliefs, and he wrote several passages of doubt into the original text of *Frankenstein*. Their social circle included Thomas Jefferson Hogg, who openly rejected religion, and William Lawrence, the materialist scientist who gained notoriety for questioning the idea of an immortal soul. Despite the formative influences of the men in her life, however, Mary Shelley never abandoned her own faith in a higher power. Her journals are filled with references to God. In 1827, for instance, she wrote, "Oh You supreme Power . . . to whom I bow—if it is your will that I may die during this year—behold me ready to obey your commands that will call me from this prison to the shining atmosphere that you inhabit."[1] Later, in the aftermath of her father's death in 1836, she asked God to protect "my adored child," to "rain evil & pain upon me but spare him!"[2] Her personal letters, too, reflect her faith. In an April 1823 letter to Jane Williams, she describes pushing back against Lord Byron's irreligious mockery: "I am growing terribly religious—LB. says—what are you a Christian? no I were not religious—if I were—but I have a firm faith—& I place my hope in those aspirations that lead me to my lost one."[3]

This volume seeks to foreground Mary Shelley as an important religious thinker of the Romantic period, one who developed a belief system that was both influenced by and profoundly different from those of her more often analyzed male counterparts. Over the past two decades, several studies have been published on religion and religious controversy in the Romantic era, notably Morton D. Paley's *Apocalypse and Millennium in English Romantic Poetry* (1999), Martin Priestman's *Romantic Atheism: Poetry and Freethought, 1780–1830* (1999), Robert M. Ryan's *The Romantic Reformation: Religious Politics in English Literature, 1789–1824* (1997), and Daniel E. White's *Early Romanticism and Religious Dissent* (2006). These books discuss Mary Shelley's work only in passing, if they mention her at all. Other authors have devoted more sustained attention to Shelley's religion. Orianne Smith's *Romantic Women Writers, Revolution, and Prophecy: Rebellious Daughters, 1786–1826* (2013) devotes a chapter to the topic, while Anne K. Mellor's *Mary Shelley: Her Life, Her Fiction, Her Monsters* (1988) examines the treatment of religion in *Frankenstein*. Surprisingly, however, no prior full-length study has been published on Shelley's religion, nor have critics treated her shifting depictions of religion across the length of her career. It is the aim of this volume to close that gap, treating her works as both a product of and an influence on her cultural moment.

Mary Shelley was born in the shadow of the French Revolution, came of age during the Napoleonic Wars, and lived to see the beginnings of the Victorian era. During her lifetime, the Industrial Revolution fundamentally changed the economic and cultural landscapes of England, and a conservative backlash destroyed her mother's legacy and hardened the doctrine of separate spheres. It was an age of religious instability, one that witnessed the spread of atheism, millenarianism, Methodism, Unitarianism, and Evangelicalism, among other belief systems, and which finally permitted full Catholic participation in Britain's political processes. Shelley's works therefore offer valuable insight into the complexity of religious views prominent in her cultural moment. It is the goal of this volume to examine both that moment and the ways in which her works reflect and engage with the religious controversies of her day.

The French Revolution precipitated in many ways a destabilization of religion in Europe. While some conservative writers reacted to the abolition of the Catholic Church in France with horror, others praised the destruction of religion as a necessary part of human progress toward liberty. William Blake's association of priests with kings as mutually evil tyrants reflects the extent to which many radical English thinkers prophesied the overthrow of organized religion as a vital human necessity. By the late eighteenth century, atheist writings, while still disdained by the culture at large, had begun to circulate in ways previously unimaginable. Philosophers such as the Baron d'Holbach openly denied the existence of God, while others, including William Godwin, criticized the repressive and regressive forces of institutional religion; according to Godwin, religion is "a tyrant perpetually controlling us with his lash."[4]

Developments in scientific knowledge also influenced early nineteenth-century views of religion. In his 1794 treatise *Zoonomia*, Erasmus Darwin proposed an early theory of evolution, challenging the biblical creation story and undermining traditional religious views. Meanwhile, the study of galvanism, the use of electrical currents to reanimate the dead, began to alter the ways that people conceptualized the relationship between body and soul. Percy Shelley was particularly interested in such experimental science; he kept an electrical machine in his quarters at Oxford, attended public presentations of galvanic experiments, and later discussed his findings with his wife. The influence of such work on Shelley's worldview can be found in *Frankenstein*, a novel in which a human uses science to usurp both the divine and the maternal functions.

Atheism was not, of course, the only religious perspective to flourish in the early nineteenth century. The period also witnessed an explosion of different forms of religious belief. From deists and Rational Dissenters to Methodists, Baptists, and free thinkers, non-Anglican religious denominations grew and thrived. Religious enthusiasm, frequently criticized in the eighteenth century for its association with political and religious radicalism, was increasingly embraced by Romantic philosophers as a form of transcendent experience of the divine. At the same time, the period witnessed the gradual weakening of restrictions placed on Roman Catholics. Long considered England's most fearsome enemy, Catholics won greater freedoms throughout the period, in part because the public sympathized with Catholic refugees displaced by the revolution in France. The move toward Catholic emancipation culminated in 1829 with the passage of the Roman Catholic Relief Act (also known as the Catholic Emancipation Act), which enabled Roman Catholics to serve as members of the British Parliament. Anti-Catholic sentiment did not, of course, disappear with emancipation; images of Catholic degeneracy, licentiousness, and violence were resurrected throughout the period. Such currents find their way into Mary Shelley's writings, as she engages with the tropes of anti-Catholic discourse and periodically undermines them.

It was not only men who debated the role and meaning of religion. Until 1803, when female preaching was forbidden, itinerant women regularly traveled the country spreading Methodist doctrine. Meanwhile, authors such as Germaine de Staël defended the power and importance of female religious enthusiasm, while others claimed the status of female prophets who spoke the word of God. Tapping into a tradition of female political and religious activism dating back to the English Civil Wars, women such as Joanna Southcott challenged the view of religion as a masculine preserve and, with their prophecies, encouraged female participation in the religious sphere. Southcott attracted thousands of followers; at the height of her popularity, upward of one hundred thousand copies of her books were in circulation. Such women sought to recover a tradition of female mysticism and enable full female religious participation. Their works also bespoke the ways in which the culture at large was attempting to mediate the relationship between organized religion and protofeminist beliefs. Such negotiations are similarly apparent in Shelley's writings, which alternate between championing feminine artistic expression and conforming to patriarchal norms. Shelley frequently invokes the memory of her mother's religious beliefs in her writings. Mary Wollstonecraft did not belong to any particular denomination, but she never abandoned her belief in God, and her faith was shaped both by her Anglican upbringing and her friendships with Rational Dissenters. Religious faith in Shelley is thus linked with maternal legacy, and a tradition of female prophecy. If organized religion is often repressive and patriarchal, faith itself may offer a refuge to women. It is this sort of contradiction—religion simultaneously as oppression and retreat—that *Religion Around Mary Shelley* seeks to trace over the length of her authorial career.

Mary Wollstonecraft Godwin Shelley was born on August 30, 1797, the only child of Mary Wollstonecraft and William Godwin. Eleven days after giving birth, Wollstonecraft died of puerperal fever contracted as a result of unhygienic medical intervention at the birth. Shelley grew up in the shadow of her deceased but infamous mother and her largely absent father, who passed care of his children on to schoolteachers and eventually to a new stepmother, Mary Jane Clairmont, with whom Shelley enjoyed a fractious relationship. Throughout her life, Shelley would mourn her absent mother and yearn for a closer relationship with her father; she famously wrote to Maria Reveley Gisborne of her "excessive & romantic attachment to my Father."[5]

In 1812, Godwin and his wife sent Shelley to Scotland for the sake of her health. Years later, in her introduction to *Frankenstein*, she would write of this time, "My habitual residence was on the blank and dreary northern shores of the Tay, near Dundee. Blank and dreary on retrospection I call them; they were not so to me then. They were the eyry of freedom, and the pleasant region where unheeded I could commune with the creatures of my fancy."[6] In November 1812, she returned to England, where she met Percy Shelley for the first time. By 1814, Percy, an admirer of William Godwin's political writings, had become a fixture in her household. Five years older than his future wife, he was already married to Harriet Westbrook and was the father of one child, with a second on the way. He was also a proponent of free love and an avowed atheist; several years earlier, his publication of a tract entitled *The Necessity of Atheism* precipitated his dismissal from Oxford. The pair became infatuated with one another, and on July 28, 1814, they ran away to the Continent accompanied by Shelley's stepsister, Clara Mary

Jane Clairmont (later called Claire). Despite his radical principles, Godwin did not approve of his daughter's love life, and he disowned the couple until the occasion of their marriage several years later.

Between July and September of 1814, Mary and Percy traveled extensively, their initial journey commemorated in the jointly authored *History of a Six Weeks' Tour* (1817). Having run out of funds, however, they returned to England, where they lived mostly apart, and Percy tried desperately to raise money and avoid arrest for debt. During this time, Percy encouraged Mary to engage in an affair with his friend Thomas Jefferson Hogg, and he may have conducted his own affair with her stepsister Claire.[7] On December 30, 1816, despite continuing friction in their household, Mary and Percy married following the suicide of his wife. The marriage earned them Godwin's forgiveness, but Shelley sank repeatedly into bouts of depression precipitated by a series of tragic losses: her half sister Fanny Imlay, who committed suicide in October 1816; her first child, a baby girl born prematurely in February 1815; her daughter, Clara, in September 1818; and her son, William, in June 1819. "I never know one moment's ease from the wretchedness & despair that possesses me," she wrote to Marianne Hunt in June 1819.[8] She also suffered a near-fatal miscarriage in 1822, saved from death only by Percy's split-second decision to immerse her lower body in ice. Her grief at these events was exacerbated by her anger at Percy for his perceived indifference to his children's deaths and her resentment at Godwin, who neither understood nor respected the depth of her grief. "You have lost a child: and all the rest of the world, all that is beautiful, and all that has a claim upon your kindness, is nothing, because a child of two years old is dead," he wrote dismissively following William's death.[9] This period resulted in the composition of her novel *Mathilda*, a work of incest and despair that so horrified Godwin that he confiscated the manuscript; the work was recovered and published only in 1959.

Shelley's life changed fundamentally on July 8, 1822, with the drowning death of her husband. Although Shelley loved Italy and did not wish to leave the places she had lived with her husband, she could not afford to support herself, and she reluctantly returned to England. At home in London once more, she could not expect financial support from Godwin, who was frequently in financial difficulty himself, nor from Percy's father, Sir Timothy Shelley, who remained implacable in his hatred of his daughter-in-law. He offered to support her child if she would give up custody, and when she would not do so, he begrudgingly offered her a small stipend, which relieved some of her immediate financial distress, but gave Sir Timothy a measure of control over her literary productions. Shelley could not produce a full biography of Percy in her father-in-law's lifetime, and she had to be careful that her works did not cause him too much offense.

Thus Mary Shelley wrote continuously, in part to express herself artistically, but in large part to support herself financially. Her novels *Valperga* (1823) and *The Fortunes of Perkin Warbeck* (1830) were designed at least in part to capitalize on the vogue for historical fiction made popular by Sir Walter Scott, and after the critical and financial failure of *The Last Man* (1826)—a postapocalyptic work of early science fiction—she turned to writing domestic novels closer in tone to the popular Silver Fork novels of the period. She also contributed short stories to *The Keepsake*, a yearly collection of stories aimed predominantly at middle-class women, and her collection of biographical essays for Dionysius Lardner were mostly written with money in mind. In 1831, she also brought out a revised edition of *Frankenstein*, now a cultural touchstone, complete with the famous preface detailing the story of its conception.

To read Mary Shelley's journals in the time following her husband's death is to experience her loneliness and bouts of depression. "I pray God I may not live to endure the vicissitudes of these years—I know that no good can come to me," she wrote in 1824.[10] Shelley frequently felt betrayed—by her best friend Jane Williams, who spread pernicious rumors about Shelley's life with her husband; by friends such as Edward Trelawney, who turned on her when she would not accept his marriage proposal or participate in his attempts to capitalize on Percy's fame; and by servants who made her the victim of several blackmail attempts. She wrestled with her parents' radical legacy, defending her own perceived failure to be an activist in their mold. "Some have a passion for reforming the world: others do not cling to particular opinions," she wrote in her journal in 1838. "That my parents & Shelley were of the former class, makes me respect it. . . . For myself, I earnestly desire the good & enlightenment of my fellow creatures . . . but I am not for violent extremes which only bring on an injurious reaction. . . . Besides I feel the counter arguments too strongly."[11] She also slowly accepted the fact that her son did not possess his father's intellect, creativity, or political drive. According to Muriel Spark, he was "a good, dull son whom she dragged all over Europe in an effort to launch him in society," but he would never live up to his father's legacy.[12]

Shelley never remarried, although she appears to have enjoyed an intense flirtation with politician Aubrey Beauclerk. In the early 1840s, she spent several years traveling with her son, seeking treatment for her health problems at various continental spas in a series of trips commemorated in *Rambles in Germany and Italy* (1844), her final published work. Throughout the 1840s, she was the target of repeated blackmail attempts, and she grew increasingly infirm, suffering from severe headaches and occasional bouts of paralysis. After her son's 1848 marriage to Jane Gibson, she settled with the couple in Sussex, where she died on February 1, 1851, at the age of fifty-three, likely from a brain tumor. Her literary legacy included one of the most famous and popular novels of all time.

*Religion Around Mary Shelley* is not a biography. Scholars have already produced several excellent biographies of Shelley, and I do not wish to recover such well-trod ground.[13] It is also my fervent wish to avoid falling into what Graham Allen calls "biographism," the tendency to read each of her works through the lens of her life experiences.[14] Scholars have often treated Shelley's work as a window into her psychological state, subsuming the political and philosophical messages of her novels beneath their emotional content. Although such readings can provide valuable insight, to reduce her work entirely to her biography is to risk creating a reductive view that I hope to avoid here. Such readings also tend to produce an unfortunately skewed view of her literary output, prioritizing her earlier works and overlooking the majority of her later corpus. In both the public imagination and much of literary criticism, Shelley has been frozen in time either as the young ingénue author of *Frankenstein* or as Percy Shelley's grieving widow. Biographies of Shelley, even recent biographies, tend to privilege her younger years and her time with Percy, paying much less attention to her life as a widow. Charlotte Gordon, for example, devotes only three chapters of twenty-one to Shelley's life post-Percy in her masterful recent biography, and even Anne K. Mellor's formative feminist work, *Mary Shelley: Her Life, Her Fiction, Her Monsters*, allots six of eleven chapters to Shelley's early life and composition of *Frankenstein*. Without diminishing the excellent scholarly contributions of these authors, I want to note that such readings privilege Percy's place in Mary's life and suggest that she is most interesting in relationship to her husband, that her works are more important for what they can tell us about second generation (predominantly male) Romanticism. In truth, Shelley was most productive as an author after Percy's death. Between Percy's death in 1822 and her own in 1851, she composed four novels, numerous short stories, a two-volume travel narrative, an edited collection of her husband's poetry, and numerous entries for Dionysius Lardner's *Cabinet Cyclopaedia*. To fixate on early Shelley, then, is fundamentally to distort her literary career.[15] In giving equal weight to her writings at all stages of her life, this volume in part seeks to correct that imbalance.

I begin in chapter 1, "Religion Around Romanticism," by outlining the political and religious culture in which Shelley wrote, a period marked by wars, controversies, and a gradual movement away from the radical principles of the French Revolutionary years. Chapter 2, "Religion Around Mary Shelley," examines the religious culture of Shelley's inner circle, along with the formative readings that influenced her intellectual development. The second half of the volume turns to Shelley's writings themselves, examining their treatment of religion and their place in the shifting culture of the early nineteenth century. Chapter 3, "Doubt," analyzes Shelley's *Frankenstein* and *Mathilda*, her first two novels, along with her short story, "Valerius: The Reanimated Roman," setting up the themes that preoccupied Shelley throughout her career. Drawing on the many different religious currents that surrounded her—from Calvinist theology to Manichaeism to atheist doubt—Shelley posits in her early works a world in which Christianity is a mutable fad, not an eternal truth, and God may be absent or even hostile to his creations. These themes grow stronger in the works Shelley wrote immediately around Percy's death. In chapter 4, "Despair,"

I turn to *Valperga*, *The Last Man*, and several of Shelley's short stories, in which anxiety over God's absence or hatred is ever present. Here, Shelley draws on images of female prophecy and, conversely, on scientific discourses that undermined the sanctity of biblical timelines. I conclude in chapter 5, "Domesticity," with Shelley's 1831 revisions to *Frankenstein*, along with her later novels, *The Fortunes of Perkin Warbeck*, *Lodore*, and *Falkner*. These novels, as multiple critics have pointed out, offer a new turn to the domestic. In their propensity to find religious truth in the home and family, however, they do not reflect such a radical break with her older works as prior critics have claimed. Even as Shelley draws on Evangelical discourses that elevated woman's role as theological and moral center of the household, she returns to the themes of her earlier novels, showing the gradual transformation of religious anxiety into love of humanity. Consolation for religious doubt may be found in family and interpersonal love.

A word on names: Mary Shelley was born Mary Wollstonecraft Godwin, and after her marriage, she referred to herself in print as Mary Wollstonecraft Shelley. It was common in early criticism for scholars to call Percy Shelley "Shelley" while referring to his wife with the more familiar "Mary," reflecting the period-typical sexism that unfortunately pervades much of the early critical work. It is my intent in this volume to continue the more recent critical trend of viewing Shelley's works apart from her husband's legacy, and of valuing her substantial literary legacy in its own right. Therefore, as Mary Shelley is the primary subject of this book, I will refer to her throughout this volume as "Mary Shelley" or "Shelley"; Percy Shelley, when referenced, will be differentiated as either "Percy Shelley" or "Percy."

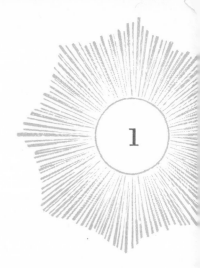

# RELIGION AROUND
# ROMANTICISM

In his 1794 poem, "The Book of Urizen," William Blake describes how Urizen, one of the Four Zoas, rises from the darkness, a "shadow of horror. . . . Self closd, all repelling."[1] Urizen separates himself from the primordial chaos that predates the human world, and immediately embarks on a process of creation: "Times on times he divided, & measur'd / Space by space in his ninefold darkness" (1:8–9). Trapped in an "intellectualistic insistence on certainty,"[2] Urizen works to divide and separate, removing the world from the oneness of eternity, imposing on it the rule of previously unnecessary law.

> Lo! I unfold my darkness: and on
> This rock, place with strong hand the Book
> Of eternal brass, written in my solitude.
> Laws of peace, of love, of unity:
> Of pity, compassion, forgiveness . . .
> One command, one joy, one desire,
> One curse, one weight, one measure
> One King, one God, one Law. (2:31–40)

Urizen subsequently separates himself from his newly created world, leaving Los, the prophet called into being by his initial act of separation, to create humanity:

> In ghastly torment sick;
> Within his ribs bloated round,
> A craving Hungry Cavern;
> Thence arose his channeld Throat,
> And like a red flame a Tongue
> Of thirst & of hunger appeard.
> And a sixth Age passed over:
> And a state of dismal woe. (4:4–11)

The creation of mankind is depicted as a terrible fall, and Los is horrified by his invention. Blake's "Book of Urizen" thus depicts the origin of mankind as an act of cruelty that brings into being both "the physical confinement of the human body and . . . the mental manacles of rational categories."[3] This is a world in which gods are repelled by their offspring and humanity would have been better off left undifferentiated from the darkness.

Urizen initially retreats from the world he has called into being, imprisoning himself for protection. When he later returns, awoken from his self-created prison by the voice of the infant Orc, he is horrified by the chaos he finds. He then "plays the role of the tyrannical ruler and bad father,"[4] trying to divide, separate, and control, and imposing on the world mathematical measurements, new forms of law, and finally, "the Net of Religion" (8:22):

> Where ever the footsteps of Urizen
> Walk'd over the cities in sorrow . . .
> a Web dark & cold, throughout all
> The tormented element stretch'd
> From the sorrows of Urizens soul
> And the Web is a Female in embrio
> None could break the Web, no wings of fire.
> So twisted the cords, & so knotted

The meshes: twisted like to the human brain
And all calld it, The Net of Religion. (8:13–22)

With the Net of Religion, Urizen creates all manner of suffering and hypocrisy, as prelapsarian oneness disintegrates into organized religion and church hierarchy.

Urizen appears throughout Blake's cosmology as the embodiment of Enlightenment reason—*your reason*—set apart from the voice of the divine.[5] The voice of restriction, of the church and the kings, of repressive institutional hierarchy, he stands apart from the power of poetic inspiration that seeks integration, intuitive passion, and universal oneness. Thus when Urizen meets John Milton in Blake's epic *Milton* (1804), the two strive to destroy one another:

> Silent they met, and silent strove among the streams of
>     Arnon
> Even to Mahanaim, when with cold hand Urizen stoop'd
>     down
> And took up water from the river Jordan: pouring on
> To Milton's brain the icy fluid from his broad cold palm.
> But Milton took of the red clay of Succoth, moulding it
>     with care
> Between his palms: and filling up the furrows of many
>     years.
> Beginning at the feet of Urizen, and on the bones
> Creating new flesh on the Demon cold.[6]

Urizen attempts to defeat Milton with a symbolic baptism that would imaginatively reintegrate him into the net of religion.[7] He is revealed to be Satan, not the evil force of biblical Christianity, but the embodiment of tyranny via religion and law that limits human imagination and unfairly demonizes bodily experience. The triumph of *Milton* occurs when Milton successfully combines with Blake, imaginatively destroying the physical barriers that separate the two poets from one another and symbolizing the moment in which Blake opens himself up to the greater consciousness that exists beyond individuality. Blake throws off the chains of Urizen and a Selfhood that "depends on reason to comprehend what it perceives"[8] and hooks into something much greater than himself. This moment, Blake suggests, will hopefully be just the beginning. He envisions a vast apocalypse that will consume the world, destroy Urizen's creation, and free humanity to be absorbed once more into a collective whole. According to Blake's *Europe: A Prophecy* (1794), God has become "a tyrant crown'd," and in the oncoming conflagration of the French Revolution, the world may finally find freedom.[9]

I begin this study of Mary Shelley's religion with William Blake because he is at once an outlier—a strange visionary printing poems and engravings that were at the time marginal to the Romantic movement—and representative of the period's complicated responses to religion. A Dissenter who rejected the mainstream Church of England, Blake celebrated what he perceived as the creative potential of the French Revolution's apocalyptic violence. In depicting a God who creates from fear and despises his creation, he also touches on themes that would preoccupy Mary Shelley throughout her own authorial career. These themes, as we shall see, reflect the complex and often contradictory attitudes toward religious faith that existed in the late eighteenth and early nineteenth centuries. Developing amid the French Revolution and Napoleonic Wars abroad and quickly shifting social and economic forces at home, views of religion were undergoing fundamental and sustained shifts throughout the period. From the proliferation of dissenting religious denominations to the explosion of millenarian prophecies and the development of atheism in its modern sense, the Romantic era offered many different ways to believe—or not to believe. This chapter will survey some of these political and social shifts, providing an overview of the major developments that influenced Mary Shelley's writings.

Throughout the seventeenth century, religious nonconformity—that is, refusal to worship in the Church of England—had both enabled and been accompanied by other forms of political and social dissent. From the Ranters and Diggers of the mid-seventeenth century to the female millenarian preachers who gained prominence during the English Civil Wars to the Puritans who briefly took control of England's government, Dissenters questioned social, political, and gender hierarchies that had previously seemed natural and immutable. As such, nonconformity was often viewed with deep suspicion, a potential revolutionary ideology in England's midst. By the 1730s, however, things had begun to change as the Evangelical and Methodist revivals began, first as movements to reform the Church of England, and later as popular movements in their own right, to the consternation of many mainstream Anglicans. Inspired by itinerant preachers such as George Whitefield, who after 1735 grew famous for his magnetic preaching style, large-scale open-air sermons, and devout following, Evangelicalism cut across denominations.[10] David Bebbington describes four central components of Evangelical belief: "conversionism, the belief that lives need to be changed; activism, the expression of the gospel in effort; biblicism, a particular regard for the Bible; and what may be called crucicentrism, a stress on the sacrifice of Christ on the cross."[11] Central to Evangelical belief was a focus on the centrality of (and later inerrancy of) the Bible, the belief that Christ had died for man's sins—what believers named "substitionary atonement"[12]—the insistence that people could achieve salvation only through faith, and an emphasis on proselytism. Henry Venn, Vicar of Huddersfield, for instance, emphasizes in his *The Complete Duty of Man* (1763), a foundational Evangelical text, "the necessity of dependence upon the righteousness and death of Christ . . . we must be declared free from that guilt and invested with a righteousness which will stand before the law of sinless perfection, and intitle [sic] us to the kingdom of heaven. And if we have it not in ourselves, where must we look for it, but as existing solely in the person of Jesus Christ?"[13]

Intimately connected with the Evangelical revival was the growth and spread of Methodism, founded by John Wesley with help from his brother Charles.[14] Wesley followed in Whitefield's footsteps, preaching the gospels and intending initially not to form his own denomination but to reform the Church of England from within. Where Whitefield adhered to the Calvinist belief in predestination, Wesley preached an Arminian view, which promoted salvation by faith alone. According to David Bebbington, "Evangelicals generally repudiated the traditional Calvinist doctrine of reprobation, that God had destined certain souls to hell.'"[15] Instead, "John Wesley was willing to describe two doctrines as fundamental: justification, the forgiving of our sins through the atoning death of Christ; and the new birth, the renewing of our fallen human nature at the time of conversion."[16] Whitefield and the Wesleys ultimately parted ways over this doctrinal difference, and the Wesleys proved intensely successful in proselytizing their beliefs. After John Wesley's death, the Methodists officially broke from the Church of England, forming their own denomination.

Central to Wesley's Methodism was the "felt experience of contact with God,"[17] the rejection of sacerdotalism (the belief that priestly intervention was necessary for forgiveness), and a privileging of the individual's relationship with God. According to Misty Anderson, "conversion was a moment of utter authenticity in which the self was, paradoxically, destroyed."[18] Sampson Staniforth (1720–1799), an early Methodist preacher, for instance, describes his conversion experience as follows: "I kneeled down, and determined not to rise, but to continue crying and wrestling with God, till He had mercy on me. How long I was in that agony I cannot tell; but as I looked up to heaven I saw the clouds open exceeding bright, and I saw Jesus hanging on the cross. At the same moment these words were applied to my heart. 'Thy sins are forgiven thee.' My chains fell off; my heart was free. All guilt was gone, and my soul was filled with unutterable peace."[19] Individuals who converted, who truly embraced their faith, found peace and assurance of their own salvation. According to John Wesley, "I never yet knew one soul thus saved, without what you call 'the faith of assurance': I mean a sure confidence that by the merits of Christ he was reconciled to the favour of God."[20] According to Bebbington, other denominations, including Roman Catholics, found "the expectation of assurance among Evangelicals eccentric, presumptuous or even pathological,"[21] but the idea that one could find true peace via conversion through the Holy Spirit was central to Methodist belief (and to Evangelical belief more broadly).

According to American Congregationalist preacher Jonathan Edwards, "Persons after their own conversion, have commonly expressed an exceeding great desire for the conversion of others," and the Methodists, too, made conversion central to their practice.[22] Wesley himself preached "more than 40,000 sermons and issu[ed] more than

400 publications" during his lifetime,[23] and he attracted huge crowds; in May 1740, ten thousand people gathered at Rose Green to hear him speak.[24] He also inspired an army of itinerant preachers—including laymen and (until 1803) women—who traveled the countryside spreading the gospel. Methodism attracted believers especially from the lower classes; its adherents' outreach in taverns and other nonnormative religious spaces, co-opting of secular ballads for religious purposes, and emphasis on theatricality and spectacle at services all appealed to people who might have felt alienated from traditional Anglican forms of worship. Methodists focused on creating "brilliant songs, cheap and diverse anthologies, emotional services rich with audience participation, and techniques for self-study and group socialization" to extend their reach.[25] As such, the religion "made its fastest gains in areas least amenable to paternalistic influence, including freehold parishes, industrial villages, mining communities, market towns, canal- and sea-ports and other centres of migratory populations."[26] The very characteristics that made it popular among the lower classes, however, alienated the middle and upper. Horace Walpole commented acerbically to his friend John Chute that he had "been at an opera, Mr. Wesley's. They have boys and girls with charming voices, that sing hymns, in parts, to Scotch ballad tunes."[27] Leigh Hunt complained that "the vulgar admire Methodism just as they do violent colours, violent noise, and violent swearing."[28] Many of Methodism's opponents mocked the religion by emphasizing its undesirable class and gender makeup. James Lackington, a Methodist who abandoned the faith, writes disparagingly in his *Memoirs* (1792), "you now see what sort of a society I was got into. In country places particularly, they consist of farmers, husbandmen, shoemakers, woolcombers, weavers, their wives, &c. I have heard Mr. Wesley remark that more women are converted than men; and I believe that by far the greatest part of his people are females; and not a few of them sour, disappointed old maids.'"[29] Methodists did not shy away from blending "biblical and theatrical language," combining in their hymns "religion and eroticism" in ways that scandalized outsiders.[30] That Methodism was also perceived, in David Hempton's words, as "predominantly a women's movement"[31] enabled its critics to levy attacks on female sexual desirousness to discredit the religion

more broadly. Despite such attacks, however, the religion flourished. By 1767, there were upward of twenty-six thousand professed Methodists in England, and by the end of the nineteenth century, that number had grown to over twenty-five million.[32]

The growth of Methodism in England was coupled with a backlash against the faith, and against Evangelicalism in general. Viewed as feminized, uneducated, and lower class, a "religion of feeling,"[33] Methodism was dismissed by many adherents of the Church of England who thought the religion was popular because of its theatricality and emphasis on irrational emotion. In 1760, Samuel Foote wrote bitterly, "religion turned into a farce is, by the constitution of this country, the only species of drama that may be exhibited for money without permission."[34] Frequently, anti-Methodist satire linked Methodist preachers with the *commedia dell'arte*'s Harlequin, signifying the theatricality and "protean mobility of character, which complements the geographic mobility of the Methodist preacher."[35] Methodist preachers, critics argued, attracted the uneducated and used the celebrity status of Whitefield and Wesley to create fans, not congregants. Methodists and Evangelicals were also frequently accused of enthusiasm, which Samuel Johnson defines as "1. A vain belief of private revelation . . . 2. Heat of imagination; violence of passion, confidence of opinion."[36] The term connoted irrationality and fanaticism, and in the eighteenth century it was frequently linked with the seventeenth-century prophets who supported parliament over king and enabled the regicide of Charles I. For many traditional Anglicans, "To hear faith lauded to the skies aroused suspicions of fanaticism, the 'enthusiasm' that the eighteenth century shunned because its seventeenth-century version had killed a king."[37] Edmund Gibson, for instance, argues that the "Madness and Enthusiasm" of the Puritans led to the "Times of Anarchy and Confusion" of the Civil Wars, a phenomenon he sees reoccurring with the Methodists.[38]

According to Jon Mee, "enthusiasm was the very anti-self of enlightenment notions of civility," and in some sources, it is likened to a form of disease.[39] According to a 1793 article in *The New London Magazine*, "enthusiasm is as catching as the plague"; it is an "epidemical distemper" that persists "against the light of true reason, or what is generally called common sense."[40] Methodists are, one poet wrote, "Mad with

Scripture, void of Sense."[41] They were also frequently associated with Roman Catholics, whose liturgy was regarded by Anglicans as similarly irrational and irreligious. Anderson explains, "This concentration of sacred or mystical experience in Methodist discourse was often read as a front for Roman Catholicism, which would drag the nation back into a 'superstitious' past and place it under papal control."[42] George Lavington, for example, draws "a Comparison between the wild and pernicious Enthusiasms of some of the most eminent Saints in the Popish Communion, and those of the Methodists in our own Country."[43] Lavington goes on to accuse both Methodists and Catholics of "the most wild Fanaticisms of the most abominable Communion, in its most corrupt Ages."[44] William Hazlitt likewise described the religion as "a bastard kind of Popery, stripped of its painted pomp and outward ornaments."[45] It is perhaps no surprise, then, that Methodists were occasionally subject to mob violence, as during the Pendle Forest riots of 1748, and the Cork City riots of 1749.[46]

If some Evangelicals and Methodists embraced the irrational aspects of religious faith, others sought to explain their beliefs through the lens of Enlightenment philosophy.[47] According to Phyllis Mack, Wesley's "insistence on the importance of reason and common sense, his acceptance of the limits of reason in understanding religious truths, and his conviction of the malleability of human nature were as much the product of Enlightenment values as they were of Pauline Christianity."[48] Wesley insisted that Methodism was inherently rational. "It is a fundamental principle with us that to renounce reason is to renounce religion, that religion and reason go hand in hand, and that all irrational religion is false religion," he wrote in a letter to Dr. Thomas Rutherford.[49]

Other dissenting sects, too, embraced rationality as an underpinning of their faith. For Rational Dissenters (now Unitarians), belief was the culmination of a process of logical argumentation. Led by Dr. Richard Price (1723–1791), a preacher, philosopher, and political pamphleteer, and Joseph Priestley (1733–1804), a preacher, philosopher, scientist, and one-time tutor at the Warrington Academy, Rational Dissenters stressed the centrality of reason to all religious belief. "The most cerebral of the Nonconformist sects," they rejected the idea of Christ's divinity, fostered a philosophy of human benevolence and individual conscience, and embraced "a vision of mankind as essentially good and inherently perfectible."[50] Emphasizing personal moral judgment and the importance of faith grounded in reason, Rational Dissenters also promoted education, for women as well as men, as a necessary prerequisite to full religious and civic engagement. Ruth Watts explains, "to be a good person and to be a Unitarian, people needed a good education . . . [T]he emphasis on knowledge and understanding led Unitarians to promote an education for females which was far wider and deeper than the contemporary norm."[51] Women, Priestley wrote, "are capable of the same improvement, and the same furniture, as those of men; and it is of importance that, when they have leisure, they should have the same resource in reading, and the same power of instructing the world by writing, that men have."[52] As Watts explains, "it was education not sex which made people what they were."[53]

Rational Dissenters believed, broadly speaking, in personal conscience, religious toleration, and the separation of church and state, up to and including "the disestablishment of the Church of England."[54] Yet Rational Dissent was not a monolith, and there were profound differences between the philosophies of Price and Priestley, the movement's two leading figures. David Nicholls explains, "Price was an Arian while Priestley was a Socinian; Price believed in free will and self-determination while Priestley was a materialist and a 'necessarian.'"[55] Price "retained a sense of Christ's divinity," while emphasizing "Christ's non-violence."[56] Priestley, in contrast, embraced Jesus's philosophy while emphasizing his essential humanity. In *A History of the Corruptions of Christianity* (1782), Priestley criticized early Christians who "were enabled to give to the soul of Christ what rank they pleased in the heavenly regions before his incarnation."[57] It was only through a lengthy process of syncretism and a corruption of the original religion that Christians "came, in the natural progress of things, to believe that Christ was, in power and glory, equal to God the Father himself."[58]

While Priestley rejected Christ's divinity, he did not reject belief in God. Still, for much of the contemporary public, Unitarians were little better than atheists. Although Priestley believed that man's "only prospect of immortality is from the Christian doctrine of resurrection," he did insist that "man is wholly material," a claim that attracted much censure.[59] To Priestley's critics, to deny the soul's innate immortality was to deny Christianity in its entirety. Thus the movement elicited from mainstream Anglicans at best distrust and at worst condemnation. The anonymous author of *An Essay on the Immateriality and Immortality of the Soul* (1778), for instance, complains, "If we are entirely material, the progress of the man who was a Christian (until convinced by Dr. Priestley that he has no spiritual principle of life) is much more rapid to Atheism, than even the progress of a Deist."[60] Likewise, according to the Methodist minister Joseph Benson, Priestley's belief that "we have no souls . . . is not far from teaching, *there is no God*."[61]

If Unitarians were controversial for their religious beliefs, by the 1790s, they had also become controversial for their political views. Because they believed that "man must not only work his personal salvation but must also take responsibility for the condition of the society in which he lives," Rational Dissenters supported the battle for abolition, promoted (to a degree) women's rights, and at least initially, celebrated the French Revolution.[62] An early supporter of both the French and American Revolutions, Price repeatedly preached the ideals of freedom and equality, and the rejection of hierarchies. In *Additional Observations on the Nature and Value of Civil Liberty, and the War with America* (1777), he argues that "free government . . . only, is just and legitimate government," that man is born with "natural equality and independence," and that "no people can lawfully surrender their liberty."[63] In his *Discourse on the Love of our Country* (1789), he writes, "The times are auspicious. Your labours have not been in vain. . . . Behold, the light you have struck out, after setting *America* free, reflected to *France*, and there kindled into a blaze that lays despotism in ashes, and warms and illuminates *Europe*!"[64] Such ideas were deeply disturbing to the conservative establishment. Edmund Burke famously responded in his *Reflections on the Revolution in France* (1790) that Price's "sermon is in a strain which I believe has not been heard in this kingdom, in any of the pulpits that are tolerated or encouraged in it, since the year 1648 when a predecessor of Dr Price, the Reverend Hugh Peters, made the vault of the king's own chapel at St. James's ring with the honor and privilege of the saints."[65] By referring to Hugh Peters, Puritan advisor to Oliver

Cromwell, Burke directly links Rational Dissent with the revolutionary chaos of the English Civil Wars. To undermine the sanctity of political hierarchies was to undermine the stability of society as a whole.

Hatred of Rational Dissent culminated in the Birmingham riots of 1791, which "began as an attack on a July 14 dinner commemorating the outbreak of the French Revolution, raged for three days and nights, destroyed three dissenting chapels and seven residences belonging to prominent religious Dissenters, cost several lives, including those of drunken rioters, and caused, in some contemporary estimates, hundreds of thousands of pounds worth of damage."[66] Priestley was an especial target of mob anger; rioters sought out and destroyed his home and laboratory. The government eventually quashed the violence, trying twelve and executing two participants, but the riots did not make Rational Dissenters more sympathetic to the public at large. George III wrote to Henry Dundas, Viscount Melville, that he felt "better pleased that Priestley is the sufferer for the doctrines that he and his party have instilled, and that the people see them in the true light."[67] The violence may have been quashed, but Unitarians remained marginalized until well into the nineteenth century.

Although he later eschewed organized religion, William Godwin was raised a Calvinist and trained as a dissenting minister. Mary Wollstonecraft, meanwhile, attended Anglican services for much of her life, but she lived among and was influenced by Rational Dissenters, including Richard Price, whose services she attended. As we shall see in greater detail in chapter 2, Mary Shelley's writings are thus marked by conflicting worldviews inherited from her parents. Her works depict faith alternately as deeply irrational and as intellectually grounded. Meanwhile, the distant, punitive deity of Calvinism that pervades her early works eventually cedes to John Wesley's loving father in her later novels.

In contrast to the Rational Dissenters, who emphasized the intellectual roots of faith, a wave of self-proclaimed prophets emerged during the years of the French Revolution, many of whom embraced irrationality and "expected the millennium to arrive in their own lifetime, preceded by apocalyptic destruction."[68] Both pro- and anti-Jacobins reacted to reports of the revolution in apocalyptic terminology, with varying degrees of excitement. Richard Brothers, a popular itinerant prophet who advertised his ability to cure the blind, for instance, celebrated the French Revolution as part of God's greater plan. In *A Revealed Knowledge of the Prophecies and Times* (1794), he insisted, "the time of the world was come to fulfil the seventh chapter of the Prophecy of Daniel, and some of the judgments of God in the Revelation; that the death of Louis the Sixteenth, and the Revolution in France for the perpetual destruction of its Monarchy, was decreed in the Scripture of Truth, and would against all human opposition, mostly surely take place."[69] Brothers was not alone in his view of the French Revolution as a biblically ordained event. The author of *The French Revolution Foreseen* (1796) cites seventeenth-century theologian Thomas Goodwin's description of Revelation's earthquake to argue that the revolution had already precipitated millennial peace: "It appears from prophecy, that while by these events"—the events of the French Revolution—"the state of man, as a member of society, will be greatly improved, religion shall appear in her native beauty and simplicity, and have a more powerful influence over the hearts of men than she has yet had."[70] Similar prophecies may be found in the work of Alexander Pirie, whose *French Revolution Exhibited* (1795) argues that "no important Revolution can happen in the European States . . . but it must have been made the subject of ancient Prophecy,"[71] and of James Snodgrass, who locates the French Revolution in the vial of the fifth angel of Revelation.[72] Even Joseph Priestley "stressed the apocalyptic, identifying the French Revolution with the earthquake of Revelation 11:33."[73] According to Priestley, "This great event of the late revolution in France appears to me, and many others, to be not improbably the accomplishment of the following part of the Revelation, chap xi. 3.'"[74]

As paranoia against Jacobins grew in England, the laws designed to repress prorevolutionary sentiment grew harsher, and prophecies of the sort that endorsed the revolution were harshly suppressed. Worried that the events in France would lead to another civil war in England, conservatives resurrected the image of Oliver Cromwell to remind the British populace what would happen if revolutionary sentiment and support for France went too far. Authorities also cracked down on the prophets themselves. According to Fulford, "Prophetic texts, as well as agitation on the streets, could put one's liberty in danger. . . . Government repression seemed to have stamped out religious radicalism."[75] Yet prophecy did not die out in the 1790s or with the collapse of the French Revolution. The early 1800s witnessed the growth of Joanna Southcott's cult, which will be discussed at length in chapter 4. At the height of her popularity, Southcott sold as many as one hundred thousand copies of her prophecies, making her one of the best-selling authors of her day. Meanwhile, the rise of Napoleon shifted the focus of prophecy away from the French Revolution. According to John Beer, "it was not the events of the Revolution that were now seen as apocalyptic so much as the declaration of war against France."[76] Early nineteenth-century prophets began to equate Bonaparte with the Antichrist or the Beast of Revelation. According to James Frere, for instance, Napoleon was "the Infidel Power" described by Daniel: "although he may not yet have so clearly manifested himself in his character as the personal enemy of the Church of Christ, as it is probable that he will do hereafter . . . he has been the bitter enemy of that nation which is peculiarly favoured by God," that is, England, itself.[77]

As late as the 1820s, self-proclaimed prophets and millenarianists continued to find audiences. In his 1828 publication, *A Discourse on the Prophecies of Daniel and the Apocalypse*, Church of Scotland minister Edward Irving continued to read the events of the early nineteenth century through the lens of biblical prophecy. He divides the period from September 1792 to September 1823 into six phases—including "the dissolution of religious and social principles by the spirit of infidelity" and Napoleon's "twelve years' reign of conquest, oppression, and change"—that correspond with the six vials of Revelation.[78] Irving was ultimately removed from his church when he refused to discourage parishioners from speaking in tongues at his services, and he died in 1834, one of the last high-profile millenarian figures of the period.[79] According to Fulford, "By 1832, with the French Revolution and the Napoleonic war long over, millenarianism was no longer a cultural force and religious mode through which young intellectuals defined themselves."[80] By the time Queen Victoria took the throne, millenarianism had waned as a cultural force. It is perhaps unsurprising, then, that Shelley's fascination with prophecy that appears so clearly in her works of the 1820s gives way in the 1830s to a more traditional under-standing of religion. Shelley grew up in the shadow of apocalypse and lived to witness the failure of biblical prophecy in the French Revo-lution and Napoleonic Wars. The depiction of religion in her works mirrors shifts in the culture more broadly.

Fervent, prophetic, or irrational expressions of faith in the eighteenth and nineteenth centuries also coexisted with a new validity afforded to unbelief. High profile atheists existed prior to the eighteenth cen-tury—Christopher Marlowe, perhaps most notably—but the sixteenth-century concept of atheism did not entail disbelief in the existence of God, as it does today. David Riggs explains, "Early modern unbeliev-ers usually did not dispute the existence of God; they denied God's capacity to intervene in their lives via the Son and the Holy Ghost . . . [A]nyone who rejected the immortality of the soul, the existence of heaven and hell (especially the latter) and the operations of Providence qualified as an atheist."[81] To be an atheist in the early modern era was to believe that God exists but does not intervene in or have a plan for human affairs. By the early eighteenth century, atheism in its modern sense had begun to emerge, but the idea remained profoundly shock-ing, even unthinkable, to many. Writing in 1737, Thomas Broughton commented, "there is room to doubt, whether there ever have been thinking men, who have actually reasoned themselves into a disbe-lief of a Deity."[82] A similar disbelief pervades an article published by the *Universal Spectator* in 1734: "A contemplative Atheist"—that is, a person who has given deep thought to the topic of God's existence before rejecting it—"is what I think impossible; most who would be thought Atheists, are so out of Indolence, because they will not give themselves Time to reason, to find if they are so or not."[83] Men (all atheists were presumed to be men) may default to what David Ber-man calls "practical atheism," acting immorally as if there is no God, or they may fall into "unthinking atheism" by giving no thought to God's existence.[84] If they were to afford themselves time for true con-templation, however, they could not accept such a position. Indeed, many theologians argued that the theist position was the only logical one. According to John Balguy, "Of all the false Doctrines and foolish

Opinions, which ever infested the Mind of Men, nothing can possibly equal that of Atheism, which is such a monstrous Contradiction to all Evidence, to all Powers of Understanding, and the Dictates of Common Sense."[85] He concludes, "Let any Man survey the Face of the Earth, or lift up his Eyes to the Firmament. . . . Will he presume to say or suppose that all the Objects he meets with are nothing more than the Result of unaccountable Accidents and blind Chance."[86] Nature offers sufficient proof of divinity.

Like many theologians of the period, Balguy denies the existence of atheists, but by the late eighteenth century, people had begun explicitly to defend atheist ideas. Writing in 1782 under the pseudonym William Hammon, physician Matthew Turner publicly proclaimed his disbelief in God to prove that atheists do exist: "But as to the question whether there is such an existent Being as an atheist, to put that out of all manner of doubt, I do declare upon my honour that I am one."[87] In the prefatory materials to Hammon's *Answer*, the publisher distances himself from the subject matter: "as [the Editor] has no desire of making converts, [he] hopes he shall not be marked out as an object for persecution."[88] He also insists that the publication of such material will shore up individual readers' faith: "Doubts upon Natural Religion have not hitherto been looked upon as attacks upon Revelation, but rather as corroborations to it."[89] Still, the publication of *Answer to Dr Priestley's Letters* marks a decisive turning point in the history of British atheism, the first time that nonbelief had been publicly and unapologetically defended in print.

The appearance of open atheism in Britain was made possible by the circulation of similar materials in France earlier in the century. The French philosophes, "the group of French thinkers including Voltaire, Denis Diderot and Baron d'Holbach," were, in Martin Priestman's words, "credited with an undermining of religious authority throughout the eighteenth century which eventually precipitated the French Revolution."[90] Michael J. Buckley names Diderot "the first of the atheists, not simply in chronological reckoning but as an initial and premier advocate and influence."[91] In his *Promenade du Sceptique* (*The Skeptic's Walk*, 1747), Diderot's skeptic mocks the concept of religion; God is "a Ruler whose name his subjects more or less agree on; but whose existence is very much in dispute. Nobody has seen him. . . .

Nevertheless, he is assumed to be infinitely wise, enlightened, and full of tenderness for his subjects; but as he has resolved to make himself inaccessible, at least for the time being, and since any communication from him would necessarily become distorted in transmission, the means he has used to prescribe his laws and to manifest his will are rather dodgy."[92] Religion is irrational, confining, and scientifically unprovable, and thus the skeptic advocates a materialist view of the universe. Because Diderot's writings were rooted in scientific rationalism, French authorities considered them especially dangerous. As Gavin Hyman explains, "he could not be dismissed as a malevolent or frivolous mind. On the contrary, Diderot's atheism was a consequence of his intellectual integrity and a disinterested quest for truth."[93] Diderot's atheism was rooted in his scientific knowledge of the universe.

The materialist position, the belief that "the universe consisted purely of matter animated by its own energies and needing no external divine input," was also shared by Paul-Henri Thiry, Baron d'Holbach, whose Paris salon became known as a hotbed of atheist thought.[94] In his *Système de la Nature* (*System of Nature*, 1770), d'Holbach seeks to "dispel those clouds of ignorance which prevent man from marching with a firm and steady pace through the path of life."[95] Man is, he argues, "in almost every climate, a poor degraded captive," made so by "error, consecrated by religion."[96] Religion is a series of irrational inherited beliefs that maintain systems of oppression, and d'Holbach complains of the "calamities that the political and religious tyranny has brought upon the earth."[97] The priests and kings work together to play on people's fears and shore up their own authority, in Peter Gay's words, "a trick imposed on the subject by the ruler for his own selfish purposes."[98]

It was to the French philosophes, then, to Diderot and d'Holbach, along with Voltaire, Jean le Rond d'Alembert, and Claude Adrien Helvétius, that eighteenth-century British nonbelievers turned as they became more open about their lack of belief. Turner specifically referenced the French tradition to support his own claims. "Modern Philosophers are nearly all atheists," he wrote in his *Answer to Dr Priestley's Letters*.[99] "I take the term atheist here in the popular sense. Hume, Helvetius, Diderot, D'Almbert [*sic*]."[100] Late-century atheists also turned to David Hume, who, Priestman points out, "famously refused to be pinned down as a deist, let alone an atheist," but whose *Dialogues on Natural Religion* (1779) launched "a devastatingly sceptical assault on deist arguments that any deity, let alone a benign one, can be deduced from the evidence available to us from the natural universe."[101] Edward Gibbon's *Decline and Fall of the Roman Empire*, too, served as a model, as Gibbon emphasized the "fanaticism and intolerance" of the early Christian Church, in contrast to the "tolerance of long-established polytheism."[102] At the conclusion to chapter 16 of his *Decline and Fall*, Gibbon writes, "We shall conclude this chapter by a melancholy truth . . . [I]t must still be acknowledged that the Christians, in the course of their intestine dissensions, have inflicted far greater severities on each other than they had experienced from the zeal of infidels."[103]

Richard Watson, a professor of divinity at Cambridge University, responded to Gibbon at length in *An Apology for Christianity* (1776). According to Watson, Gibbon's work "had made upon many an impression not at all advantageous to Christianity," and he felt compelled to reply, lest "the silence of others, of the Clergy especially, began to be looked upon as an acquiescence in what you had therein advanced."[104] The actions Gibbon ascribes to the "inflexible" and "intolerant zeal" of early Christians,[105] Watson attributes to their "love of God, which was in Christ Jesus their Lord."[106] Watson concludes with an open letter to atheists in which he proclaims more broadly the dangers of nonbelief. "Suppose the mighty work accomplished, the cross trampled upon, Christianity every where proscribed, and the religion of nature once more become the religion of Europe; what advantage will you have derived to your country, or to yourselves, from the exchange?" he asks.[107] Watson chastises nonbelievers for "freeing" the world from the stability and hope of the Christian religion: "You will have freed the world . . . from it's [sic] abhorrence of vice, and from every powerful incentive to virtue . . . you will have robbed mankind of their firm assurance of another life; and thereby you will have despoiled them of their patience, of their humility, of their charity, of their chastity."[108] Without Christianity, there can be no virtue or morality.

As the number of open atheists increased, so did the reaction against nonbelief. According to the author of "An Essay Against

Atheism" (1773), individual morality is dependent on religious faith: "To destroy the notion of a God is to destroy the end, and support, and security of human society. . . . There can be no restraint of conscience where there is no fear of God; and in this case virtue and vice would be things indifferent."[109] That Edmund Burke attributed the French Revolution to a "deep-laid atheist conspiracy" reflects the extent to which Christianity was seen as necessary to political stability.[110] According to Burke, "atheism is against, not only our reason, but our instincts"; were the British to abandon their religious faith, they would also lose "one great source of civilization amongst us."[111] Atheism "gnaws at the very foundations of society"[112] and leads directly to political chaos. Hannah More adopts a similar view in her *Remarks on the Speech of M. Dupont* (1793). According to More, "anarchy and atheism" go hand and hand as "monsters" that would "soon slay tens of thousands."[113] Even Thomas Paine worried in his *Age of Reason* (1794) that abandonment of religion might lead to chaos. Although he believed that "all national institutions of Churches . . . appear to me no other than human inventions set up to terrify and enslave mankind, and to monopolize power and profit," he cautioned, "lest, in the general wreck of superstition, of false systems of government, and false theology, we lose sight of morality, of humanity, and of theology that is true."[114] For some, atheism had the power to free humanity from tyranny and a false and oppressive moral system. For others, to abandon Christianity was to abandon stability, morality, and restraint. It was at the height of this debate that Mary Shelley was born, and she spent many years surrounded by self-proclaimed atheists, including her father, Godwin, and her husband, Percy Shelley.

Although Mary Shelley is best known as the author of *Frankenstein*, the bulk of her work was composed after much of Romanticism's second generation had passed on. She lived many years into Queen Victoria's reign, and thus existed in a very different world from the one in which she grew up. By the mid-1810s, England was a country unsettled, as the violence occasioned by the Napoleonic Wars was matched by economic and political unrest at home. The British government had spent "a staggering £800 million" on the wars, and "had sucked dry the profits of both the old industries and the new technologies."[115] Wages among

the working class began to fall, the result of mechanization, "disrup-
tions in trade" caused by the war, and the "wildly fluctuating patterns of
supply and demand that it engendered."[116] According to historian Ian
Hernon, Lancashire weavers saw their wages fall from fifteen shillings
per week in 1803 "to 5 shillings or even 4s 6d" in 1818.[117] The effect
of falling wages was compounded by cuts to funding for Poor Relief, a
high inflation rate, and mass unemployment as three hundred thousand soldiers were sent home from the Continent without pension or
provision for their support. It was also exacerbated by food shortages
and fears of famine, driven in no small part by newly imposed restric-
tive governmental policies. As the Napoleonic Wars drew to a close, a
series of bumper harvests led to a greater corn supply than demand,
and the price of corn began to fall. In response to economic losses suffered by farmers, the government imposed in 1815 a series of measures
known as the Corn Laws, which, Boyd Hilton explains, "were designed
to ensure, through a mixture of import duties and export bounties, that
English farmers grew sufficient grain."[118] The 1815 Corn Laws created a
price floor, forbidding foreign imports until the price of domestic corn
reached "twenty-seven shillings for oats; forty shillings for barley, beer
and bigg; fifty-three shillings for rye, peas, and beans; and, most hated
of all, eighty shillings for wheat."[119] Such prices were prohibitively high
for many, and by 1816–17, the "economic situation rapidly deterio-
rated . . . throughout the nation" and was "made worse in the English
Northwest by acute food shortages and soaring grain prices."[120]

In this "postwar era of economic dislocation and popular unrest,"[121]
protests began to break out in manufacturing areas across the country. Between 1811 and 1813, the Luddites famously destroyed factory
machinery perceived to be replacing human workers and driving down
wages, leading in 1812 to the passage of the Frame Breaking Act, which
made "the destruction of industrial machinery a capital offence."[122] In
March of 1818, as many as forty thousand people, the so-called Blanketeers, named for the blankets they brought for warmth on the trip,
attempted to march from Manchester to London with the intent of
petitioning the Prince Regent for redress from "(1) excessive government spending and high taxes, the latter allegedly having quadrupled
during the war; (2) high rents which were said to have doubled during

the war; (3) the Corn Law of 1815; (4) the Libel Laws; (5) the suspension of *habeas corpus*; and (6) the Prince Regent's ministers, whose dismissals the petition demanded."[123] Robert Poole describes the gathering as "a last-ditch appeal for constitutional reform, not to parliament but to the crown,"[124] but only one man successfully completed the journey to London. After the magistrates read the Riot Act, the leaders of the march were arrested and the crowd disbanded.

The outbreaks of unrest came to a head on August 16, 1819, with the so-called Peterloo Massacre. On that day, approximately "60,000 marched to St. Peter's Field" in Manchester "to demand universal suffrage and parliamentary reform."[125] They were met by fifteen hundred troops, who were prepared to break up the crowd. At 1:35 p.m., when the crowd had grown beyond capacity, Reverend Charles Ethelston read the Riot Act, and when the crowd did not disperse, the cavalry charged. Within a few minutes, "fourteen people died, and 654 were injured, as a direct consequence of the actions of soldiers and police."[126] Included among the casualties were women and children, many of them discovered after the fact suffering from "sabre wounds."[127] According to Robert Poole, the Peterloo Massacre was one of the "defining events of its age."[128] It became "a byword for repression under the old regime, a shorthand term for the political dark side of the industrial revolution."[129] The massacre inspired widespread shock and outrage across the country, and it inspired Percy Shelley to write *The Mask of Anarchy*. It also cemented the role of women in radical movements. According to Michael Bush, "the driving force was predominantly working women. They had been suddenly transformed into a potent and disturbing political force not by the feminist message of Mary Wollstonecraft but by the process of industrialization, which opened up for them sources of employment outside domestic service."[130] Bush speculates that the presence of women at the protest may have prompted the barbaric governmental response: "the women at the meeting appeared to express a taunting forwardness, a triumphal confidence and a message of militancy that enraged the magistrates and aroused the cavalry's blood-lust."[131]

The economic and political demands of an increasingly radical lower class were met with a conservative middle-class backlash, one that reshaped the social and religious worlds of nineteenth-century

England. Anglican Evangelicals—"staunch members of the Church of England who believed in reform from within rather than in following the example of John Wesley"[132]—set themselves up in opposition to the lower-class enthusiasm of the Methodists, the radical philosophy of the Jacobins, and the perceived excesses of aristocratic culture. By the early nineteenth century, an influential group of Evangelical Anglicans, the so-called Clapham Sect, which included such figures as William Wilberforce, Henry Venn, and Hannah More, sought to foster change within the Church of England. For Evangelical Anglican reformers, the purpose of religion was to foster introspection and to encourage society to behave in more moral and humane ways. "The nation," late-century Evangelicals believed, "was suffering from moral degeneracy. Events in France were a warning of what was to come if individuals did not inspire a revolution in the 'manner and morals' of the nation, a transformation which must begin with individual salvation."[133] Evangelical leaders such as John Angell James (1785–1859) explicitly rejected lower-class calls for reform. He attributed lower-class protests in Birmingham to "drunkenness and swearing rather than the problems of wages and labour,"[134] preached against utopianism and Owenite socialism,[135] and attributed social unrest to personal moral failings. The foundation of reformation societies such as the Society for the Suppression of Vice (founded 1802) were thus the product of the Evangelical Anglican emphasis on personal reform and attempts to diminish revolutionary potential among the poor.

Such groups also sought to improve the morals of society at large. Evangelicals and other Dissenters led the charge against the slave trade, treating it as a sin perpetrated by the English nation. "Judgment was expected on nations as well as individuals if they persisted in corporate sins like tolerating the slave trade," and it fell to the devout to encourage the nation to reform legally and morally.[136] Anna Letitia Barbauld, a lifelong Dissenter, depicts in her *Epistle to William Wilberforce* (1791) the consequences of the slave trade in England. In its deliberate choice to turn away from the suffering of the African slaves, England commits a horrible sin and knowingly stains its own soul: "The spreading leprosy taints ev'ry part, / Infects each limb, and sickens at the heart . . . / By foreign wealth are British morals chang'd."[137] The abolition movement gained momentum and legitimacy as dissenting sects lobbied for freedom; abolition was finally decreed throughout the empire in 1833.[138]

Throughout the nineteenth century, the power of the Evangelical movement grew as the English middle classes became increasingly devout. According to Davidoff and Hall, "by mid century adherence to Evangelical protestant forms had become an accepted part of respectability if not gentility,"[139] and it fell to individual Christians to monitor themselves, to be constantly vigilant in "valiantly confronting their weaknesses and denying their baser impulses."[140] As William Wilberforce wrote in his *Practical Christianity* (1797), Christianity "is a state into which we are not born, but into which we must be translated. . . . This is a matter of labour and difficulty, requiring continual watchfulness and unceasing effort, and unwearied patience."[141] The Christian had a duty to self-survey, to negate personal will and embrace God's plan. Within this world view, the home was an important site of worship, and family life a vital forum for devotion. According to Davidoff and Hall, "The shift to family worship across all denominations, even in preference to individual prayer, the spread of 'parlour' as well as cottage worship, marked the growing prominence given to the family. The family would collectively pray over each member's successes and failures, each individual would be collectively called to account. Family prayer stood between public worship and private devotion."[142]

As the doctrine of separate spheres became more codified in the nineteenth century, women paradoxically became both more important to and less powerful in organized religion.[143] Although women were presumed to be spiritually equal to men, they were required to be submissive in this life. From 1803 on, Methodist women were restricted from preaching, and women of all denominations were pressured to remain within the household. Within the domestic sphere, however, they increasingly controlled the spiritual life of the family; women were not allowed to participate in the public world of men, but "Christianity was thought to give enormous scope to woman as wife and mother."[144] This shift, what Callum Brown calls the "feminisation of piety," privileged women's supposedly innate religiosity.[145] Women were tasked with ensuring male morality and with transforming the domestic sphere into an attractive paradise that would encourage male fidelity.

According to Wilberforce, "The wife, habitually preserving a warmer and more unimpaired spirit of devotion, than is perhaps consistent with being immersed in the bustle of life, might revive [her husband's] languid piety."[146] They were also expected to oversee the religious upbringing of children. As Gail Malmgreen explains, they "left the home in droves to conduct Sunday schools and prayer-meetings," and many began to write religious texts aimed at children; "religious writing offered middle-class women a chance to be self-supporting."[147] Through the feminized province of religious instruction, women participated in the public sphere, even as they were encouraged to restrict themselves within the domestic realm. As we shall see, Mary Shelley's later writings would internalize many of these newly emergent cultural ideologies. Her late works are marked both by a longing for domestic harmony and by a clear belief in the religious sanctity of the household. These novels are markedly different in tone and genre from the works that made her famous, and they reflect the new dominance of Evangelical morality.

Thus far, we have been discussing developments within Protestantism. Central to the late eighteenth and early nineteenth centuries, however, was the continued debate over the status of Roman Catholics in England. Since the sixteenth century, Catholics had been treated as the greatest threat to British national security, an insidious, often invisible army of potential traitors who owed loyalty to pope over king. Texts like John Foxe's *Acts and Monuments*—after the Bible, the best-selling work of the sixteenth and seventeenth centuries—constructed a myth of British Protestant martyrdom that offered proof of Godly favor through the Church of England's triumph over the Catholics. This chain of events—Queen Elizabeth I surviving her Catholic sister, Bloody Mary, the destruction of the Spanish Armada, the failure of the Gunpowder Plot, and the success of the so-called Glorious Revolution of 1688–89—enabled British Protestants to tell a story of their own superiority and triumph over Catholic treachery.[148]

Coupled with tales of British Protestant might was a strand of atrocity narrative that demonized Catholics by accusing them of all manner of unthinkably violent behaviors. Jesuit priests were looked on with particular suspicion in such tracts. According to the author of *A Bloody Tragedie, Or Romish Maske* (1607), "They say the Iesuites are bloody, and stirrers up [sic] sedition in Christian kingdomes, that they are lyars, that they are proude, that they delight in rich apparell . . . that they are Epicures, and make their belly their god, that they are lascivious, and love women, having Gentlewomen for their chamber-maides and young wenches for their bedfellowes."[149] Irish Catholics were also treated as a physical threat; stories of over-the-top violence supposedly committed during the 1641 Irish rebellion were resurrected to prove the dangers posed by allowing Catholics too much freedom. In such tracts, they are violent, subhuman in their animalistic willingness to rape, maim, rob, and kill, even engaging in acts of cannibalism and vampirism to assuage their master, the pope. According to the author of *The Kings Majesties speech On the 2. day of December, 1641*, for instance, Irish rebels enact horrific violence on the body of a young Protestant Parliamentarian: they "drew their swords & cut off, first, her right arme, then her left, then both her legs, then they tied a rope about her middle, and drag'd it about, which having done they ript ope her belly, and saved as much of her blood as they could, saying that her puritane sisters should be glad of that to drinke."[150] Such stories were resurrected during the 1820s, as British politicians debated the merits of religious toleration. According to Linda Colley, "In Surrey, an anti-emancipation tract called *Queen Mary's days* circulated, full of grisly pictures of the burnings at Smithfield. In the West Country, magistrates had to confiscate pictures of 'infants quartered and . . . young girls impaled alive and naked' at the hands of Catholic priests."[151]

Because Catholics were seen as such a fearsome threat, a series of laws was passed throughout the period to keep them in their proper place. In 1672, parliament forced through the Test Act against the will of King Charles II, legally requiring government officials to swear allegiance to the Church of England, and forcing the future King James II to step down as head of the British navy. Other restrictions were passed in the wake of the Glorious Revolution. By the mid-eighteenth century, Catholics were forbidden by law from educating their children in their faith, holding public office, inheriting or purchasing property, and, after 1689, living within ten miles of London or Westminster. As the eighteenth century progressed, there was some movement toward toleration. The 1778 passage of the first Act for Catholic Relief allowed Catholics to own and inherit property, and priests were no longer prosecuted, provided they took an oath of loyalty to the British government, but the act led to an immediate anti-Catholic backlash in the form of the Gordon riots, "the largest, deadliest, and most protracted urban riots in British history."[152]

By the beginning of the nineteenth century, however, anti-Catholic sentiment had begun to dissipate. Irish Catholics were allowed to serve in the British military during the American Revolution, and after 1793, the army and navy were opened to all Catholics, meaning that "opponents of emancipation" increasingly appeared "unappreciative of the patriot dead and out of touch with Great Britain's current grandeur and expansiveness."[153] Subsequently, in 1800 the Act of Union incorporated Ireland into the United Kingdom, increasing "the percentage of Roman Catholics in the kingdom to thirty percent."[154] Public sympathy was also roused by the news of Catholic refugees fleeing France. A series of bills thus further decreased discriminatory practices. The 1791 Roman Catholic Relief Act legally allowed Catholics to become lawyers and to practice their faith openly, and in 1811, Catholic soldiers were permitted freedom of worship. In the late 1820s, the battle for full emancipation gained steam, culminating in the Roman Catholic Relief Act of 1829. The debate leading up to the act was unsurprisingly passionate, and the so-called Catholic Question became "the most explosive political issue in Britain in the early years of the century."[155] Robert Southey published *The Book of the Church* (1825) to illustrate "the errors and crimes of the Romish Church."[156] He followed up those claims in *Vindiciae Ecclesiae Anglicanae* (1826), in which he wrote that "the Romanish Church is inherently, incurably, and restlessly intolerant"; its followers seek to undo "the work of the Reformation and of the Revolution" and reestablish "that system of superstition, idolatry, and persecution, from which the sufferings of our martyrs, and the wisdom of our ancestors, by God's blessing delivered us."[157] Southey was not alone in this assessment. According to Irene Bostrom, "in the final debate on the subject" in parliament, the Protestant "Lord Eldon declared that if the Emancipation Bill passed, 'the sun of England was set forever!' and he wept in public at the outcome."[158] The "poorer, more marginal and less literate folk" also remained "stridently and devotedly anti-Catholic."[159] Yet as Linda Colley points out, there was no repeat of the Gordon riots in 1829. "There were no major riots on the British mainland on account of the Catholic Emancipation Act. No one seems to have been killed opposing it; and no Catholic chapels were burnt to the ground in retaliation. Toleration was growing."[160] Throughout her career, as we shall see, Shelley vacillates between adopting anti-Catholic imagery, especially when she criticizes the oppression of women by organized religion, and expressing sympathy for the long-standing oppression of Catholics. She is also often supportive of Italian Catholic independence. Shelley's response to Catholicism is thus both indicative of the anti-Catholic climate in which she grew up and remarkably progressive on the subject of toleration.

It is, of course, impossible to offer an exhaustive analysis of nineteenth-century religious, political, and social culture in a single chapter. British religious practice was shaped not only by the forces described above, but by developments in continental European politics beyond France, by encounters with non-Christian religions such as Judaism and Islam, and by the proliferation of many other religious dominations that I don't have room to survey here. Taking all of these currents together, however, the early nineteenth century, the era in which Mary Shelley grew up, was a period in flux, one that reshaped understandings of gender, family, social structure, and religious belief. Her writings reflect multiple sources of influence: her mother's engagement with Rational Dissent; her father's Calvinism; her husband's fervent atheism; her culture's reactions to Evangelicalism, millenarianism, and Catholicism. And as subsequent chapters will explore, questions of faith and salvation would preoccupy her throughout her literary career, even as her understanding of what deity means and how one should worship shifted over time.

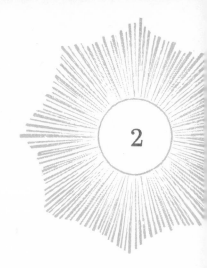

# RELIGION AROUND
# MARY SHELLEY

Any study of Mary Shelley's immediate religious context must begin
with her parents, whose "ghosts . . . are visible and audible in her
writing to the end of her life."[1] Born in 1756, William Godwin came
from a family of Calvinist Dissenters. His father, John Godwin, was a
dissenting minister, and from a young age, William Godwin intended
to join the church, as well. "I will be a minister," he wrote in a poem
entitled "The Wish," which he composed at the age of five.[2] Godwin
attended religious schools as a child, and at the age of eleven, he was
sent to Norwich to study with the Reverend Samuel Newton, a follower
of Robert Sandeman, "the most radical Calvinist in the eighteenth century."[3] Sandeman was known for adopting "the most literal interpretation of the New Testament," and he "restricted the possibility of grace
to a tiny minority."[4] Years later, Godwin would write of Sandeman's
beliefs, he "contrived a scheme for damning ninety-nine in a hundred
of the followers of Calvin."[5] He also called Samuel Newton "the most
wretched of pedants."[6] In his youth, however, he remained firm in
his faith, training as a dissenting minister at Dr. Coward's Dissenting
Academy of Hoxton.

After graduating in 1778, Godwin attempted, largely unsuccessfully, to find steady work as a minister. By 1782, however, he had begun to read works that challenged his religious faith, a "Cromwellian puritan . . . suddenly confronted with the full blaze of the European Enlightenment."[7] The works of d'Holbach, Helvétius, and Rousseau, coupled with his introduction to radical political circles in which organized religion was viewed with suspicion, all contributed to shake his faith, and by the mid-1780s, Godwin was vacillating between the "strict Christianity of his upbringing and the near agnosticism of the age of reason."[8] By the late 1780s, he had begun to proclaim "his disbelief in the immortality of the soul,"[9] and in 1788, he wrote in his *Autobiography*, "I took my last farewel of the Christian faith."[10] By the early 1790s, Godwin was calling himself an atheist, although in truth, he was probably "more of a rational deist."[11] Still, by 1797, the year in which Mary Shelley was born, Godwin was well known for his Jacobinism, his rejection of Christianity as the basis of human perfection, and his belief in the progressive evolution of modern politics. "Perfectibility is one of the most unequivocal characteristics of the human species, so that the political, as well as the intellectual state of man, may be presumed to be in a course of progressive improvement," he wrote in his *Enquiry Concerning Political Justice* (1793).[12] Within this belief system, humanity need not await paradise in the afterlife, as "man could achieve a form of earthly paradise rather than wait for a promised Christian afterlife."[13] In addition, Godwin argued that man was born neither good nor bad, rejecting the doctrine of election: "We bring into the world with us no innate principles: consequently we are neither virtuous nor vicious as we first come into existence."[14] He spurned "the notion of any tyrannizing God or Ultimate Authority."[15] The God of the Christian Bible is a tyrant that can never be overthrown or escaped. "He is acquainted with all our secret motions," Godwin wrote mockingly, "and sits like Jeremy Bentham, perched on top of his Panopticon, to spy into our weaknesses."[16]

If Godwin explicitly rejected the Calvinist faith of his youth, his worldview was nonetheless "heavily tinctured with Calvinist stoicism and immaterialism."[17] Daniel White attributes his "lifelong principle that any form of institutional coercion of the private judgment constituted an impediment to human progress" to a Calvinist perspective on "the primacy of the individual conscience."[18] His fictions, too, reflect a Calvinist sensibility; Falkland's persecution of Caleb Williams bespeaks Godwin's Calvinist understanding of God, the all-seeing being whose anger is implacable and from whom escape is impossible. Mary Shelley's works, as we shall see, were marked both by Godwin's political optimism and by his darker view of a universe governed by an inescapable and unloving deity. From *Frankenstein* to *The Last Man*, Shelley constructs a world in which God's voice is either absent or actively ill-intentioned toward his creations. As Victor Frankenstein proves, there is no guarantee that God must love his creation. Perhaps, like Frankenstein, he recoiled in horror from his invention and now, like Falkland, actively seeks the destruction of humankind.

While Godwin is best known for his lack of faith, he reconsidered his agnosticism as he aged. Godwin wrote in his *Autobiography*, "In my forty-fourth year, I ceased to regard the name of Atheist with the same complacency I had done for several preceding years, at the same time retaining the utmost repugnance of understanding for the idea of an intelligent Creator and Governor of the universe, which strikes my mind as the most irrational and ridiculous anthropomorphism. My theism, if such I may be permitted to call it, consists in a reverent and soothing contemplation of all that is beautiful, grand, or mysterious in the system of the universe."[19] If Godwin never returned to the faith of his youth, he did adopt a more deist understanding of the universe. He also placed new emphasis on family. In *Political Justice*, Godwin insisted that "radical individualism is crucial to both personal felicity and corporate progress,"[20] and he rejected marriage as the worst of social evils: "Cohabitation is not only an evil as it checks the independent progress of mind; it is also inconsistent with the imperfections and propensities of man."[21] Following his marriage to Wollstonecraft, however, he became more sympathetic to family life, and in *St. Leon* (1799) wrote, "Man was not born to live alone. He is linked to his brethren by a thousand ties; and, when those ties are broken, he ceases from all genuine existence."[22] In Weston's words, "social and domestic relations *are* the whole of our existence."[23] The domestic sphere creates meaning and contentment.

Mary Shelley enjoyed a close relationship with her father throughout much of her life, and her views of religion were shaped both by and in opposition to her father's. As we shall see, her works follow a similar ideological trajectory to Godwin's, from the rejection of interpersonal relationships in *Frankenstein* to the embrace of domesticity in *Falkner* as a basis for all human happiness. She could never fully accept her father's political optimism, however. If Godwin believed in the perfectibility of human nature, that a time will come in which "there will be no war, no crimes, no administration of justice as it is called, and no government,"[24] *The Last Man* abandons Godwinian optimism for a Malthusian dystopia, "a nightmare world of overcrowding, depleted resources, and human suffering."[25] Shelley thus registers both support for and criticism of her father's philosophies at various points of her career; she cannot embrace uncritically Godwin's optimistic view of human social evolution.

Mary Shelley never knew her mother, Mary Wollstonecraft, who died of septicemia days after her birth, but she was shaped religiously and philosophically by her mother's writings, which she read frequently throughout her life. In *History of a Six Weeks' Tour*, Shelley mentions reading her mother's *Letters Written During a Short Residence in Sweden, Norway, and Denmark* for inspiration, and as Jacqueline Labbe points out, "*History* in many ways mirrors her mother's travel narrative."[26] She was also particularly influenced by Wollstonecraft's lesser-known *Mary, A Fiction*, a novella that "has been given short shrift in Romanticist and even Wollstonecraftian criticism."[27] As we shall see, Shelley returns time and again to the imagery of her mother's works, responding to and adapting their religious content in different ways throughout her career.

According to William Godwin, Mary Wollstonecraft did not adhere to a specific religious denomination. In his *Memoirs of the Author of A Vindication of the Rights of Woman* (1798), written to commemorate his wife after her death, Godwin explains that "Mary had been bred in the principles of the church of England. . . . Her religion was, in reality, little allied to any system of forms."[28] According to Godwin, Wollstonecraft's conception of God elicited only joy because she was not raised in any particular faith tradition: "she had received few lessons of religion in her youth, and her religion was almost entirely of her own creation. . . . She could not recollect the time when she had believed the doctrine of future punishments. The tenets of her system were the growth of her own moral taste, and her religion therefore had always been a gratification, never a terror, to her."[29] Unlike Godwin, who was raised with the idea of a vengeful and distant deity, Wollstonecraft found solace in her self-created vision of the Almighty. She also took, Godwin claims, a quasi-deist pleasure in the natural world. "She found an inexpressible delight in the beauties of nature. . . . When she walked amidst the wonders of nature, she was accustomed to converse with her God."[30] Wollstonecraft finds happiness in the promise of a merciful God whose love is apparent in nature.

According to Godwin, Wollstonecraft's "opinions" on religion "approached much nearer to the received ones, than mine."[31] Yet he also claims that she eschewed religion on her deathbed: "During her whole illness, not one word of a religious cast fell from her lips."[32] As the result of such passages, Wollstonecraft's critics labeled her an atheist, and thus while Godwin apparently wrote his *Memoirs* with good intentions, he succeeded only in destroying her reputation for generations to come. "She died on the 10th of September, and her husband boasts that during her whole illness not one word of a religious cast fell from her lips. Rare philosophy!" the reviewer for *The Scots Magazine* sneered.[33] Critics used the salacious details reported in *Memoirs*—the story of Wollstonecraft's affairs, illegitimate pregnancy, and suicide attempts—to discredit her as a philosopher, functionally succeeding in discrediting early feminism. Jane Moore points out that the Tory *Anti-Jacobin Review and Magazine* called Wollstonecraft Imlay's "concubine" and "indexed Godwin's book under 'Prostitution: see Mary Wollstonecraft.'"[34] The *European Magazine* named her a "philosophical wanton,"[35] and even the generally sympathetic reviewer of *The Critical Review* commented, "It is . . . not without disgust that we have read these 'Memoirs' and some of the posthumous pieces, because we are convinced that they are not calculated to do honour to her memory, although this may have been the sincere intention of the writer and editor."[36] Godwin had unintentionally destroyed his late wife's reputation; after the publication of *Memoirs*, to identify publicly with Wollstonecraft or to espouse her ideas was to align with perceived immorality and heresy. Hannah More, for instance, refused to read Wollstonecraft on principle, even though their educational ideas were not dissimilar.

It is perhaps ironic, then, that Wollstonecraft was not, in fact, an atheist as many of her critics implied. In 1800, Mary Hays, Wollstonecraft's friend and fellow feminist, published her own version of Wollstonecraft's biography, disputing Godwin's account and recasting Wollstonecraft's "allegedly extreme passions . . . as part of a larger picture of personal and spiritual growth."[37] Hays concurs with Godwin that Wollstonecraft's faith was unaffiliated with any specific denomination: "Her religion, for she laid no stress on creeds and forms, was a sentiment of humility, reverence, and love."[38] Like Godwin, Hays also links Wollstonecraft's love of God with her appreciation for the natural world. "She believed in a being, higher, more perfect than visible nature," and she "adored the Creator in the temple of the universe, worshipped him amidst the beauties of nature."[39] Unlike Godwin, however, Hays insists that Wollstonecraft's belief was strong and that she took comfort in her religion on her deathbed: "The religious sentiments she had imbibed in her youth, had in them no terrours that could discompose a dying hour."[40] According to Hays, "her imagination had embodied images of visionary perfection, giving rise to affections in which her sensibility delighted to indulge,"[41] an account substantiated by Wollstonecraft herself, who complained in a letter to Godwin, "how can you blame me for taken [sic] refuge in the idea of a God, when I despair of finding sincerity on earth?"[42] Written on July 4, 1797, mere months before her death, this letter reaffirms Wollstonecraft's belief in a higher power, suggesting that Godwin's vision of her atheism was more wishful thinking than truth.

According to Kari Lokke, Wollstonecraft "developed her own religious creed," a creed influenced by her engagement with multiple Protestant denominations.[43] Raised in the Church of England, she attended Anglican services until the 1780s, when she began to eschew institutional religion. In 1784, she moved to Newington Green, where she became acquainted with Richard Price. According to Hays, Price had a formative impact on her intellectual development: "Some valuable connexions which she now formed, gave a tincture to her future views and character; among the most distinguished of these she accounted Dr. Richard Price (equally respected for his talents and virtues), for whom she conceived a sincere reverence and friendship, and on whose public instruction she occasionally attended."[44] Within the social world of Newington Green, she was surrounded "culturally, intellectually, and politically with the progressive and reformist elements of English religious Dissent."[45] She attended sermons preached by Price—whom she calls in *Vindication* "one of the best of men"[46]—and she regularly interacted with the circle that included Joseph Priestley and the Unitarian publisher Joseph Johnson, an early supporter of her works.

This is not to suggest that Wollstonecraft herself identified as a Rational Dissenter. Indeed, she speaks critically of Rational Dissenters in *Vindication*, where she compares the effects of oppression on women with those on Dissenters:

> From the tyranny of man, I firmly believe, the greater number of female follies proceed; and the cunning, which I allow, makes at present a part of their character, I likewise have repeatedly endeavoured to prove, is produced by oppression. Were not dissenters, for instance, a class of people, with strict truth characterized as cunning? And may I not lay some stress on this fact to prove, that when any power but reason curbs the free spirit of man, dissimulation is practised, and the various shifts of art are naturally called forth? Great attention to decorum, which was carried to a degree of scrupulosity, and all that puerile bustle about trifles and consequential solemnity, which Butler's caricature of a dissenter brings before the imagination, shaped their persons as well as their minds in the mould of prim littleness. I speak collectively, for I know how many ornaments to human nature have been enrolled amongst sectaries; yet, I assert, that the same narrow prejudice for their sect, which women have for their families, prevailed in the dissenting part of the community, however worthy in other respects; and also that the same timid prudence, or headstrong efforts, often disgraced the exertions of both.[47]

Wollstonecraft does not defend Dissenters from attacks on their "prim littleness" of mind, their "cunning," or "timid prudence." Rather, she attributes their perceived failings to cultural subjugation, likening the effects of oppression on Dissenters to the deleterious effects of patriarchy on female intellect.

Wollstonecraft would again speak critically of Rational Dissenters in her *Letters Written During a Short Residence in Sweden, Norway, and Denmark* (1796). Wollstonecraft complains that Christiania (now Oslo) "is a clean, neat city; but it has none of the graces of architecture, which ought to keep pace with the refining manners of a people."[48] The city's lack of grandeur calls to her mind "the meeting-house of my respected friend, Dr. Price," which, she argues, suffers from a similar architectural plainness.[49] Appreciation of beauty, Wollstonecraft argues, both natural and manmade, can lift the individual closer to God, and thus she criticizes the austerity of dissenting worship spaces: "I am surprised that the dissenters, who have not laid aside all the pomps and vanities of life, should imagine a noble pillar, or arch, unhallowed. Whilst men have senses, whatever sooths them lends wings to devotion."[50] Wollstonecraft turns away from the perceived sterility of Rational Dissent and looks instead to the natural world for proof of divine presence: "The beauties of nature . . . force even the sorrowing heart to acknowledge that existence is a blessing; and this acknowledgement is the most sublime homage we can pay to the Deity."[51]

Still, despite the fact that Wollstonecraft criticized some aspects of Rational Dissent, she was taken seriously as a philosopher and intellect among the social circles of Newington Green. She honed her argumentative skills and developed her feminist philosophy among Rational Dissenters, and their egalitarian beliefs deeply influenced her own. According to Caroline Franklin, "Though she never formally embraced Unitarianism, it was Rational Dissent which had a particularly strong influence on the development of first her education and then her political thinking."[52] Of particular interest to Wollstonecraft was the Unitarian rejection of original sin and the belief espoused by Price that "only those free to think and act for themselves will take their place by God's throne."[53] As Franklin explains, in Price's theology, "every individual has a right to use his reason to ascertain where his duty lies; to subject laws and precepts to sceptical criticism; and . . . to follow his conscience if sincerely convinced, even if later proved incorrect."[54] It was therefore imperative for Price that women as well as men learn to reason, that they develop the capacity for moral judgment and pious self-improvement, an idea that Wollstonecraft would internalize.[55] Such views underpin *Vindication*'s insistence that "reason alone established human preeminence over the rest of creation," that "private reasoned judgment is the foundation of true religion," and that women were not only capable of but obligated to develop that moral capacity.[56] The influence of Rational Dissenting discourse is also apparent in *Vindication*'s claim that women "are rendered weak and wretched" not by mental incapacity, but by "a false system of education."[57] Just as Godwin's beliefs were inflected by his early Calvinism and later engagement with deism and atheism, Wollstonecraft's work was marked by her engagement with Unitarianism.

Wollstonecraft's religious beliefs are also apparent in her fictions, and especially *Mary, A Fiction*. As a young woman, Mary is rejected both by her father, who is uninterested in female minds, and by her mother, who cannot love a daughter.[58] Isolated and desperate for companionship, Mary retreats to the natural world. "Neglected in every respect, and left to the operations of her own mind, she considered every thing that came under her inspection, and learned to think. She had heard of a separate state, and that angels sometimes visited this earth. She would sit in a thick wood in the park, and talk to them."[59] According to both Hays and Godwin, contact with the natural world reinforced Wollstonecraft's faith, and Mary, too, sees in nature evidence of God's love. "Sublime ideas filled her young mind—always connected with devotional sentiments; extemporary effusions of gratitude, and rhapsodies of praise would burst often from her, when she listened to the birds, or pursued the deer. . . . She began to consider the Great First Cause, formed just notions of his attributes, and, in particular, dwelt on his wisdom and goodness."[60] The love she cannot receive from her parents she attempts to find in God's natural beauties.

When Mary finds herself alone, friendless and miserable, she retreats to the mountains near her house. "When her mother frowned, and her friend looked cool, she would steal to this retirement, where human foot seldom trod—gaze on the sea, observe the grey clouds, or listen to the wind."[61] In her "Temple of Solitude"—a deliberately religious descriptor—Mary consoles herself with her reading, with "Thomson's Seasons, Young's Night–Thoughts, and Paradise Lost."[62] It is significant that Wollstonecraft's Mary occupies herself with one of the same works, *Paradise Lost*, that would later fascinate Frankenstein's creature, who also reads while isolated in nature. The creature is thus the first in a series of Shelley's characters who, reminiscent of Wollstonecraft's Mary, seek solace in the natural world when they are rejected by the human community. *The Last Man*'s Lionel, *Perkin Warbeck*'s Edmund, and the eponymous Mathilda and Falkner are all by turn isolated in nature with only books for companionship, and they find varying degrees of peace therein. Shelley re-creates over and over a scene from her mother's first novel, reflecting the central importance of Wollstonecraft's work to her own corpus.

While many male Romantic authors would find solace in the natural world—Byron writes in *Childe Harold*, "to me / High mountains are a feeling, but the hum / Of human cities torture: I can see / Nothing to loathe in nature"[63]—neither Wollstonecraft nor Shelley is able to find real comfort in the absence of human ties. When Wollstonecraft's Mary is denied the love first of parents and later of husband—when the nuclear family structure fails her—she turns instead to the performance of good works. Just as Frankenstein's creature becomes fascinated with the De Lacey family, whom he observes from his forest solitude, Mary finds herself watching over the "huts of a few poor fishermen, who supported their numerous children by their precarious labour."[64] While the creature can love the De Laceys only from afar, Mary is able to reach out to these impoverished families, finding joy in service to others. "In these little huts she frequently rested, and denied herself every childish gratification, in order to relieve the necessities of the inhabitants. Her heart yearned for them, and would dance with joy when she had relieved their wants, or afforded them pleasure."[65] Mary learns to love charitable pursuits, "the luxury of doing good," and she defines herself entirely through her philanthropy.[66] "Her benevolence, indeed, knew no bounds; the distress of others carried her out of herself; and she rested not till she had relieved or comforted them."[67] For Mary, these charitable acts are also acts of devotion: "Enthusiastic sentiments of devotion at this period actuated her; her Creator was almost apparent to her senses in his works; but they were mostly the grand or solemn features of Nature which she delighted to contemplate."[68] Mary's sense of religion, her understanding of God, combines a deist focus on nature with a benevolent pursuit of good works.[69]

In contrast to the Calvinist vision underlying Godwin's works, in which no amount of charity can comfort those whom God has forsaken, *Mary* offers the possibility of contentment in helping others. The novel does not have a happy ending. Mary cannot be with the man she truly loves and instead must look forward to the afterlife, "where there is neither marrying, nor giving in marriage."[70] Yet there is the sense that in performing good works, she can be "not happy, but content," to borrow a line from her daughter.[71] Mary Shelley likewise returns to the image of the outcast throughout her career, allowing her characters to find contentment in kindness, charity, and good works. Indeed, the trajectory of her career will reflect a movement from Calvinist isolation to an Evangelically inflected version of Wollstonecraftian charity. *Frankenstein*'s creature's isolation and misery will finally be resolved in *Falkner*, when the title character is reincorporated into the domestic sphere. Human happiness may be fleeting, but there is power in human love and benevolence.

In 1811, Percy Shelley was expelled from Oxford University for coauthoring with Thomas Jefferson Hogg a pamphlet entitled *The Necessity of Atheism*. According to this pamphlet, religious belief is inherently irrational. "God is an hypothesis, and, as such, stands in need of proof."[72] Such proof may come from "the evidence of the sense," from "Reason," or from external "Testimony," but "having no proof from either of the three sources of conviction, the mind cannot believe the existence of a creative God."[73] Fear of death, the authors argue, animates all religious belief, giving rise to a faith that cannot otherwise be rationalized: "The desire to be forever as we are . . . is, indeed, the secret persuasion which has given birth to the opinions of a future state."[74] Percy positioned religious faith as an irrational bulwark against despair at nothingness, and he remained committed to the belief that religion was a fiction that enabled oppression, at considerable personal cost. A self-styled "Atheist-monster,"[75] he lost custody of his children by his first wife, Harriet, for his (ir)religion, and his relationship with his father did not survive the scandal. Even so, in 1816, he inscribed in a hotel visitors' book the Greek words for "Democrat, Philanthropist, and Atheist" alongside his own name.[76]

If Percy Shelley views religious faith as a fiction developed by those too afraid to face a universe of nothingness, he also decries the deep social evils promulgated by Christianity and the institutionalized church. "I can scarcely set bounds to my hatred of Xtianity," he wrote to Hogg.[77] "The delusions of Christianity are fatal to genius and originality; they limit thought," he told Trelawny.[78] Religion is also a means of institutionalizing social and economic inequity, he wrote in a letter decrying Richard Carlile's imprisonment. "They know that the Established Church is based upon the belief in certain events of a supernatural character having occurred in Judaea eighteen centuries ago; that but for this belief the farmer would refuse to pay the tenth of the produce of his labours to maintain its numbers in idleness; that this class of persons if not maintained in idleness would have something else to do than to divert the attention of the people from obtaining a Reform of their oppressive government . . . a consummation incompatible with the luxurious idleness in which their rulers esteem it their interest to live."[79] A similar philosophy underlies his 1813 poem, *Queen Mab*; recalling William Blake's complaints against the priests and kings, Percy writes,

> From kings and priests and statesmen war arose . . .
> Kings, priests and statesmen blast the human flower
> Even in its tender bud; their influence darts
> Like subtle poison through the bloodless veins
> Of desolate society.[80]

The fear of God is used to control the populace, to reinforce inequalities, and to perpetuate tyranny.

Critics have long debated the extent of Percy's atheism. Carlos Baker writes that "the title of his college pamphlet should have been

*The Necessity of Agnosticism* rather than *The Necessity of Atheism*," while according to Hopps, "he was passionately attached to the founder of the system he hated so much," viewing Christ as a reformer and political radical, if not the son of God.[81] If Percy rejects the idea of the Christian deity, he never fully disdains the idea of a universal consciousness larger than humankind, a "Spirit of Nature," an "all-sufficing Power" that, "Unlike the God of human error . . . / Requirest no prayers or praises."[82]

At the same time, Percy holds out the possibility that the universe may be governed not by a benevolent, if distant, unknowable nature, but by a much more malevolent force. *Queen Mab*'s Ahasuerus describes "an almighty God, / And vengeful as almighty."[83] This God figure hates his own creation and seeks to make humans miserable, punishing people for crimes he enticed them to commit.

> I, God, awoke; in seven days' toil made earth
> From nothing; rested, and created man;
> I placed him in a paradise, and there
> Planted the tree of evil, so that he
> Might eat and perish, and my soul procure
> Wherewith to sate its malice and to turn,
> Even like a heartless conqueror of the earth,
> All misery to my fame.[84]

A similar view of God appears in Percy's *A Refutation of Deism* (1813), in which the deist Theosophus challenges the Christian Eusebes's understanding of biblical narratives and wonders why God created evil, punishing innocent people for sins they did not commit. "You assert that the human race merited eternal reprobation because their common father had transgressed the divine command, and that the crucifixion of the Son of God was the only sacrifice of sufficient efficacy to satisfy eternal justice. But it is no less inconsistent with justice and subversive of morality that millions should be responsible for a crime which they had no share in committing, than that, if they had really committed it, the crucifixion of an innocent being could absolve them from moral turpitude."[85] Theosophus defamiliarizes biblical narrative to make it look ridiculous, but in the process, he implicitly poses an important theological question: If God does exist in the vengeful form of the Old Testament, then what guarantee does humanity have that God is good, or that he cares about his creation?

Several critics have likened *Queen Mab*'s Ahasuerus to Milton's Satan, but his words also reflect the influence of Manichaeism and dualist philosophy.[86] Percy Shelley was fascinated with dualist beliefs, the idea that the universe was caught in a battle between two equally powerful deities, one good, one evil. According to Emily Paterson-Morgan, "Absolute Dualism, such as Gnosticism, presents the deities as perfectly matched adversaries, whereas monarchian Dualism, like Catharism, has a more powerful being and a lesser. These two deities are locked in a struggle for dominion over the material world."[87] That material world was itself constantly suspect. Within Zoroastrianism, it emanated from the Good Principle, but Manichaeism and Catharism perceived "the material world as the inherently and irrevocably corrupt creation of the Evil Principle, designed to sully the pure soul."[88] Such ideas were circulating broadly in Shelley's circle. James Rieger explains, "Through Peacock, Volney, and John Frank Newton, Shelley knew of the Zoroastrian deadlock between Ahriman and Ormuzd, the personifications of the darkness and the light."[89] He was also familiar with dualist ideas through Byron, who touches on Manichaean principles in his play, *Cain* (1821). Byron's Lucifer describes the "two Principles" that control the world, locked in an eternal battle:

> And world by world,
> And star by star and universe by universe
> Shall tremble in the balance, till the great
> Conflict shall cease, if ever it shall cease,
> Which it ne'er shall, till he or I be quench'd![90]

*The Quarterly Review* criticized the play for such passages, lamenting a worldview that "holds out God to the abhorrence of his creatures as a capricious tyrant, and which regards the Devil . . . as the champion of all which is energetic and interesting and noble. . . . This deification of vice; this crazy attachment to the worser half of Manicheism, we long since lamented to find . . . in some of the most powerful lines which have proceeded from Lord Byron's pen."[91] Byron himself rejected the appellation, writing in an 1820 letter to Murray that he was "not a Manichean—nor an Any-chean."[92] Still, his writing reflects the extent to which Manichaean and dualist philosophy were in vogue amongst Percy Shelley's circle.

Percy himself directly addressed Manichaean philosophy in his essay *On the Devil and Devils* (ca. 1819): "To suppose that the world was created and is superintended by two spirits of a balanced power and opposite dispositions is simply a personification of the struggle which we experience within ourselves, and which we perceive in the operations of external things as they affect us, between good and evil."[93] According to Shelley, dualist beliefs reflect the desire to externalize an inherently internal conflict. Within any given individual, "the Evil Spirit and the Good meet and contend."[94] Thus his works display not only a distaste for organized religion, but unresolved questions about the nature of the divine. After all, if "Christianity is violent, oppressive, and unconducive to human flourishing, this does not mean that its God does not exist."[95]

Mary and Percy Shelley were together for only a few short years, but his intellectual influence can be found throughout her works. In the early years of their relationship, Mary and Percy bonded deeply over intellectual pursuits. They apparently spent much of their time reading aloud to one another, and as Jennifer Wallace argues, they bonded romantically over their shared love of reading: "Literary and private passions were intimately connected in their relationship, so that learning Greek and reading classical texts were both public acts of rebellion and private gestures of erotic play for Mary."[96] In the early years of their relationship, Mary and Percy collaborated on intellectual projects, and Mary Shelley both learned from and was edited by her husband.[97] Thus her approach to religion developed alongside Percy's beliefs, which alternately influenced and clashed with her own. Like her husband, Mary Shelley considers in her writings what it would mean to live in a godless universe, and like her husband, she grapples with the concept of a malevolent deity. *Frankenstein* and *The Last Man* depict in stark terms the consequences of divine hatred, finally positioning human companionship as the antidote to divine vengefulness. In her novel

*Valperga*, she also explores both the possibilities and the limitations of dualism, considering in Beatrice the implications of Manichaean philosophy in an age of institutional Christianity. Her depictions of religion therefore draw on many different sources, including her father's Calvinist upbringing and deistic leanings, her mother's engagement with Rational Dissent, and her husband's anti-Christian sentiment and interest in alternative belief systems. Unlike her husband and father, however, she never abandoned a general faith in God.[98]

Beyond her immediate familial circle, Shelley was also deeply influenced by early nineteenth-century advances in science. The discovery of electricity in the mid-eighteenth century enabled the rise of a new branch of medical science, "medical electricity," or "the therapeutical application of electricity" to treat diseases resistant to other remedies.[99] In the 1740s, Benjamin Franklin postulated that electricity was a single fluid, and his theories circulated broadly in Italy, where they were applied to the study of anatomy. Prior to the 1750s, scientists believed in "the existence of a fluid matter, named 'animal spirits' or 'nervous fluid,' which was produced in the brain. Animal spirits flew from the brain through nerves to produce muscular contractions."[100] By the 1750s, however, scientists like Albrecht van Haller (1708–1777) had begun to differentiate between nerve impulses and voluntary muscular contractions, while anatomist Tommaso Laghi (1709–1764) argued that "muscular contractions were brought about by a fluid flowing through nerves and having an electrical nature."[101] This "neuro-electrical theory" was also promoted by Luigi Galvani (1737–1798), chief of the Bolognese College of Physicians. According to Galvani, death resulted when the blood no longer circulated, ceasing "its friction on the brain and nerves which produces the electrical fluid."[102] Life is thus explained by a series of electrical impulses, mechanical processes divorced from a conception of the soul or divinity.

By the mid-1780s, Galvani had become famous for his electrical experiments on frogs, which, he wrote in his *Commentaries*, were "cut transversally below their upper limbs, skinned and disemboweled," and then attached to a metal hook on an iron railing.[103] During electrical storms, the frogs would begin to twitch, proving, for Galvani, the existence of the "vital fluid that circulated within their bodies," as he proudly demonstrated during public dissections in 1780 and 1786.[104] His findings were challenged, however, by Alessandro Volta (1745–1827), inventor of the electric battery. Volta re-created Galvani's experiments, only to discover that "it was not the frogs that possessed the so-called vital fluid. . . . What actually made them twitch was the metal of the outside apparatus that Galvani used."[105] As Richard Sha explains, "Where Galvani believed that he had discovered a new form of electricity, Volta insisted that such animal electricity was merely artificial, a man-made electricity caused by the connection between two metals. Thus what Galvani equated with life was from Volta's perspective only mechanical electricity."[106] Galvani and Volta argued publicly until Galvani's death in 1798, but Volta eventually won out. Galvani died in disgrace, his most well-known theory disproven, and his academic titles stripped away by the French, to whom he refused to swear allegiance.

If Volta disproved the theory of "animal electricity," Galvani's nephew, Giovanni Aldini, was determined to redeem his uncle's legacy. In 1802, he traveled to London, where he sought permission to experiment on a human cadaver, with the goal of resuscitating the dead. The desire to resurrect the dead had been a preoccupation of British scientists since 1774, when physicians William Hawes and Thomas Cogan founded the Royal Humane Society (initially the "Institution for affording immediate relief to persons apparently dead from drowning"). The Humane Society promulgated techniques for saving the recently deceased, including warming the body and performing mouth-to-mouth resuscitation.[107] Such techniques had a direct impact on Shelley's life; her mother was apparently saved by a member of the society after her second suicide attempt. Aldini approached the Humane Society for help with his experiments. He "hoped that the men of the society would provide him much-needed validation for his contraptions, as well as support, and introductions to the even more refined society of London."[108] Aldini was successful in his plan, and in 1803 he arranged to perform a public experiment on the body of George Forster, a convicted murderer executed for killing his wife and infant child.

A strong distrust of scientific research pervaded the culture of the later eighteenth and early nineteenth centuries. As dead bodies could be procured legally only in cases of execution, grave robbing and even murder for hire provided avenues for continued research. "We murder to dissect," Wordsworth would write in 1798.[109] Despite the fact that the evidence against George Forster was largely circumstantial, and his confession likely coerced, the Royal College of Surgeons took possession of his corpse on January 17, 1803. In front of a large audience, "Aldini attached metallic rods to the corpse's face and body."[110] Electricity was then applied, with immediate results. According to the *Newgate Calendar*, "on the first application of the arcs the jaw began to quiver, the adjoining muscles were horrible contorted, and the left eye actually opened."[111] The crowd witnessed a "convulsive action of all the muscles of the face."[112] The sight was so horrifying to spectators that "Mr Pass, the beadle of the Surgeons' Company, who was officially present during this experiment, was so alarmed that he died soon after his return home of the fright."[113] Despite these encouraging (albeit terrifying) signs of life, however, Forster was not restored to the living, leading Aldini to conclude that his galvanic instruments were not strong enough: "With a much stronger apparatus we might have observed muscular actions much longer," he wrote in his notes.[114]

Percy Shelley was still a child when Aldini conducted his experiments, but he was fascinated from a young age with scientific and electrical experiments. According to Hogg, Percy kept in his rooms at Oxford "an electrical machine, an air pump, the galvanic trough" and "a solar microscope."[115] He attended scientific lectures and "knew passages from" Humphrey Davy's "published lectures almost by heart."[116] Mary Shelley records in her journal on December 28, 1814, that she attended a lecture on electricity with Percy: "Shelley and Clary out all the morning. Read French Revolution—in the evening. S. & I go to Gray's Inn to get Hogg—he is not there—go to arundel Street—cant find him—go to Garnerin's lecture—on Electricity—the gasses—& the Phantasmagoria—return at ½ past nine Shelley goes to sleep."[117] This lecture was delivered by Andrew Crosse, a scientist who studied "the formation of crystals under the influence of electricity," and who in the 1830s would become infamous for observing "the appearance of life in immediate connection with his voltaic arrangements."[118] Mary Shelley was therefore quite familiar with the scientific developments of her day, although she downplays her knowledge in her preface to the 1831 *Frankenstein*; she describes herself as a witness to her husband's conversations with Byron on the topics of galvanism and "the principle of life": "Many and long were the conversations between Lord Byron and Shelley, to which I was a devout but nearly silent listener. During one of these, various philosophical doctrines were discussed, and among others the nature of the principle of life, and whether there was any probability of its ever being discovered and communicated. . . . Perhaps a corpse would be re-animated; galvanism had given token of such things" (*Frankenstein* [1831], 179). The themes underlying *Frankenstein*—the power of humans to usurp God's authority through science, the power of electricity to create and sustain life, and the power of science to discover the source of living motion—all draw on the scientific currents that so fascinated both Shelley and her husband.[119]

Given Crosse's influence on Shelley's novel, it is ironic that in the late 1830s, Crosse would be "accused of being a Frankenstein";[120] the character that Crosse once influenced became a weapon used against his own research. The *Leader and Saturday Analyst* wrote of his experiments that "the general public felt a thrill of horror at the idea of a Frankenstein asserting that he had 'created' a Louse."[121] Crosse's work, like that of Galvani and Aldini, was viewed as threatening in part because it challenged religious understandings of the world. Developments in late eighteenth- and early nineteenth-century science gave rise to a contentious controversy between materialists—people who believed that life was the product of biological processes, chemical reactions, and electrical impulses—and vitalists, who believed in some divine spark, an ineffable soul existing apart from anatomical realities. When the members of the Royal Humane Society promoted resurrection techniques, for instance, they promulgated the idea that life was rooted in biology and that it could be restored by skillful aid. One pamphlet printed in 1786 offered the following instructions for reviving the recently drowned, an early form of CPR: "Apply the pipe of a common sized bellows up the nostril, and blow with some force, closing the other nostril and mouth, while a third person gently presses the chest with his hands as son [*sic*] as the lungs are inflated."[122] Were such techniques proven successful, the religious implications would be profound. In 1777, a reader queried the *Gentleman's Magazine*, "Now, as it is the general received opinion, that when a man dies, the instant he becomes dead his soul quits the body, and departs into a state of spiritual existence; how, or by what cause, or means, does the emptying these bodies of the water, and warming and diluting the blood so as to get it into circulation yet again . . . bring back the *soul* from its state of spiritual existence and be united with the body again?"[123] Readers wanted to know: Where did the soul go between death and resurrection? Was life simply the result of biological processes, or was there a spirit that existed independent of the body, without which humans were just so much meat?

For vitalists of the early nineteenth century, the materialist focus on biology was profoundly disturbing and reminiscent of French atheism. In *Consolations in Travel* (1830), Humphry Davy writes, "The doctrine of the *materialists* was always, even in my youth, a cold, heavy, dull and insupportable doctrine to me, and necessarily tending to atheism."[124] In 1808, therefore, the Animal Chemistry Society "was founded by Royal Society members, including Humphry Davy, who shared reactionary and conservative political views."[125] In contrast to the Royal Humane Society, the Animal Chemistry Society devoted itself to the study of organic chemistry from a vitalist perspective. According to David Knight, members of the Animal Chemistry Society shared the belief that "the phenomena of life cannot be 'reduced' to or fully explained by the laws of chemistry."[126] As Davy wrote, "The laws of dead and living nature appear to be perfectly distinct: material powers are made subservient to the purposes of life, and the elements of matter are newly arranged in living organs; but they are merely the instruments of a superior principle."[127] Without the soul, without some spark that exists beyond human comprehension, there can be no life.

In the second decade of the nineteenth century, the conflict between vitalist and materialist science played out in a very public battle between John Abernethy, "a prominent member of the Royal College of Surgeons," and his "erstwhile pupil," William Lawrence.[128] Drawing on the work of Scottish surgeon John Hunter, Abernethy argued in an 1814 lecture that life was more than the sum of its biological parts: "The matter of animals and vegetables is . . . common matter, it is inert; so that the necessity of supposing the superaddition of some subtile and mobile substance is apparent."[129] Two years later, William Lawrence responded to Abernethy with the argument that bodily reality is all, that "there was no separate 'principle of life' independent of the body."[130] According to Lawrence, "The vital properties of living bodies correspond to the physical properties of inorganic bodies; such as cohesion, elasticity, &c. . . . Life is the assemblage of all the functions, and the general result of their exercise."[131] Lawrence's lecture was perceived as an attack on the religious underpinnings of Abernethy's beliefs. Caldwell explains, "The conservative press caricatured the debate as a duel between transcendentalist religion and materialist science. Abernethy was promoted as a believing scientist, protecting the domain of the immaterial soul, whereas Lawrence was denounced as a French-influenced materialist, hostile to religion."[132] Ultimately, Lawrence was suspended from the Royal College of Physicians, and his membership was reinstated only when he retracted his writings publicly. "Further experience and reflection have only tended to convince me more strongly that the publication of certain passages in these writings was *highly improper*; to increase my *regret* at having sent them forth to the world; to make me satisfied with the measure of withdrawing them from public circulation; and consequently firmly resolved, not only never to reprint them, but also never to publish any thing more on similar subjects," he wrote in a letter printed by the *Monthly Repository of Theology and General Literature*.[133]

Lawrence's career recovered; he went on to serve as personal physician to Queen Victoria, regaining his position within the conservative medical establishment. In the early nineteenth century, however, Lawrence's lectures were deeply challenging to religious orthodoxy, and the controversy surrounding his work left its mark on Mary Shelley, who was undoubtedly familiar with the dispute. Percy Shelley "attended Dr. John Abernethy's lectures in anatomy at St. Bartholomew's Hospital with his cousin John Grove," and Lawrence was personal physician and "close friend" to both Percy and Mary Shelley.[134] Mary Shelley's familiarity with Lawrence's work is also reflected in *Frankenstein*. Lawrence "served as one of the models for" *Frankenstein*'s Professor Waldman, and the creature's construction may be viewed as philosophically materialist, a collection of discrete biological processes assembled to create life.[135] Yet Shelley was equally influenced by the vitalist works of Davy and Galvani, and unlike Lawrence, Mary Shelley does not adopt a fully materialist position. There is a spark in the creature that gives him life apart from his assembled parts. The novel also lays bare the "horrific consequences" of "Victor's materialism," which "sees merely *with* the eye, devoid of a conscience."[136] In this way, *Frankenstein* reflects Shelley's awareness of contemporary scientific debates and their religious implications.

Shelley was a prodigious reader, and she recorded exhaustive reading lists in her early journals. Central to her readings were the works of John Milton, which were popular with many writers of Shelley's generation. In the late seventeenth century, Milton was known more for his radical politics than for his poetry; as James Winn explains, upon its 1667 publication, *Paradise Lost* was "regarded by many as an odd effusion from a notorious regicide."[137] By the eighteenth century, however, his poetry was being celebrated as England's answer to the classical epic, and by the end of the century, conservatives and radicals alike were claiming him as an intellectual forebear. Conservatives embraced Milton's Christian orthodoxy, distancing him "from the revolutionary turmoil of the past" and insisting to readers that he "had been a saintly man with few real interests except writing religious poetry, defending 'liberty,' and loving God."[138] For supporters of the French Revolution, by contrast, Milton's politics modeled defiance in defeat and the triumph of individual will over despotism. In the wake of the French Revolution's failure, his works offered both "consolation for the thwarted liberal aspirations of a post-revolutionary era" and a model for continued resistance.[139]

Second generation Romantics particularly venerated Milton's Satan as *Paradise Lost*'s true hero, rebelling against a cruel, arbitrary, and illegitimate God. "The reason Milton wrote in fetters when he wrote of Angels & God, and at liberty when of Devils & Hell, is because he was a true Poet and of the Devil's party without knowing it," William Blake famously wrote of *Paradise Lost*.[140] A generation later, Percy Shelley took a similar approach to Milton in his "Defence of Poetry" (1821), expounding at length on Satan's sublimity and God's wickedness:

> Nothing can exceed the energy and magnificence of the character of Satan as expressed in Paradise Lost. It is a mistake to suppose that he could ever have been intended for the popular personification of evil. . . . Milton's Devil as a moral being is as far superior to his God, as one who perseveres in some purpose which he has conceived to be excellent in spite of adversity and torture, is to one who in the cold security of undoubted triumph inflicts the most horrible revenge upon his enemy, not from any mistaken notion of inducing him to repent of a perseverance in enmity, but with the alleged design of exasperating him to deserve new torments.[141]

Milton's God is defined by his maliciousness toward his creations and his lust for vengeance. By contrast, with his claim that "the mind is its own place, and in it self / Can make a Heav'n of Hell, a Hell of Heav'n," and his declaration that in Pandaemonium, "Here at least / We shall be free," Satan embodies heroism in defeat and a refusal to submit, in mind if not in body.[142]

According to Peter L. Thorslev Jr., Satan appealed to the late Romantics for a number of reasons: "Some of the doctrines closest to the romantic's heart have a philosophical or psychological affinity with Satanism: the doctrine of the self-sufficiency of the individual mind . . . the doctrine of the creativity of mind . . . and, finally, the doctrine of the ultimate freedom of mind, not merely in its independence of time or place, but in that ultimate (and existentialist) sense in which the mind is free to create itself, to exist beyond good and evil."[143] Satan came to represent artistic creativity unshackled, individual subjectivity celebrated. He was also increasingly "associated with romantic rebellion in the name of the new humanist self-assertion."[144] In Romantic discourse, he was often entwined with the figure of Prometheus, another popular avatar of heroic suffering in defeat. Prometheus, the Titan who stole fire from the gods only to be punished by Zeus with eternal torment, was "a fundamentally political icon" for the later Romantics.[145] The Prometheus myth provided a vocabulary for understanding the horrific violence of the Napoleonic Wars, and Byron and Percy Shelley both depicted Prometheus as "a spokesman for the oppressed."[146] "Thy Godlike crime was to be kind," Byron writes in his poem "Prometheus"; the Titan sought "To render with thy precepts less / The sum of human wretchedness," and in return, is rewarded with "A silent suffering, and intense / . . . All that the proud can feel of pain," forbidden "even the boon to die."[147] Rejecting the longstanding Christian emphasis on eternal life as a triumph over death—the "O death, where is thy sting? O grave, where is thy victory?" of 1 Corinthians[148]—Byron instead locates victory in resistance despite pain, and in the nothingness that exists beyond the grave. Byron's Prometheus maintains

> a firm will, and a deep sense,
> Which even in torture can descry
> Its own concenter'd recompense,
> Triumphant where it dares defy,
> And making Death a Victory.[149]

Just as Milton's Satan embraces hellish suffering in the name of freedom, Prometheus defies Zeus by accepting his pain and anticipating oblivion. In both cases, separation from the tyrant is not a punishment but a form of victory.

Milton's Satan and Prometheus, his "brother rebel against God," are the artistic precursors to the Byronic hero that became so popular in the early nineteenth century.[150] They were also deeply influential on Shelley's *Frankenstein*. Shelley records in her diary multiple evenings spent reading *Paradise Lost* with Percy, and it is clear from both the novel's subtitle—"the Modern Prometheus"—and its Miltonic epigraph that she had Prometheus and Satan in mind when she composed her famous text. According to Burton Hatlen, "*Frankenstein* is at least in part a commentary on and amplification of *Paradise Lost*."[151] Frankenstein's monster is at once Milton's Satan, Milton's Adam, and Milton's

Eve, while Victor alternately stands in for the mythological Zeus and Milton's distant, cruel God. As we shall see in chapter 3, however, Shelley's commentary is refracted both through her experiences as a woman in nineteenth-century England and through her own personal interest in the concept of divine cruelty and neglect.[152]

Also central to this study is Mary Shelley's engagement with the works of Constantin François de Chasseboeuf, Comte de Volney, whose *Les Ruines, ou méditations sur les révolutions des empire* was published in France in 1791 and translated into English as *The Ruins of Empire* by James Marshall, a good friend of Godwin's.[153] Written during the turbulent years of the French Revolution, Volney's *Ruins* radically undermines religious understandings of the universe and attributes the rise and fall of empires not to a divine plan but to human viciousness, self-interest, and greed. The text begins with an unnamed narrator who "journeyed in the empire of the Ottomans, and traversed the provinces which formerly were kingdoms of Egypt and of Syria."[154] Everywhere he travels, he sees devastation, "fields abandoned by the plough, villages deserted, and cities in ruins," along with the "wrecks of temples, palaces, and fortifications; pillars, aqueducts, sepulchres."[155] As the speaker mourns the loss of a once great civilization, he questions the religious significance of the devastation. Why would God, he wonders, allow the destruction of his true believers? "Why . . . is this race, beloved of the Divinity, deprived of the favours which were formerly showered upon the Heathen? Why do these lands, consecrated by the blood of the martyrs, no longer boast their former temperature and fertility?"[156] The narrator is then attended by an apparition, who announces that devastation is caused not by divine decree, but by man's own inhumanity. "How long will man importune the heavens with unjust complaint? How long, with vain clamours, will he accuse Fate as the author of his calamities?"[157] Man would blame something outside himself—fate, God, nature—for the evils that befall him, when in fact, his own disposition is to blame: "The source of his calamities is not the distant heavens, but bear to him upon the earth: it is not concealed in the bosom of the Divinity; it resides in himself, man bears it in his heart."[158] Suffering comes not from a distant God but from man's predatory constitution.

Volney's *Ruins* traces "the inauguration of utopia through a gradual, intellectual revolution,"[159] but in the process, it evinces doubts about human nature and adopts an atheist view of the world. The natural world, here personified as a sentient force, takes no pleasure in protecting the human race but instead leaves man to his own devices. Nature is not a benevolent mother, offering her bounty to her children with love. "I owe you nothing, I give you life," she says.[160] Nor is there a benevolent father-God watching over man's actions. Indeed, humans believe in God only because they are inculcated with such beliefs as children: "Imposed by force and authority, inculcated by education, maintained by the influence of example, [religious dogmas] were perpetuated from age to age."[161] There is no Mother Nature or God the Father to protect us.

For Volney, "all religious systems were products of history and culture rather than the hand of God."[162] Thus he adopts in *Ruins* the perspective of a non-Christian outsider to defamiliarize belief, retelling Bible stories in a tone of deep incredulity.

> God (after having passed an eternity without doing any thing) conceived at length the design (without apparent motive) of forming the world out of nothing . . . that these first parents having yielded to temptation, all their race (as yet unborn) were condemned to suffer the penalty of a fault which they had no share in committing: that after permitting the human species to damn themselves for four or five thousand years, this God of compassion ordered his well-beloved son, engendered without a mother and of the same age as himself, to descend upon the earth in order to be put to death, and this for the salvation of mankind, the majority of whom have nevertheless continued in the road to sin and damnation: that to remedy this inconvenience, this God, the son of a woman, who was at once a mother and a virgin, after having died and risen again, commences a new existence every day, and under the form of a morsel of

dough is multiplied a thousand-fold at the pleasure of the basest of mankind.[163]

Read in this light, biblical narrative sounds incredible, even ridiculous, a fact Volney emphasizes further by pointing out that there is no one left alive who witnessed the miracles of the Bible. "As we are none of us certain of what passed yesterday, of what is passing this very day before our eyes, how can we swear to the truth of what happened two thousand years ago?"[164] What man mistakes for God is simply a series of natural, scientifically explainable phenomena, "the physical powers of nature, the elements, the winds, the meteors, the stars, all of which have been personified by the necessary mechanism of language."[165] There is no God, merely science and nature and a human race left to thrive or die on its own merits.

The themes of Volney's *Ruins*, the absent God and hostile Mother Nature, the reduction of religious concepts to scientific principles, and man's inhumanity to man, all deeply influenced the first part of Shelley's career.[166] *Ruins* shows up explicitly in *Frankenstein* when the creature overhears Felix de Lacey instructing Safie from the text. "The book from which Felix instructed Safie was Volney's *Ruins of Empires*. . . . Through this work I obtained a cursory knowledge of history and a view of the several empires at present existing in the world." The creature learns from Volney about human nature and human government: "Was man, indeed, at once so powerful, so virtuous and magnificent, yet so vicious and base? He appeared at one time a mere scion of the evil principle and at another as all that can be conceived of noble and godlike."[167] Ultimately, then, *Frankenstein* dramatizes some of the themes of *Ruins*. As we shall see in chapter 3, *Frankenstein*'s is a world in which God is absent, religion has been replaced by science, and ruination stems not from divine retribution but from human fallibility. Victor's failure of compassion for his creature precipitates the novel's tragedy. For Shelley, as for Volney, man destroys himself.

To read Mary Shelley's works is to see religious beliefs drawn from and shaped by many sources—the writings of her (quite philosophically distinct) parents and peers, the philosophy and literature she consumed, and the religious and scientific controversies of her day. In the chapters that follow, we will trace in her works a pathway from doubt to despair to domestic contentment. This path correlates with an increasing trend of gender conservatism in nineteenth-century England. It is also reflective, we shall see, of Shelley's increasing embrace of the feminine religious heritage of her mother over the doubts of her father and husband.

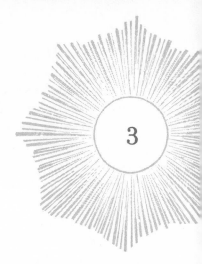

# DOUBT

Mary Shelley's *Frankenstein* is a novel of religious doubt. In building his creature, Victor Frankenstein usurps the functions of both the maternal and the divine, and in the process, he raises questions about the nature of God himself. What if, the text asks, God is not the loving father described in the New Testament, but instead a Victor disgusted by his own creation? What if he has fled humanity, leaving us alone in a world of chaos and injustice? What if he actively seeks our destruction? *Frankenstein* is, of course, Shelley's most famous work. It has been the subject of hundreds of critical studies, ranging from examinations of gender roles, post-Revolutionary politics, and the depiction of science and nature, to treatments of the legal system, the Romantic ethos, and imperial expansion.[1] It also sets up the religious themes that would preoccupy Shelley throughout her career. In the story of Justine, she criticizes patriarchal organized religion, which uses the threat of divine retribution to manipulate, control, and punish female bodies. In the story of Victor and his creature, she draws on both the atheist beliefs that preoccupied her husband and the Calvinist milieu in which her father was raised, emphasizing the prospects of divine neglect or malevolence. She also considers the possibility for human happiness in a world without divine love, suggesting that in the absence of religious sureties, the ways in which humans treat one another become all the more important. Human relationships and kindness are paramount when God's love is no longer assured.

These themes—distrust for organized religion, especially in regard to women; doubt about the nature and role of the divine; and an emphasis on interpersonal relations—will characterize Shelley's work throughout her career. This chapter thus examines three of Shelley's early works, *Frankenstein* (1818), "Valerius: The Reanimated Roman" (written ca. 1819), and *Mathilda* (written 1819–20), all of which examine in different ways the concept of divine absence. "Valerius," like *Frankenstein*, tells the story of an unnatural creature, in this case, a Roman soldier brought back to life in Shelley's contemporary moment. Amid the ruins of ancient Rome, Valerius mourns the family and friends he has lost, the Roman Republic that has fallen to dust, and the remnants of a once-dominant religion now supplanted by Christianity. While the Vatican historically encouraged the preservation of Roman ruins as proof of the church's triumph over paganism, "Valerius" instead employs them as a symbol of mutability. Just as the Roman religion gave way to Christianity, that religion, too, may one day pass. There is no eternal truth in the Christian God, just a constantly shifting series of belief systems.

Written in the wake of several personal tragedies, *Mathilda*, a story of patriarchal failure, also subtly develops the themes put forth in *Frankenstein* and "Valerius." The characters of *Mathilda* live in a peculiarly unreligious world; neither Mathilda nor her father receives any sort of religious education, and God offers no aid or protection to either in their sufferings. *Mathilda* is thus a novel about absence, the lacunae left behind by Mathilda's deceased mother, her missing and later dead father, and the absent God who fails to protect them. It is also a novel about writing, about a search for human connection via the pen. In one sense, Mathilda is writing into a void; she knows that her words will not change her past or alter her future. On the other hand, as *Frankenstein*'s Walton finally discovers, there is consolation in human connection and the sharing of human language; Mathilda triumphs over the void by writing into it, a theme that will reappear in many of Shelley's works. By the time of *Mathilda*, then, Shelley had fully formulated the concerns that would preoccupy her throughout her literary career.

Mary Shelley lived among atheists and agnostics, and *Frankenstein* is marked by her interest in their ideas. *Frankenstein*'s characters do not live in a world of divine oversight. The characters refer occasionally to the devil—Victor views the creature as an infernal monster, his "demoniacal enemy"[2]—but God is largely absent. Religious language is instead repurposed. Victor's journey to the arctic to kill the creature is a "horrible pilgrimage" (*Frankenstein* [1818], 156), and both the monster and Victor refer to themselves as Miltonic fallen angels. Victor tells Walton, "like the archangel who aspired to omnipotence, I am chained in an eternal hell" (161), while the creature describes his relief at finding the De Laceys' cottage: "It presented to me then as exquisite and divine a retreat as Pandaemonium appeared to the daemons of hell after their sufferings in the lake of fire" (79). Here, biblical stories are made flesh, their mystical properties stripped away in the absence of a divine cosmology or the promise of an afterlife. Later, when little William dies, he is described as "livid and motionless" (51). There is no sense that he has gone to a better place, nor is there comfort to be found in proof of his heavenly reward.

Critics have long debated the extent of *Frankenstein*'s atheism, and the ways in which Percy Shelley altered the religious content of the text. Charles E. Robinson estimates that Percy wrote "over 4,000 (and probably over 5,000) of the novel's 72,000 words."[3] Anne K. Mellor describes his contributions: "He made many technical corrections and several times clarified the narrative and thematic continuity of the text; on other occasions he misunderstood his wife's intentions and distorted her ideas. Throughout he tried to elevate her prose style into a more Latinate idiom."[4] Certainly, Percy made a number of edits that influenced the religious ideology of the manuscript. To Mary Shelley's description of Victor's final pursuit of the creature as "a task enjoined by heaven" (*Frankenstein* [1818], 160), Percy added the phrase, "as the mechanical impulse of some power of which I was unconscious" (156), diminishing Victor's religious conviction. When Mary Shelley wrote of Victor's "daily prayers . . . for revenge," Percy struck the word "prayers," replacing it with "vows" (106). He also reworked his wife's description of the creature's demise. Mary Shelley described the creature's belief that by consigning himself to the funeral pyre, "the flame that consumes my body will give rest & blessings to my mind." Percy changed "rest & blessings" to "enjoyment or tranquility," stripping out the promise of God's forgiveness.[5] He subsequently returned to that passage, adding an additional layer of religious uncertainty. "My spirit will sleep in peace; or if it thinks, it will not surely think thus" (170), the creature exclaims in the final published version, suggesting that the creature does not accept the certainty of a Christian afterlife.[6]

Nature, too, is stripped of religious significance in the novel. Certainly, the natural world provokes in many of the characters the experience of the sublime. Victor says of the valley of Chamounix, "Mont Blanc, the supreme and magnificent Mont Blanc, raised itself from the surrounding *aiguilles*, and its tremendous *dome* overlooked the valley" (*Frankenstein* [1818], 71). But that experience is not linked with religious devotion. Indeed, there is an emptiness to nature that runs throughout *Frankenstein*, one that will be tempered in later works like *The Last Man* (where nature is a malevolent mother, "a menacing figure with the agency for apocalyptic revenge"[7]) and *Lodore* (where nature is linked with a sanctified maternal spirit). Victor finds comfort in nature—at Lausanne, "the waters were placid; all around was calm. . . . By degrees the heavenly scene restored me" (53)—and he tries to find meaning in natural events. As a thunderstorm rages, Victor "clasped my hands, and exclaimed aloud, 'William, dear angel! this is thy funeral, this thy dirge!'" (54). Victor wants to believe that nature responds to his moods and mourns his brother alongside him, but the text offers no external confirmation of this belief. Nature simply is, beyond Victor, beyond intentionality, beyond religious faith.

Shelley's interest in nature reflects a broader cultural interest in the relationship between nature and man. The eruption of Mount Tambora in 1816 led to the coldest summer in recorded British history and precipitated a series of crop failures. Percy Shelley describes in the preface to the 1818 *Frankenstein* the "cold and rainy" season that accompanied the composition of his wife's novel (*Frankenstein* [1818],

8), while Shelley herself described the unseasonable Genevan weather in a letter written to Fanny Imlay on May 17, 1816: "The spring, as the inhabitants informed us, was unusually late, and indeed the cold was excessive; as we ascended the mountains, the same clouds which rained on us in the vallies [sic] poured forth large flakes of snow thick and fast."[8] As Lord Byron wrote in his poem "Darkness," produced during the summer of 1816, "Morn came and went—and came, and brought no day."[9] In this context, many were convinced that the end was nigh, that the apocalypse was approaching, and that nature was conspiring with God to wipe out humanity.[10] It functions apart from biblical timelines, a series of scientific phenomena that elude man's understanding, but which are not necessarily linked with a supervising deity.

Shelley's interest in stripping nature of its religious significance is reflective not only of her cultural moment or her husband's beliefs, but of the scientific developments of the early nineteenth century.[11] Mary Shelley clearly draws on her husband's knowledge of and interest in galvanism, discussed in chapter 1, depicting the power of electricity to create life. She also draws on the Lawrence-Abernethy debate discussed in chapter 2, ultimately creating in the novel a materialist view of life that earned her criticism in the popular press. At the same time, Calvinist overtones pervade the text, echoes of the belief system in which her father had been inculcated, even if it was one to which he no longer subscribed. According to Jane Goodall, "The premises of Calvinism set a complex and inescapable trap for the anxious mind. Every human life was predetermined by God to set a course toward salvation or damnation. The saved or 'the elect' were a tiny minority (statistics are given variously as one in a hundred, one in a thousand and one in a million) and the damned or 'reprobate' could do little about their predicament, which had been decided before birth."[12] As Goodall has persuasively argued, Calvinist beliefs resonate throughout *Frankenstein*. When, for instance, Victor and his creature both speak of the hell they nurse within, they refer not only to Milton, but to the words of William Perkins, an early proponent of English Calvinism: the reprobate "carrieth an hell about him in his life."[13] *Frankenstein*'s Calvinism is thus filtered through the lens of both Godwin's upbringing and Milton's Puritanism. That Victor views himself as preternaturally destined for destruction also invokes a Calvinist worldview. "Some destiny of the most horrible kind hangs over me, and I must live to fulfil it," he tells his father (*Frankenstein* [1818], 139), gesturing toward Calvin's insistence that some people are "devoted from the womb to certain death, that [God's] name may be glorified in their destruction."[14] Victor is the victim not only of his own uncontrollable urges, but of a destiny he cannot avert. Likewise, the creature's malevolence is the product both of Victor's negligence and of the creature's own reprobation. As Goodall points out, Calvin refers repeatedly to reprobates as "monsters" in his *Institutes*, and he emphasizes their physical ugliness, suggesting that the creature may have been predestined to behave as he did.[15]

It is not possible within Calvinism to know conclusively whether one has been born elect or damned, and Calvin discourages the individual from probing God's will. According to Goodall, "God's reasons for selecting one person to be saved and another to be damned were beyond human comprehension; seeking to penetrate the secrets of divine reasoning was itself a sign of reprobation."[16] The result for some was an overwhelming sense of despair; as Goodall points out, the suicide rate in Europe sharply increased as Calvinist doctrine spread.[17] When Frankenstein's creature cries out to the father who has abandoned him, then, he speaks for all of the reprobate, the seemingly arbitrarily rejected. Read in this light, *Frankenstein* expresses a profound fear not of the excesses of scientific creation, but of a world in which God's love is neither guaranteed nor able to be earned. Underlying Shelley's depiction of religion is a Calvinist fear of a distant or spiteful God, whose hatred for individual creatures cannot be understood by human logic.

As a stand-in for the Calvinist God or, in Leslie Tannenbaum's words, "a distorted version of Milton's God," Victor Frankenstein proves himself a bad patriarch.[18] Horrified by his creature's ugliness, he abandons his creation, abjuring his responsibility to love the being to whom he gave life. "I ought to be thy Adam; but I am rather the fallen angel, whom thou drivest from joy for no misdeed" (*Frankenstein* [1818], 74), the creature chastises Victor. The creature cries out for his father's love, turning evil only in the absence of human kindness. "I was benevolent and good; misery made me a fiend. Make me happy, and I shall again be virtuous" (74). As the unwanted, unloved child of a cruel creator, the creature likens himself to Milton's Satan, rebelling against the God that gave him life.

> Like Adam, I was created apparently united by no link to any other being in existence; but his state was far different from mine in every other respect. He had come forth from the hands of God a perfect creature, happy and prosperous, guarded by the especial care of his Creator; he was allowed to converse with, and acquire knowledge from beings of a superior nature: but I was wretched, helpless, and alone. Many times I considered Satan as the fitter emblem of my condition; for often, like him, when I viewed the bliss of my protectors, the bitter gall of envy rose within me. (97)[19]

In his encounters with Victor, however, he raises a troubling possibility for readers: What guarantee is there, the text implicitly asks, that our own universe is overseen by a benevolent deity? What if our world is overseen by a being that looks on humanity as Victor Frankenstein looks on his monster? What if we, too, are a mistake, an abomination? Shelley would return repeatedly to these questions throughout the first decade of her career.

If the "narrative of *Frankenstein* is . . . acted out in the absence of God," and fathers are ineffectual or malign, then mothers are displaced entirely, often violently.[20] As many critics have argued, *Frankenstein*'s is a world in which mothers do not survive, and where women's bodies are destroyed at the hands of men.[21] Victor Frankenstein's mother dies at a young age, leaving behind Elizabeth Lavenza, a beloved cousin, to fulfill the maternal function. "Elizabeth, my love, you must supply my place to your younger cousins" (*Frankenstein* [1818], 29), Caroline instructs.[22] Through union with Elizabeth, that "predictable self-sacrificing female entity which preserves domestic bliss,"[23] Victor could reconstruct the loving family circle lost with his mother's death. With Elizabeth, he could also eschew the masculine world of monstrous science and reembrace natural modes of procreation. Instead, in creating his monster, in procreating without a mother, Victor precipitates Elizabeth's death.

Her body is destroyed, "her head hanging down, and her pale and distorted features half covered by her hair" (150), a vicious response to Victor's decision to dismember the body of his female creature. Victor "tore to pieces the thing on which I was engaged" (129). According to Erin Hawley, "a female monster—a woman born of unnatural means, a creature both desirable and horrible—would have been too *much* of a boundary crossing, even within this tale about monstrosity and otherness," and as such, she must be destroyed.[24] *Frankenstein* thus tells the story of a failed patriarch doing violence to female bodies, another theme underlying many of Shelley's works.

If Victor Frankenstein as a malevolent God directly precipitates the destruction of the feminine, the novel also protests the treatment of women by organized religion. The priests and kings of Blake's cosmology are replicated in Shelley's work, leading to the deaths of innocent women at the hands of male power structures. *Frankenstein*'s Justine is one of the novel's biggest victims, failed first by the legal system, and later by a priest who coerces her into a false confession. "Ever since I was condemned," Justine explains, "my confessor has besieged me; he threatened and menaced, until I almost began to think that I was the monster that he said I was. He threatened excommunication and hell fire in my last moments, if I continued obdurate. Dear lady, I had none to support me; all looked on me as a wretch doomed to ignominy and perdition. What could I do? In an evil hour I subscribed to a lie; and now only am I truly miserable" (*Frankenstein* [1818], 62). Here, Shelley invokes the memory of her mother's work, as Wollstonecraft's Maria is also disbelieved in a court of law (in one potential ending at least), treated as an unreliable witness to her own experiences. Shelley's novel also recalls Godwin's skepticism toward the church and his discomfort with religious power structures. Shelley would revisit this skepticism of organized religion throughout her career—in *Valperga*, where the ethereal prophetess Beatrice is raped by a priest and condemned to death by men who do not listen to or understand female religious expression; in *The Last Man*, where a Methodist preacher takes advantage of the plague survivors' fears and gullibility; and in *Perkin Warbeck*, where the church becomes the center of political machinations against Richard, the rightful king. Justine's treatment at the hands of the priests thus represents Shelley's earliest protest of organized religion, in this case of female oppression at the hands of a structure designed by and for men.

At the end of the novel, the creature, disgusted by the world and finding that "there is no religious consolation, and there can be no salvation," removes himself from humanity by fleeing to the emptiness of the arctic wastes.[25] Victor, too, rejects humanity. With his family and friends destroyed, he is as isolated as the monster, and he removes himself from humankind to preserve what remains of his race. As a result, when he meets Walton, he is a man seeking nothingness. He rejects the possibility of friendship, and he desires only the violent death of his creation, followed by the end of his own existence. "I thank you," he tells Walton, "for your kind intentions toward so miserable a wretch; but when you speak of new ties, and fresh affections, think you that any can replace those who are gone? Can any man be to me as Clerval was; or any woman another Elizabeth?" (*Frankenstein* [1818], 161). Walton, like Victor, has eschewed family and friends in favor of scientific exploration and a desire to probe the secrets of the divine. Unlike Victor, however, Walton seeks communion with like minds. He has come to the arctic to test his own limits but has not relinquished his desire to find a friend, "someone to participate in his joy, whose eyes would reply to his, whose tastes would be like his own."[26] He tells his sister, "I bitterly feel the want of a friend. I have no one near me, gentle yet courageous, possessed of a cultivated as well as of a capacious mind, whose tastes are like my own, to approve or amend my plans." (13). Thus despite his grief at abandoning his "ideas of glory and honour" (164), he agrees to turn his ship back toward home. He tells Victor of his men, "I cannot lead them unwillingly into danger, and I must return" (165), finally locating meaning in service to and protection of others. Similar characters will appear in Shelley's later works: *Perkin Warbeck*'s Katherine will satisfy her religious duty through service to Henry VII's wife, while *Lodore*'s Ethel and *Falkner*'s Elizabeth will both find religious peace in family and friendship. Like Walton, they reject the idea of self-isolation, seeking value in human connection. This opposition, the beauty of humanity in the face of protonihilist nothingness, will follow Shelley throughout her career.

Central to Shelley's musings on humanity is a meditation on what it means to be an author in a world of uncertain divine presence. If, as Robert James LeCussan writes, "God, the creator, has so long abandoned us that he no longer takes any role in the story," then humanity must find meaning in other ways.[27] Walton is not merely a sailor; he is also a writer and a self-described failed poet. He tells his sister, "I also became a poet, and for one year lived in a Paradise of my own creation; I imagined that I almost might obtain a niche in the temple where the names of Homer and Shakespeare are consecrated. You are well acquainted with my failure, and how heavily I bore the disappointment" (*Frankenstein* [1818], 11). When he writes to his sister, he does so both to express his creative consciousness and to seek connection with another human mind, despite the vast expanse of the artic and the possibility that his writings will never make it to their intended targets: "I write to you, encompassed by peril, and ignorant whether I am ever doomed to see again dear England, and the dearer friends that inhabit it" (162). He writes his memoirs into what he recognizes may be a void, not knowing if his words will ever be read by another human being. "You will not hear of my destruction," he muses, "and you will anxiously await my return" (162). Still, he writes anyway, seeking that connection, that proof of mutual existence.

The power of writing as proof of humanity in a godless world is another motif that will run throughout Shelley's work. Mathilda, eponymous heroine of Shelley's next novel, will also write to connect, even without hope of an audience beyond Woodville. Most urgently of all, *The Last Man*'s Lionel will write his memoirs, knowing that no human beings remain to read what he has produced. The hope, of course, is that someone, someday will exist to acknowledge that Lionel—the human race itself—once existed and had value. Human minds matter, and consolation may be found in artistic creation. This is not writing as consolation in the (Percy) Shelleyan sense; Mary Shelley evinces no belief that writing will change the world. But there is value in artistic creation nonetheless, another theme she will develop over the course of her career.

In 1819, not long after the completion of *Frankenstein*, Mary Shelley turned her literary attentions to another sort of unnatural creature. "Valerius: The Reanimated Roman" tells the story of a man brought back to life thousands of years after his death, and it follows him as he marvels at and mourns the loss of his family and friends, nation, culture, and way of life. Valerius's story is conveyed twice, first as he relates his story to "an Englishman of rank" who meets him on his journey, and second by Isabell Harley, a married woman who serves as a protector of and mother figure to the Roman.[28] The story's tone is elegiac; Valerius can never return to the Rome he knew and recapture what he has lost, and the text ends without a conclusion. Valerius's story is a fragment as he himself is a fragment, a single remaining piece of a world that has passed on.

Central to Mary Shelley's depiction of Valerius is her interest in Roman ruins as remnants of the culture that was. The story begins with a description of a bay "formed by the extreme point of Cape Miseno and the promontory of Bauli," in which "you saw . . . the remnants of the palaces of the Romans now buried under the waters" ("Valerius," 332). Ruins are thus foregrounded from the beginning of the story, physical proof of the world Valerius left behind, and a jumping off point for his internal meditations. The Coliseum in particular plays a central role in Valerius's world as the landmark that most clearly emblematizes Rome's fall. "The Coliseum is the Type of Rome," he explains (335). Mary Shelley was not alone in her fascination with Roman ruins. As early as the fifteenth century, European authors had treated "the sight of Roman ruins" as an "occasion for reflection on the folly of human pride and the vanity of worldly hopes."[29] The Roman Catholic Church, by contrast, interpreted those same ruins as proof of the church's triumph over paganism. In April 1472, Pope Pius II issued a bull forbidding the desecration of Roman ruins, in part because they served as a "continuous reminder that human works are fragile," and in part because they were useful visual symbols of the power of the church.[30]

By the mid-eighteenth century, the co-option of Roman ruins by the Catholic Church had become a commonly accepted phenomenon. According to the Vatican Museum's website, "The Popes viewed themselves as the legitimate heirs of Roman history. . . . The monuments of the Roman civilisation therefore had to be preserved, safeguarded and revered *ad maiorem Dei gloriam* and for the honour and glory of the Church."[31] Originally founded in the sixteenth century by Pope Julius

II (1503–13), the Vatican Museum was expanded significantly in the eighteenth century by Popes Benedict XIV (1740–58), Clement XIV (1769–74)—who founded the Pio-Clementine Museum—and Pius VI (1775–99), who oversaw multiple excavations throughout Rome. Central to the papal preservation of ruins was the desire to celebrate the might of Christianity, and to glorify the union of the church and the arts in Rome. As Alessandro De Sanctis wrote in a 1795 sonnet praising the excavation of Augustus's "sundial" obelisk, "Rome for eternity will be in the Vatican the mistress of the unconquered Faith, and the venerable seat of the arts."[32] Another anonymously authored sonnet of 1773 praised the discovery of a Roman sarcophagus: "A generous and lofty thought brings you to the happy protection of the Sovereign Pastor, thanks to whom, having shaken off the black and silent horror, you now shine forth bright and famous in the Vatican."[33] The Vatican represents the realization of the divine plan; through its incorporation of and triumph over the ruins of ancient Rome, the church "has finally prevailed over the vicissitudes of history."[34]

According to Carolyn Springer, authors interested in Roman ruins roughly wrote in three modes: the "encomiastic mode of the Church," popular among pro-Vatican authors who proclaimed the might of the church through the presence of ruins; "the exhortatory mode of the democratic opposition," authors who saw in the ruins the remnants of Rome's republican past; and elegiac authors, for whom the fall of Rome symbolized the temporality of all things. In England, the elegiac mode most frequently held sway, as an interest in Roman ruins swept the culture.[35] So great was the interest in archeological ruins that in 1816, the future George IV imported Roman ruins from Libya to create a facsimile of a ruined Roman temple in Windsor Great Park, part of an aristocratic fad for creating "fake ruins out of real ones."[36] For Romantic poets, the image of ruins offered an opportunity to meditate on "the relationship between the historical and the personal, the anxiety about permanence and ephemerality, the haunting of memory and melancholia, the experience of solitude and the sublime, and the conflict of tradition versus innovation."[37] From Percy Shelley's *Ozymandias* to Byron's *Childe Harold*, poetry featuring classical ruins proliferated, as authors used the decay of past civilizations alternatively to glorify or criticize the present moment. When Percy Shelley's traveler views the remnants of Ozymandias's once great and terrible empire, he reminds readers of the temporality of civilizations. "Round the decay / Of that colossal Wreck," the great symbol of the emperor's fearsome authority, "The lone and level sands stretch far away."[38]

Byron expounds on a similar theme in the fourth canto to *Childe Harold*. "The Niobe of nations," Rome is a monument to a civilization lost, collapsed under the weight of its own "Wealth, vice, corruption,— barbarism at last."[39] According to Mark Sandy, "For Byron both the posthumous reputations of cities or poetic selves are conditioned by a past that can never be fully known and are solely reliant on the whim of the historian to determine their glorious or inglorious legacies."[40] Rome thus serves as cautionary tale of the rise and fall of empires, and a reminder of an eternal cycle of individual insignificance. Byron, like Valerius, finds himself at the Coliseum, where he mourns Rome's ruin. "While stands the Coliseum, Rome shall stand; / When falls the Coliseum, Rome shall fall," Byron writes, paraphrasing Edward Gibbon's *The Decline and Fall of the Roman Empire*. Yet the Coliseum has collapsed to ruin, and with it the promise of Roman might. In the moonlight, the spectator can imagine that Rome carries on: "When the light shines serene but doth not glare, / Then in this magic circle raise the dead: / Heroes have trod this spot."[41] Yet in truth, "'t is on their dust ye tread."[42] The Coliseum remains a symbol of fallen might, the mutability of human enterprise, and like Ozymandias's statue, a monument to pride.

In contrast to Byron and Percy Shelley, other eighteenth-century authors used the image of ruins to warn their countrymen of oncoming doom. In 1742, clergyman Conyers Middleton wrote in his *Life of Cicero*,

> One cannot help reflecting on the surprising fate and rev-
> olutions of kingdoms; how Rome, once the mistress of the
> world, the seat of arts, empire and glory now lies sunk in
> sloth, ignorance and poverty . . . while this remote coun-
> try, the jest and contempt of polite Romans, is become the
> happy seat of liberty, plenty and letters; flourishing in all
> the arts and refinements of civil life; yet running perhaps

the same course which Rome itself had run before it, from virtuous history to wealth; from wealth to luxury; from luxury to an impatience of discipline and corruption of morals: till by a total degeneracy and loss of virtue, being grown ripe for destruction, it falls a prey at last to some hardy oppressor, and with the loss of liberty, losing every thing that is valuable, sinks gradually into its original barbarism.[43]

A similar concern underlies Anna Letitia Barbauld's *Eighteen Hundred and Eleven*, in which she stresses the cyclical nature of history and reminds her contemporaries that no empire lasts forever. As William Keach explains, she begins the poem "with critical alarm at the ruins of war and out of this shapes an elegiac future for British culture as ruin."[44] "Still the loud death drum, thundering from afar, / O'er the vext nations pours the storm of war," she begins ominously.[45] She then looks forward to a time in which the British Empire has gone the way of the Roman, in which only broken fragments of Englishness remain, and "London's faded glories" serve as a testament to what was lost.[46] In this future time, tourists visit the remnants of imperial England, treating the ruins of the city with the same combination of curiosity and veneration they now reserve for ancient Rome. "With throbbing bosoms shall the wanderers tread / The hallowed mansions of the silent dead, / Shall enter the long isle and vaulted dome / Where Genius and where Valour find a home."[47] The image of London's ruined future thus serves as a warning to Barbauld's contemporaries, a reminder of the fleetingness of imperial might; "while the ruins described in the poem may be projected into a distant future, the process of ruination has already begun in the present of the poem's composition."[48]

When Mary Shelley turned to the ruins of Rome in "Valerius," she drew on this broader cultural interest in the city as a symbol of mutability. The great and small alike fall before the effects of time, one empire giving way to the next, a truth Valerius confronts when he looks out on the ruins of his society. "When I died," he explains, "I was possessed by the strong persuasion that, since philosophy and letters were now joined to a virtue unparalleled upon earth, Rome was approaching that perfection from which there was no fall" ("Valerius," 336). What he discovers, however, is that no society, not even a virtuous, intellectual utopia, is safe from the ravages of time. Even during his own lifetime, Valerius admits, Rome was a city in decline. He was a soldier during the time of the second Cataline conspiracy, placing him historically just before the rise of Caesar and the fall of the Roman Republic. Valerius explains, "I did not live to see my country enslaved by Caesar, who during my life was distinguished only by the debauchery of his manners. I died when I was nearly forty-five, defending my country against Cataline" (333). But he acknowledges that the republic was already in trouble; Valerius lost both his father and his uncle in the civil wars of the previous generation: "Marius and Sulla had already taught us some of the miseries of tyranny, and I was accustomed to lament the day when the Senate appeared an assembly of demigods" (333). Valerius thus elegizes a Rome that had already functionally ceased to exist. All civilizations, even the best of civilizations, eventually fall, giving way to the next empire that ascends.[49]

In constructing her reanimated Roman, Shelley focuses heavily on the religious aspects of his loss, and in particular, she rejects the Vatican's propagandistic interest in claiming the fall of Rome as the church's triumph. For Shelley, the Vatican's victory is proof of mutability, not immortality. As he sits among the ruins of the Coliseum, it is not only Rome as a political entity that Valerius mourns, but the loss of Rome's ancient religious beliefs. He calls out to Jupiter, "who hast beheld so many triumphs," and begs Minerva to "protect thy Rome" ("Valerius," 334), but before him, only fragments of his religion remain, "the fallen images of the gods still left to decay in a spot where I had formerly worshipped them" (335). He also views the Elysian Fields, "the spot which was chosen by our antient and venerable religion, as that which best represented the idea oracles had given or diviners had received" (332–33), but the religious significance of the location has long since fallen away. Rome has been thoroughly Christianized, temples to Roman gods torn down and churches to Christ raised in their stead. The people "have lost all the characteristics of Romans; they have fallen off from her holy religion" (337). Worst of all, "Modern Rome is the Capital of Christianity" (337). From the top of the Coliseum, Valerius looks down on the Vatican and realizes that his world will never return:

"From its height, I beheld Rome sleeping under the cold rays of the moon: the dome of St. Peter's and the various other domes and spires which make a second city" (336). As Pope Pius II intended, the dome of St. Peter's towers over the remnants of the Elysian Fields. Thus Valerius parts company with the priest who has been his guide, determined to strike off on his own and be alone with his loss.

The theme of Valerius's lost religion returns again in Isabell's narrative, when she attempts to hearten Valerius by taking him to the Pantheon.[50] While she knows that "its conversion to a Catholic Church, although it had probably preserved it, would be highly disgusting to him" ("Valerius," 342), she hopes that sight of the mostly intact building will lighten Valerius's heart. Initially, it is a good moment, as the two sit and commune silently, he with his gods, she with God's presence in nature. Isabell describes the beauty of the Pantheon in terms very different from Valerius's. "If the work was human, the glory came from Nature; and Nature poured forth all her loveliness above this divine temple. The deep sky, the bright moon, and the twinkling stars were spread over it, and their light and beauty penetrated it" (342). Her description of the natural world is implicitly deist, as she feels "the existence of that Pantheic Love with which Nature is penetrated" (342). But the effect is spoiled, at least for Valerius, when Isabell unthinkingly points out to him the cross on an altar. Isabell admits that the "cross did not alter my feelings" (343), but for Valerius, it is proof again of his temporal displacement and Rome's fall. "The spell was snapped. The moon-enlightened dome, the glittering pavement, the dim rows of lovely columns, the deep sky had lost to him their holiness. He hastened to quit the temple" (343). Valerius does not, like Isabell, find a deistic peace in nature. The Roman gods are gone, and only Christianity remains.

While Valerius mourns the church's triumph, the story itself concludes with a very different insight into the religious symbolism of ruins; far from a symbol of Christian might, they actually undermine the church's claim to permanence. Christianity in Valerius's world has triumphed—for now. But if Valerius's religion, a religion that also once seemed immortal, has passed away, what is to ensure that the Catholic Church, or indeed, Christianity as a whole, will prove any more enduring?[51] Perhaps one day, the text forces its reader to imagine, an Englishman will awaken in an unforeseen future and find a new religion's officiant on the steps of St. Peter's where the popes were wont to tread. Maybe in that distant future, Christianity, too, will have become a relic, a quaint superstition. Implicit in that possibility is a diminishment of the significance of Christianity as a whole. If religion is not permanent, if it may one day grow or change or pass away from the earth, then it cannot lay claim to eternal truth and perfect wisdom. In this way, Shelley undermines Christian understandings of time and eternity; this is not a world moving inexorably toward a biblical apocalypse and millennium, but a world of cyclic triumphs and replacements. One religion disappears, ceding its place to the next ad nauseum in a world that does not anticipate a Christian conclusion.

Mary Shelley's "Valerius" threatens a world in which Christianity will be replaced, its claims to truth effaced. True religion, if such a thing exists, may be found only in the natural world. When Isabell communes with nature at the Pantheon, it is a more authentic moment of religious devotion than either pagan or Christian religious ceremonies. Mary Shelley would return to this theme in *The Last Man*, a novel that imagines the end of the world in terms that are neither Christian nor biblical. The natural world neither understands nor respects biblical timelines.

In 1819, Shelley began work on *Mathilda*, her first full-length work since the completion of *Frankenstein*. Conceived shortly after the June 1819 death of her son, William, *Mathilda* is a tale of grief and anger, of lonely mourning and comfortless sorrow. It is also a story in which God's absence is never mentioned, but it is palpably felt. No one can save Mathilda from her sad fate—death by slow suicide—not her father, who occasioned her misery, nor the poet, Woodville, who tries to cheer and redeem, nor even God himself, who becomes the implicit, unacknowledged third in a triad of male figures who fail adequately to lead and protect. *Mathilda* is a story of the failure of male leadership. It is also a story of a woman screaming into a void. There is no succor for her sufferings, and only writing provides a rudimentary form of peace.

Mary Shelley wrote *Mathilda* in a period of deep depression. At this point in time, Shelley was deeply angry with her husband, blaming him for her child's death and seeming failure to share in the depth of her grief. She was also disgusted with her father, William Godwin, who chastised her for what he considered an immoderate display of grief. It is therefore tempting to read *Mathilda* autobiographically as a novel of rage at Shelley's inability to change her world.[52] Godwin was so horrified by the content that he suppressed it, refusing to return the manuscript or submit it for publication, suggesting that he recognized that it was likely to be read through the lens of biography in its own day. Despite her personal tragedies, however, the novel should be read apart from her biography. *Mathilda*, as we shall see, develops themes that first appeared in *Frankenstein*, suggesting that Shelley had an intellectual purpose in the text that was not solely linked with personal suffering.

*Mathilda* is a novel characterized by absence. Mathilda, like Frankenstein's creature, grows up in what E. J. Clery calls "radical isolation."[53] Her parents' loss, her mother's death and father's abandonment, loom large over her youth. "I was a solitary being," she explains.[54] Mathilda's father's life is equally defined by absence, the loss of the wife whom he loved to the point of obsession. "He loved her with passion and her tenderness had a charm for him that would not permit him to think of aught but her. . . . He discarded his old friendships. . . . Diana filled up all his heart" (*Mathilda*, 9). Throughout the novel, lingering bits of language call attention to the absence of their composers. Growing up, Mathilda knew her father only through his portrait and his letters, which she treasured. "I copied his last letter and read it again and again. Sometimes it made me weep; and at other times, I repeated with transport those words" (14). Mathilda loves her father's writing as a stand-in for the man himself. Later, after his suicide, his final letter becomes a symbol of his physical absence and overwhelming emotional presence. "Farewell for ever!" he writes. When Mathilda's father dies, she is left with only his words and her memories.

Diana, too, is reduced to text, language serving as evidence that she once lived. When Mathilda and her father return to the countryside, a vestige of Diana's presence remains in her abandoned books. "Although more than sixteen years had passed since her death nothing had changed; her work box, her writing desk were still there and in her room a book lay open on the table as she had left it" (*Mathilda*, 22). The novel still open on her nightstand proves that Diana once existed. It also serves as a reminder of her sexual relationship with her husband. During their courtship, Diana and Mathilda's father read to one another constantly, their romantic and sexual desires mediated through the sharing of words. "They studied, they rode together; they were never separate and seldom admitted a third to their society" (9). Later, when Mathilda and her father read to one another, the activity is arousing to Mathilda's father in a way that Mathilda does not recognize. She writes, "We walked together in the gardens and in the evening when I would have retired he asked me to stay and read to him; and first said, 'When I was last here your Mother read Dante to me; you shall go on where she left off.'—And then in a moment he said, 'No, that must not be; you must not read Dante. Do you choose a book.' I took up Spencer and read the descent of Sir Guyon to the halls of Avarice; while he listened his eyes fixed on me in sad and profound silence" (23). There is nothing overtly salacious about *The Faerie Queene*—indeed, Sir Guyon is the knight of temperance—but the act of reading, of sharing language, is sexually charged for Mathilda's father, and he cannot separate the eroticized act of reading with his wife from the theoretically innocent act of reading with his daughter. Language is both proof of existence and reminder of absence.

It is perhaps all the more significant, then, that God's word is so singularly absent throughout the novel. Mathilda, we are told, is a prodigious reader. Because she has no friends or family beyond her disinterested aunt, she turns to books for companionship. "As I grew older books in some degree supplied the place of human intercourse: the library of my aunt was very small; Shakespear [*sic*], Milton, Pope and Cowper were the strangley [*sic*] assorted poets of her collection" (*Mathilda*, 13). She is also a consumer of plays, acting out the roles of "Rosalind and Miranda and the lady of Comus" (13). She reads "Livy and Rollin's ancient history" (13), but religious materials are conspicuously absent. Her education is thus nontraditional and incomplete, especially for a time in which arguments raged over the contours of female education. For Rousseau, whose *Emile* (1762) was highly influential on middle- and upper-class educational practices, the purpose of female education was to create attractive and pleasing wives. "A woman's education must . . . be planned in relation to man," he wrote.[55] "To be pleasing in his sight, to win his respect and love, to train him in childhood, to tend him in manhood, to counsel and console, these are the duties of woman for all time, and this is what she should be taught while she is young."[56] Female education should be practical, calculated to improve domestic life. Rachel Fuchs and Victoria Thompson explain that "rather than acquire an abstract knowledge of humanity," girls "were to learn what made those with whom they lived happy or sad, virtuous or corrupt."[57] It was against this "false system of education" that Mary Wollstonecraft railed in A Vindication of the Rights of Woman, a system created "by men who, considering females rather as women than human creatures, have been more anxious to make them alluring mistresses than affectionate wives and rational mothers."[58] For Wollstonecraft, education that focused solely on a woman's superficial qualities produced vapid wives, unfit for the important domestic labor of child rearing.

Hannah More considered Wollstonecraft immoral and refused to read Vindication on principle, but like Wollstonecraft, she criticized the Rousseauian style of education so popular for women of the time. As Anne Stott explains, "A political conservative, deeply hostile to the French Revolution, More was eager to distance herself from the language of women's rights. Nevertheless, there was a considerable overlap of agendas."[59] In her Strictures on the Modern System of Female Education (1799), More writes, "It is a singular injustice which is often exercised toward women, first to give them a most defective education, and then to expect from them the most undeviating purity of conduct."[60] She would later repeat this sentiment in her novel Coelebs in Search of a Wife (1809): "The education of the present race of females is not very favorable to domestic happiness. For my own part I call education not that which smothers a woman with accomplishments, but that which tends to consolidate a firm and regular system of character . . . and, more especially, that which refers all actions, feelings, sentiments, tastes, and passions to the love and fear of God."[61] Writing from an Evangelical perspective, More insists that education is necessary for girls, and that it should center on instilling morality and piety.

That view was echoed by Church of Scotland clergyman James Fordyce, who insisted that girls must be educated into "the spirit of Christian sobriety."[62] They must read widely in history, geography, astronomy, and natural philosophy, that they might better appreciate God's creation, and they may seek out poetry in which "Nature, Virtue, Religion, are painted and embellished with all the beauty of a chaste yet elevated imagination."[63] Above all, they should learn "the duty and advantage of reading the Scriptures."[64] "Novels and Romances" are acceptable only if they "expose vice and folly," which many do not.[65]

That Mathilda is raised on plays rather than scripture reflects the extent to which her father and aunt neglected her education. Despite the contemporary ubiquity of religious instruction for young people, and especially girls—according to Mary Hilton, "Women writers had crowded into the educational market where they expressed their views in a range of popular texts . . . educational treatises, conduct books, popular guides, stories and handbooks"[66]—Mathilda reads Pope and Shakespeare, not the Bible or Fordyce. Even her readings from Milton are irreligious in nature, encompassing *Comus*, not *Paradise Lost*. It is perhaps no surprise, then, that religion plays no role in Mathilda's father's consciousness either. Raised by a "weak mother with all the indulgence she thought due to a nobleman of wealth," Mathilda's father learns how to succeed as a young libertine, but he is not exposed to Christian morality (*Mathilda*, 6). Later, when he falls in love with Diana, he becomes more intellectual, as Diana is relatively well educated for a woman. She is "acquainted with the heroes of Greece and Rome or with those of England who had lived some hundred years ago," and her reading list "was very extensive" (8). Yet if Diana reads the classics of Greece and Rome, she does not appear to read the Bible. That Dante lies open in Diana's bedroom links religious writings with the couple's lust, not their piety. That Mathilda's father prays to the "Spirits of Good," not God, to protect his daughter, further underscores his irreligiosity (35).

Taken together, it might be possible to view *Mathilda* as a critique of atheist education. Critics of atheism insisted that individual morality could not exist in the absence of belief in a deity. According to "The Danger and Inutility of Atheism," an article printed in 1813 in *The*

*Universal Magazine*, atheists "declare, without hesitation, that there is no God, consequently no essential difference between good and evil . . . they would call you *brother* while cutting your throat."[67] If male atheists are depicted as unrestrained hedonists, female atheists are assumed to be prone to depression. "What shall prop up this reed, if religion doth not sustain her?"[68] Mathilda and her father conform to these stereotypes; he lacks the religiously instilled ability to restrain his inappropriate ardor, while she sinks into suicidal despair. "Farewell, Woodville," she tells him at the end of her tale (*Mathilda*, 67). "The turf will soon be green on my grave; and the violets will bloom on it. *There* is my hope and my expectation" (67). In the end, however, patriarchy, rather than atheism, is the real target of Shelley's anger. Mathilda is systematically failed by the men in her life—by her father, who should protect her, Woodville, who cannot console her, and God, who does not intervene in her sufferings. She is thus torn, brutally angry with a system that falsely promises male protection in exchange for female submission, yet simultaneously nostalgic for an imagined world of masculine protection. Underlying both feelings is God's absence. As the ultimate patriarch, the top-most point of the Great Chain of Being, God should offer a crucial sense of safety, and his absence leaves Mathilda profoundly vulnerable and uncomforted. Mathilda emerges as another version of Frankenstein's creature, abandoned by the patriarchs who should protect her, uncertain why she suffers, and alone in a world that offers no justice or possibility for recovery.

Frankenstein's creature eventually seeks to isolate himself from humankind, and Mathilda, too, finds comfort first in self-imposed isolation and eventually in self-abnegation.[69] She ends the text with the intention of killing herself. It is all the more significant, then, that she creates a written record of her existence before she dies. Frankenstein's creature lives on in text, but not by his own choice; readers encounter him through Frankenstein's eyes as reported by Walton. His memory survives because Walton turns back to humanity and reaches out to others through the medium of letters. In contrast, Mathilda tells her own story, piercing the walls of her isolation by opening up to Woodville in print. Her writing will not change her fate; despite the critical tendency to read Mathilda's story as triumphant, an act of recovery and self-assertion—according to Betty T. Bennett, for instance, Mathilda "achieves a kind of redemption through her last act"[70]—she will die nonetheless. But in the act of penning her narrative, Mathilda replicates one of the final themes of *Frankenstein*: Mathilda reaches out not to save herself, but to leave behind some trace of her existence and briefly via friendship to experience respite from the void. She engages in an act of self-commemoration, acknowledges the physical woman who will soon cease to be, and reduces herself to language that will remain behind when her physical form is gone.

In writing without hope, Mathilda—and by extension, Shelley—establishes a different understanding of literature's purpose than that frequently adopted by the male Romantics of her time.[71] In his *Defence of Poetry* (written ca. 1821), Percy Shelley writes, the "most unfailing herald, companion, and follower of the awakening of a great people to work a beneficial change in opinion or institution, is poetry."[72] For Percy, the author is the ultimate creator and judge of culture, and he has the unique capacity to reform the world with his pen. *Mathilda*'s Woodville, generally viewed as a stand-in for Percy, espouses a similar philosophy. Already a successful poet, he feels the weight of his responsibility to society. "From my youth," Woodville tells Mathilda, "I have said, I will be virtuous; I will dedicate my life for the good of others; I will do my best to extirpate evil.... I have powers" (*Mathilda*, 59). He later refuses to form a suicide pact with Mathilda, in part because he will not abandon his family and friends, and in part because he has a very powerful sense of his creative responsibility to the world. He tells Mathilda,

> Let us suppose that Socrates, or Shakespear, or Rousseau had been seized with despair and died in youth when they were as young as I am; do you think that we and all the world should not have lost incalculable improvement in our good feelings and our happiness thro' their destruction. I am not like one of these; they influenced millions: but if I can influence but a hundred, but ten, but one solitary individual, so as in any way to lead him from ill to good, that will be a joy to repay me for all my sufferings, though they were a million times multiplied. (59)

As I have written elsewhere, however, *Mathilda*'s narrative continuously confronts Woodville with his own artistic powerlessness.[73] Despite initially believing himself a character in a romance, Woodville cannot save his beloved Elinor, nor write her back to life. Nor can he save Mathilda, take away the pain of what she has suffered, or convince her that life is worth living. Despite his best efforts, Mathilda will die, reflecting what William Brewer calls Shelley's "somewhat skeptical attitude toward the power of words."[74] His poetry, however good it may be, does not have the moral or social force he would claim.

In the end, therefore, Mary Shelley offers a different view of writing from that of her male romantic colleagues, one that is more personal and ultimately tied to her religious doubts. In a world in which patriarchs fail and God is absent, writing becomes a way of proclaiming one's existence and making connections across the moral and spiritual void. Mathilda is both Frankenstein's creature fleeing to the ice, and Walton, drawn back to humanity. She also presages *The Last Man*'s Lionel Verney, for whom writing—the proof of human minds and human intellect—is all that matters. By the end of the 1810s, then, Shelley had already introduced into her writings the religious themes that would preoccupy her throughout her career.

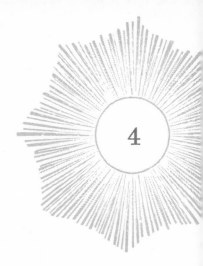

# DESPAIR

In 1820, Mary Shelley began work on her second full-length novel, *Valperga, or the Life and Adventures of Castruccio, Prince of Lucca* (published in 1823). A fictionalized history of the Ghibelline-Guelph conflict of early fourteenth-century Italy, the novel explores Shelley's profound doubts about the nature of religion as first developed in *Frankenstein* and *Mathilda*. On the one hand, Shelley depicts convent life as an acceptable refuge for women, a place in which they can be content, if not happy, and she constructs in the characters of Wilhelmina, Beatrice, and Euthanasia an alternative feminine religious tradition that provides solace to women apart from the evils of patriarchy. Simultaneously, however, organized religion is depicted as oppressive of and destructive to women. Men fetishize female suffering—and especially female religious suffering—while using the institutional authority of the church to maintain the structures of gender oppression. Nor is there a reassuring sense of divine justice in the novel. The evil triumph while the good are destroyed, leaving the reader with the uncomfortable suspicion that this is all there is; there is no divine plan or justice, no supreme patriarch to save the good and punish the guilty.

Perhaps, the novel posits, Beatrice is right in her heresy; perhaps we live in a world not of order but of injustice and entropy.

Critics traditionally view *The Last Man* (1826) as, in Samantha Webb's words, "the transitional work in [Shelley's] career."[1] Her first novel written after her husband's death, *The Last Man* is frequently viewed as an expression of her deep sense of grief, and her feelings of guilt and loneliness as a survivor of the Shelley circle. "The last man! Yes I may well describe that solitary being's feelings, feeling myself as the last relic of a beloved race, my companions extinct before me," she wrote in her journal on May 14, 1824.[2] If *The Last Man* is a transitional work, however, it is also a climactic one, the culmination of the religious doubts she had been nursing as early as the composition of *Frankenstein*. This chapter examines the theme of religious despair in the second portion of Shelley's career. Beginning with the composition of *Valperga* and culminating with the publication of *The Last Man*, this period witnessed Shelley questioning the assumption that divinity must be good, and the belief that biblical timelines must be accurate. Drawing on Calvinist, Manichaean, and atheist belief systems, Shelley creates a world in which God might be actively malevolent—if he exists at all—and religion is at best a fairy tale, at worst a tool of oppression. The benefits of religion as a potentially feminist force fall away, leaving behind the certainty that all is mutable, even the idea of God. In such a world, the only things that matter are human creativity and human minds, and it is this belief, this turn toward love for humanity, that will characterize the final portion of Shelley's literary career.

Eighteenth-century English Protestants were, generally speaking, united in their view of the convent as a cultural evil, a prison for surplus women. In 1716, Lady Mary Wortley Montagu famously wrote of her visit to a young woman in an Austrian convent, "I have been several times to see her, but it gives me too much melancholy to see so agreeable a young creature buried alive. . . . I never in my life had so little charity for the Roman Catholic religion as since I see the misery it occasions so many poor unhappy women!"[3] Convents were viewed alternatively as spaces of imprisonment and of debauchery, featuring heavily in pornography of the period. As Ana M. Acosta explains, "The eminently Roman Catholic convent was a highly charged and complex literary topic throughout the century, appearing time and again as a place of imprisonment, synonym of forbidden love, a metaphor for dangerous sexual practices, an excuse for seduction, elopement, rape, abortion, madness, suicide, and murder: the epitome of injustice, arbitrary power, and inhumanity."[4] The convent served throughout the seventeenth and eighteenth centuries as a sign of Catholic tyranny, "patriarchal despotism" epitomized in the imprisonment of healthy young women.[5] Indeed, according to Carmen M. Mangion, by mid-century, "Catholic anti-nun literature published in Britain, North America, and Australia was unequalled in its vitriol."[6] The Shelleys likewise took a dim view of convent life. Percy described Teresa "Emilia" Viviani, the aristocratic young woman and "captive bird" to whom he dedicated *Epipsychidion*, as an "unfortunate lady . . . now imprisoned in the Convent of—," while Mary wrote to Leigh Hunt that "it is grievous to see this beautiful girl wearing out the best years of her life in a[n] odious convent where both mind and body are sick from want of the appropriate exercize for each."[7] Viviani was placed in the Convent of St. Anna until her father could arrange a marriage for her, a practice the Shelleys viewed as barbaric and antifeminist, and they protested vociferously—and to no avail—for her release.

If Mary Shelley criticized convent life in her letters, her fictions often present it as a homosocial refuge, a retreat from patriarchy and the maltreatment of women. "The Convent of Chaillot," a short story written for the 1828 edition of *The Keepsake*, for instance, tells the story of Louise de la Vallière, one of the principal mistresses of King Louis XIV of France. At the beginning of the story, Louise is a deeply religious young woman who inadvertently falls in love with Theodore Blanzac, the intended of her good friend, Clemence. Avoiding the temptation to fall into sin and hurt her friend, Louise removes herself to the court, where she catches the eye of Louis XIV. Despite her deep religious convictions, she cannot refuse the king, and she becomes his mistress, while Clemence marries her beloved Blanzac. Eventually, however, Blanzac dies, and Clemence is shocked to find that her friend has been replaced in the king's affections by the infamous Madame de Montspan and has retreated to a nunnery. There, Louise once again rejects homosocial rivalries; when Mme. de Montspan visits her, seemingly for no other reason than to taunt her fallen rival, Louise will not engage in the competition. She tells Montspan, "I am not happy, but content."[8] In the nunnery, she has formed a community of female friendships that sustain her once Louis's affections have fled.

A similar view of the convent appears in another of Shelley's historical fictions, the 1835 short story "The Trial of Love," also written for *The Keepsake*. In this story, Angeline and Ippolito have sworn an oath to his father: they promise to have no contact with one another for one year, with the understanding that if at the end of that time they still wish to wed, he will support the match. Angeline takes the oath very seriously, retiring to a convent and refusing contact with Ippolito, despite his fervent and increasingly angry pleas. Ippolito, however, is not so strong of character, and he ultimately abandons Angeline for Faustina, a rich young girl for whom Angeline feels maternal affection. Homosocial hatreds briefly surface, but eventually, Angeline, like Louise, retires to a convent, renouncing her claim to Ippolito and reestablishing her bond with Faustina. As the years pass, Angeline comes to realize that Ippolito would have made her miserable. Her love would not have survived the defects of his character, as he was never the person she believed him to be: "She saw with calm and altered feelings; he was not the being her soul had loved; and if she had married him, with her deep feelings, and exalted ideas of honour, she felt that she should have been even more dissatisfied than Faustina."[9] From the security of the convent, she comforts Faustina, marveling at the sinfulness of aristocratic marriage and counting herself lucky to have escaped Faustina's fate. As is true of Louise, Angeline ends the story "cheerful, if not happy" ("Trial of Love," 243), the convent an acceptable, if not ideal, alternative to suffering in heterosexual marriage.

Shelley thus depicts the convent as a retreat from unreliable men. No longer invested in their lovers, Louise and Angeline have no more homosocial battles to fight, and they can now be friends with their erstwhile rivals. Likewise, in the aftermath of great suffering, *Valperga*'s Beatrice finds comfort in the idea of becoming a nun. She tells Euthanasia, once her rival for Castruccio's love and now her only friend, "I shall make my peace with the church. . . . I shall enter myself as a novice, and afterwards become a nun."[10] Beatrice is happiest when she is imprisoned because she and Euthanasia "find solace in their shared experiences of Castruccio"; once enemies, "they develop a friendship that transcends such competition."[11] In prison, Beatrice and Euthanasia re-create the female bonds destroyed by the world of men.[12]

At the same time, what Shelley depicts over and over—in Louise, in Angeline, in Beatrice, in Euthanasia—is the emotional struggle of the woman who no longer recognizes the man she once loved. Each woman loves the memory of a man she knew, while acknowledging that that man no longer exists (if indeed he ever did). Upon seeing Castruccio for the first time in many months, Euthanasia realizes, "He was no longer her lover, scarcely her friend . . . she saw no likeness between the friend of her youth, beaming with love, joy, and hope, and the prince who now stood before her" (*Valperga*, 197). If she still cares for the man she once knew, Euthanasia does not care for this stranger, and quite strikingly, she realizes that romantic love is not all. "Her old feelings of duty, benevolence, and friendship returned; all was not now, as before, referred to love alone; the trees, the streams, the mountains, and the stars, no longer told one never-varying tale of disappointed passion" (191). It is possible to recover from a love affair gone wrong, to find contentment, if not happiness in homosocial bonds. Shelley thus separates the convent from its religious function, privileging its capacity for enabling feminine communion.

If the convent unintentionally offers a space for female self-actualization within the bounds of institutional religion, the characters of Beatrice and her mother, the deceased prophetess and "papess" Wilhelmina, represent the creation of a subversive, solely female religious tradition. A long tradition of female prophecy existed by Shelley's time. "Baroque piety," a form of devotion "defined by passion and emotion, its manifestations sensuous and theatrical," legitimated in continental Europe physical expressions of female spirituality that would have been deemed heretical or dangerous in England.[13] Prophets such as the Spanish Teresa of Avila and the French Marguerite-Marie Alacoque rose to prominence in the early modern era and were taken seriously by many as religious authorities. As Mita Choudhury explains, "Despite their lack of theological training and despite their sex, these women now became chosen vehicles for God's voice. On occasion, mystical women even acquired a certain authority *over* other believers, including male clerics."[14] Indeed, Teresa of Avila has since been canonized by the Roman Catholic Church.

In England, female prophets were looked on with more suspicion, as female religious experience was easily dismissed with the label of enthusiasm. Still, numerous female prophets—including Eleanor Davies, Elizabeth Poole, Elizabeth Hooten, Barbara Blaugdone, Ann Audland, Mary Gadbury, Anne Wentworth, Margaret Fell, Mary Cary, Anna Trapnel, and Jane Lead, among others—came forward during the English Civil Wars to proclaim their political visions and prophecies for the future.[15] While such visionaries were much less common by the end of the eighteenth century, the rise of Methodism mid-century and the outbreak of the French Revolution at the end again loosened women's tongues. Deborah M. Valenze has traced at length the proliferation of nineteenth-century female preachers among the laboring classes of England and points out that in the southwest of England alone, there were twenty-eight prominent female preachers active in the 1820s and 1830s. Determined "to obey God rather than man," these women rejected the patriarchal emphasis on female silence in favor of public service and the promotion of their religious beliefs.[16] Originating among the lower classes, they were mocked and derided by political conservatives for being "vulgar and undisciplined," yet they reached a broader audience than ever before.[17] The creation of the press and the growth of the publishing marketplace allowed these women "greater visibility than their Civil War counterparts . . . [H]undreds of men and women read a millennial tract, followed the careers of itinerant prophets in the daily newspapers, or attended large open-air assemblies where obscure men and women warned of the dangers to come in the 1780s or 1790s."[18]

Two female prophets are particularly relevant to an understanding of Shelley's Beatrice. While Dorothy Gott (ca. 1748–1812) is largely unknown today, she published three moderately successful millenarian tracts and was a formative influence on William Blake.[19] A widow writing in the aftermath of a bad marriage, Gott depicted herself as a font of maternal religious wisdom, and she used her prophecies to react against the class and gender structures that oppressed her. "My Husband was made an instrument to strip me of man and the love of this world," she writes in *Christ the Standard of Truth Set Up* (1798), and she blames man for Eve's fall.[20] Had God and Adam sufficiently instructed Eve, she "would have been fortified against his attack of the subtilty [*sic*] of the Devil in the serpent."[21] In assuming the role of prophet, then, Gott offers a new, better, female vision of God and eternity.

More famous than Gott was Joanna Southcott, who rose to prominence in the early nineteenth century for printing her visions, and with whose works Shelley was undoubtedly familiar.[22] Southcott was not a likely prophetess, an aging lower-class domestic servant who depleted her life's savings to print and disseminate her works.[23] Yet Southcott's prophecies held particular appeal among "the dispossessed farm laborers and weavers of the West Country," along with people nationwide affected by the "political and social unrest and social dislocation caused by the French Revolution, the wars with France, and widespread famine in England during the mid 1790s."[24] Her prophecies sold, and she quickly found a following; critics estimate that by the time of her death in 1814, as many as one hundred thousand copies of her works were in circulation, and as Jasper Cragwall points out, between 1802 and 1815, she "humbled the circulation figures of most everyone other than Byron and Scott."[25] These works contained a mélange of jeremiad against the current state of the world, millenarian visions of the future, and admonishments to her sister (who very much opposed her plan to spend her life's savings on printer's fees).[26] Kevin Binfield explains, "throughout the prophecies, Southcott combines Christianity and English nationalism in eulogies for England," which she "tempers . . . with stern warnings of disasters to befall the nation if it fails to repent."[27] They also contain substantial feminist commentary, embedded especially in her complaints against a masculine hierarchy that blames woman for the fall of man and does not accept woman's prophetic capacity. In *A Warning to the World*, for instance, she describes an argument with a man who would place all responsibility for suffering on Eve, while absolving the devil of guilt: "Finding him determined to clear the Devil, and cast the *whole blame on the woman*, contrary to the Scriptures, as he would not allow that a curse cast on the Serpent *must ever take place*. I then told him to quit the room, as he was a *friend to the Devil*."[28] Satan, not Eve, is behind the fall, Southcott insists, proclaiming "the emancipation of women from the burden of the Fall" and positioning herself as "a deliverer from the inferior status bequeathed to them by the Christian tradition."[29]

Ultimately, Southcott proclaims that she herself will redeem the world from sin: "And this due time bringeth in the long-wished-for REVOLUTION, when the enmity is kindled in the woman's breast against the serpent that betrayed her at first. . . . This is the revolution that bringeth in the end, when the Lord will come to fulfil his promise, which he made to the woman, to bruise the serpent's head."[30] Positioning herself as the "metaphorical 'bride' of Revelation," and declaring herself pregnant at the age of sixty-four with "a divinely conceived child named Shiloh,"[31] she treats salvation as a product of the female body and insists that women be "redeemed and granted their rightful position within the priesthood of believers."[32] As such, her "revisionary female theology implicitly challenged the established religious and patriarchal traditions of late eighteenth-century England and redetermined the female body as an important textual medium."[33] What Southcott offers is a female religious tradition and a female religious power disconnected from masculinist church hierarchies.

In recent years, Southcott has become the subject of some critical attention, and several have identified Southcott as a model for *Valperga*'s Wilhelmina. According to Orianne Smith, Wilhelmina "bears more than a passing resemblance to . . . the notorious female visionary Joanna Southcott."[34] The bishop of Ferrara describes Wilhelmina's beliefs, which also bear more than a passing resemblance to Southcott's: "Outwardly professing the Catholic religion and conforming in the strictest manner to its rules, she secretly formed a sect, founded on the absurd and damnable belief, that she was the Holy Ghost incarnate upon earth for the salvation of the female sex" (*Valperga*, 131). Referring to God using feminine pronouns—"She has revealed Her will to me, and by Her command I now confide to you the treasure of my soul" (133)—Wilhelmina confesses that she has given birth to a daughter, her maternity a sign of her bodily power and connection to the divine. While Southcott only spoke of her miraculous pregnancy—she died before she could "give birth"—Wilhelmina has actually become a mother, and she passes her religious beliefs on to her daughter and heir. That she refuses to name the father implies that Beatrice, like Southcott's Shiloh, is the product of Wilhelmina's body and (the female) God's power alone, conceived without the aid of any man. Magfreda tells the bishop, "I cannot tell you who was the father of this child; for although I believed that her conception partook of the divinity, she never confirmed my faith" (133). Wilhelmina's religion thus restores to the female body a divine power of creation that transcends patriarchal conceptions of religion. It also taps into a lost tradition of female prophecy, a matrilineal tradition controlled not by popes, but by papesses, "threaten[ing] the very religious, social, sexual, and ethical codes of the culture, as well as of the church itself."[35]

Beatrice's religious power, too, affords her an unfeminine level of cultural authority. When she first appears in the novel, she has gained fame as a prophetess, accruing followers of all social classes who worship her. Her "followers are numerous," believing, like Beatrice herself, that she is "the *Ancilla Dei*, the chosen vessel into which God has poured a portion of his spirit" (*Valperga*, 136). The Viscountess di Malvezzi surprises Castruccio by telling him, "God has been gracious to us, in bestowing on us his visible assistant through this sacred maiden, who by her more than human beauty, the excellence of her dispositions, and above all, by her wisdom beyond that of woman, and her prophecies which have ever been fulfilled, demonstrates, even to the unbeliever and the Gentile, that she is inspired by the grace and favour of the blessed Virgin" (130). It is no real surprise, then, that Wilhelmina and Beatrice, mother and daughter alike, are persecuted by the institutions of the church, which perceives feminine power as a threat to its own authority. Wilhelmina's and Beatrice's teachings question "male domination predicated upon the submission of women," and thus they must be hunted down and destroyed.[36]

If *Valperga* tells the story of a female religious voice, it also tells the story of the foreclosing of that voice, what Orianne Smith calls "the rise and fall of the tradition of female prophecy."[37] Throughout *Valperga*, Shelley conveys her skepticism of organized religion's treatment of women, insisting that the church is set up to control and repress through the power of the Inquisition. When Beatrice usurps the authority of the institutional church by preaching successfully after mass—"Her discourse was long and continued. . . . Every eye was fixed on her" (*Valperga*, 137)—she is immediately arrested: "As this enthusiasm was at its height, some Dominican inquisitors came forward, surrounded her, and declared her their prisoner" (137). Beatrice, like Wilhelmina and Magfreda, cannot be allowed to exist, cannot be permitted to challenge the hierarchies of church control. Through force in the case of the Inquisition, whose agents call Beatrice "an impostor, a misleader of the people, a dangerous and wicked enthusiast" (138), or through kindness in the case of the bishop of Ferrara, who encourages her to renounce her mother's beliefs voluntarily, men demand that women abandon their claims to prophecy or risk imprisonment or execution.

According to Ann M. Frank Wake, Shelley depicts in Beatrice "women in collusion with the male Romantic tradition. They serve the role that we might now call 'co-dependent,' in that they encourage and support the desires of someone else at their own expense, but without finding happiness or fulfillment."[38] I think, however, that Shelley uses the story of Beatrice to develop a multifaceted criticism of religious culture. Throughout many of her historical fictions, Shelley depicts scenes of female religious suffering, scenes in which women's religious devotion and existential despair serve to enhance their beauty and heighten their sexual appeal. Louise de la Vallière, for instance, is at her prayers when Louis forces her to succumb to him sexually. The text lingers lovingly on the image of Louise at prayer: "The kneeler did not wear the monastic habit; she seemed in deep agitation; her face was concealed" ("Convent of Chaillot," 276). Louis then disturbs her devotions with an attempted sexual assault: "She sprung from the embrace of Louis, and flinging herself once more at the foot of the cross, 'Holy mother of God!' she exclaimed, 'help me or I perish!' She twined her arms round the pedestal of the cross, and, pressing it to her breast with almost phrensied violence, she wept bitterly and intensely" (278). It is clear in this scene that Louis is aroused by the spectacle of Louise's pious resistance; her religious devotion inflames his passions, and he succeeds in overcoming her resistance: "The conquest of love over virtue was accomplished" (278). In the process, he fetishizes female piety and female emotional distress.

Similar scenes appear throughout Shelley's corpus. In "The Mourner" (1830), Horace Neville becomes fascinated with the forlorn Ellen Burnet because "there was an enchantment in her sorrow."[39] More famously, Victor Frankenstein's father falls in love with his wife, Caroline Beaufort, as she mourns her father's death. He keeps in his living room a portrait of Caroline as she mourns over her father's coffin, commemorating both her father's death and her beautiful display of daughterly sorrow. Writing of Victorian "death culture," Deborah Lutz describes the nineteenth-century fascination with what she terms "secular relics": "Bodies left behind traces of themselves, shreds that could then become material for memories. Such vestiges might be found in objects the body had touched as it advanced through existence: clothing worn, letters written, utensils handled. . . . More concretely, the body itself or its parts functioned for the Victorians as mementos: the snippet of hair made into jewelry or even a bone or desiccated organ kept in a special container."[40] For the Victorians (and to a lesser extent, the Romantics—after all, Shelley was rumored to have preserved Percy's heart), the secular relic preserves the memory of the dead, a piece of the departed retained in this life. What is interesting about Caroline Beaufort's portrait, however, is that it seeks to preserve not the dead but the experience of *mourning* the dead. According to Christopher Rovee, it "perpetuates Alphonse's original performance of benevolence," memorializing eternally the moment in which he rescued his wife from poverty.[41] It also suggests that for Alphonse, Caroline is at her most appealing as a mourner, fetishizing her piety and sorrow. Read in the context of the experiences of Louise, Ellen, and, later, Beatrice, Caroline's portrait reveals Shelley's discomfort with the link between religion, female suffering, and male desire.

Beatrice, too, is treated as a religious spectacle when she first appears in the text, and Castruccio is drawn to her, fetishizing her religious devotion as a complement to her ethereal beauty. Like Louis XIV, who is unable to separate Louise's act of worship from her physical form, Castruccio is fascinated with Beatrice's "divine beauty" (*Valperga*, 129), and he later marvels, "How beautiful she is! . . . she is the *Ancilla*

*Dei*, a maiden vowed to God and chastity; yet her eyes seem penetrated with love" (149). Later in the text, the sexually violent overtones of Louis's pursuit of Louise are made more explicit in Tripalda's implied rape of Beatrice. His desire to assert power over her, coupled with a similarly fetishistic interest in her beauty, compel Tripalda to assault her. Beatrice won't speak in detail of her lengthy captivity in Tripalda's house—as Leanne Maunu describes, "Her narrative reveals, while it cloaks; it informs, while remaining obscure in its references"[42]—but it is clear that she suffered profoundly in what Jeffrey Cox calls a "Sadean nightmare."[43] According to Beatrice, "I have said enough, nor will I tell that which would chill your warm blood with horror. I remained three years in this house; and what I saw, and what I endured, is a tale for the unhallowed ears of infidels. . . . It has changed me, much changed me, to have been witness of these scenes" (257). Beatrice's story is one of martyrdom, and it condemns men who cannot perceive value in women or their religious faith beyond their sexual desirability. Read through this lens, it is all the more important that Beatrice loses her looks prematurely. By the end of the text, she has grown, by her own admission, "grey, old and withered" (257), and her religious struggles are valued more once her beauty is gone.[44]

Initially, Beatrice finds power in religion. She tells Castruccio, "I am commanded by the Power who has so often revealed his will to me. Can I penetrate his hidden designs?" (*Valperga*, 150). Beatrice is masculinized by her imagined relationship with God, metaphorically penetrating the divine plan. This power ultimately proves illusory, however, as Castruccio and Tripalda find a power in religion that exceeds her own. Tripalda commits "unspoken crimes" (286), presumably gang rape and sexual torture; his office in the church affords him both physical control over unwilling female bodies and protection from the repercussions of his crimes. No one will believe the mad prophetess over a respected cardinal.

In creating Tripalda, Mary Shelley taps into the long-standing tradition of anti-Catholic discourse described in the first chapter of this volume, a tradition that dated back to the sixteenth century, was reinforced in Irish Rebellion documents, and was redeployed in novels such as Matthew Lewis's *The Monk* (1796) and the Marquis de Sade's *Justine*, or *The Misfortunes of Virtue* (1791). In her depictions of Tripalda and Beatrice, however, Shelley invokes not only the general anti-Catholic imagery of the period, but the case of Mary-Catherine Cadière, whose 1730 accusations against her confessor, Father Jean-Baptiste Girard, fascinated the English public. Although the Cadière affair is largely unknown today, it was an international sensation in the eighteenth century, and descriptions of the resultant trial were reprinted as late as 1893. In 1728, eighteen-year-old Mary-Catherine Cadière was well known in her community for her beauty, goodness, and intense piety. She chose as her primary spiritual advisor and confessor Father Girard, a Jesuit priest who was new to her area and in great demand among women, despite his advanced age of forty-seven. Within a year after their spiritual relationship began, Cadière began to suffer from fits and convulsions, which she and Girard attributed to divine inspiration. She also began to show evidence of stigmata on her body, and she supposedly performed miracles. Soon, she had gathered a cult following of people who believed in her visions, awaited her prophecies, and proclaimed her destined for posthumous canonization.

As Cadière's fame grew, church officials became suspicious, and she was moved to a convent near Toulon. Initially, Girard continued to visit her in the convent, spending many hours alone with her in prayer, even as she continued to suffer from horrible physical ailments. Eventually, however, Girard's visits tapered off, and Cadière came forward to lodge a complaint, first with civil authorities and later with the church itself. Girard, she claimed, had raped her repeatedly, and by breathing into her mouth, he had bewitched her into experiencing visions. He also preached to her the doctrine of Quietism—the heretical belief that one needed to abandon oneself body and soul to God's will—and when she would come out of the trances he induced, she would find herself engaged in lewd behaviors at his behest. She claimed that their forced relationship continued even inside the convent, and that he compelled her to have an abortion at great risk to her body and soul. Girard for his part denied the affair entirely and accused Cadière of demonic possession and witchcraft. After much wrangling over jurisdiction and several attempts to get Cadière to recant, the state brought both up on charges, Cadière of witchcraft, false testimony, and defamation, Girard of rape, spiritual incest, and abortion. Were Cadière to be found guilty, she would burn; were Girard, he would hang. The trial dragged on for almost a year, a remarkably protracted period at the time, probably motivated, modern historians such as Jason Kuznicki have argued, by the Jansenist desire to embarrass the Jesuits.[45] Ultimately, however, the magistrates returned a split verdict: twelve judges voted in Cadière's favor, twelve in Girard's, and both were acquitted. Two years later, Girard died. Cadière, meanwhile, disappeared from the annals of history.

Although several critics have examined French reactions to the Cadière affair,[46] very little attention has been paid to English reactions to the trial, which were also considerable. Between 1731 and 1732, no fewer than fifteen separate publications were released recounting the trial, some of which were reprinted as many as eleven times, and versions of the trial continued to be resurrected as late as 1893. The pamphlets, like the magistrates, were split in their sympathies, several taking Cadière's side, others championing Girard. Pamphlets supporting Cadière were often pornographic and clearly designed with prurient interests in mind. Unlike the pro-Girard documents, which tend to elide the details of his alleged crimes, the pro-Cadière tracts report in painstaking detail the indecent acts of which he was accused, including scenes of sexualized whipping. According to the author of *Memoirs of Miss Mary-Catherine Cadiere*, for instance, "as he spoke [he] began to lay bare her Neck and Shoulders; as soon as she was naked to the Waste, he struck her two or three gentle Blows with his Whip of Discipline; after which he kissed each Place where the Blows fell (if you will believe it) with a religious fervour."[47] Often accompanied by explicit engravings, these tracts fit into the category of courtroom documents described by Peter Wagner as "a most peculiar genre of eighteenth-century English erotica."[48] Secondly, and perhaps equally obviously, the pro-Cadière documents are designed as anti-Catholic propaganda. The author of *The Case of Mrs. Mary Catherine Cadiere* (1732), for example, writes that readers "will see by what villainous and diabolical arts the Romish Priests, but especially the Jesuits, usurp and maintain an absolute dominion over the Consciences as well as the Persons of their devotees . . . here they will see what they may justly expect will be the fate of their Wives, their Daughters, and their Sisters, should they for their sins be delivered up to the Infatuations of Popery."[49] It is no accident that the tract's author invokes the political language of usurpation and dominion in describing priestly evils; it is a staple of anti-Catholic propaganda both to emphasize priestly sexual violence and to treat that violence as a metaphor for the Jesuit order's political aims. If allowed free reign in a kingdom, the Jesuits will rape women and overthrow the rightful government, to the detriment of all British Protestant men.

In contrast, pamphlets critical of Cadière sought to defend the Jesuit order by demonstrating the extent to which Girard's reputation was unfairly besmirched. Underlying many of these tracts is a fear of female verbal power, an anxiety not only about false accusations (what Antony Simpson calls the "blackmail myth"[50]), but about the feminine usurpation of religious authority. Cadière's religious visions gave her a cultural authority not normally afforded women in this period. She attracted an actual cult following (albeit a small one) of people who believed she was divinely inspired and who worshipped her as one might a saint. Indeed, the nuns in her convent collected the sweat from her body and "the water used to clean her blood" for preservation in healing rituals, suggesting the extent to which she was seen as semidivine.[51] Such power was frightening to authorities and deemed heretical for a woman; it was only when she became famous that the church hierarchy took notice of her or her interactions with Girard.

Beyond pamphlet literature, the story of Cadière's trial found its way into works by several authors with whom Shelley was familiar. Henry Fielding based his play *The Debauchees: or, the Jesuit Caught* (1732) on the Cadière trial, and this play later proved influential for both Horace Walpole and Matthew Lewis. As Diane Long Hoeveler writes, "Given the knowledge that both of them had of Fielding's works as well as the extensive visits that they both made to Paris, it is more than probable that they would have been familiar with [Cadière's] story."[52] Hoeveler also posits that the trial formed "part of the impetus for Matthew Lewis's depiction of Ambrosio's rape of Antonia in *The Monk*,"[53] and thus it is likely that Shelley, too, would have been familiar with the story, through Lewis if not independently. Mary Shelley read *The Monk* on September 22, 1814, and Percy met Lewis in person in Geneva in 1816. That Shelley may have known of the trial is apparent in the similarities between

Cadière's story and Beatrice's. As was true for Cadière, Beatrice's most violent religious torments occur after she has been the victim of sexual violence. Her visions are both empowering, the impetus for her loyal following, and proof of her oppression; she cannot articulate what has been done to her but can only feel her body tormented by a faceless evil she cannot resist. And just as Girard is never punished, there is no justice for Beatrice. Tripalda is never made to confess his crimes, and he escapes the text unharmed. Indeed, it is Bondelmonti's unwillingness to heed Euthanasia's warning about Tripalda that leads to the unraveling of their assassination plot. He views Tripalda's crimes against Beatrice as inconsequential to battles between men, and Euthanasia is proven correct too late when Tripalda betrays their plans. The men who justify crimes against female bodies ultimately suffer, punished harshly for their disbelief. It is telling, however, that Euthanasia suffers with them; women die when men will not hear them.

In invoking the trial of Mary-Catherine Cadière, Mary Shelley creates a link between female prophecy and sexual violence, between female religious expression and the institutional oppression of women. For Beatrice, as for Cadière, there is power in enthusiasm, a power that disrupts the church's patriarchal hierarchy and claims to absolute truth. For Beatrice, as for Cadière, that power is accompanied by the loss of bodily autonomy, and it is ultimately effaced from historical memory. Despite the myriad ways that the church abuses women in *Valperga*, however, Shelley's criticism of religion is not solely gendered, nor is it rooted solely in anti-Catholicism. Like Tripalda, Mandragola trades the appearance of faith for power—unlike Beatrice, she does not believe her own hype[54]—and like Tripalda, she expresses that power through acts of violence against Beatrice. Thus while some critics view Mandragola as an antifeminist caricature, "the embittered crone or witch,"[55] Mandragola and Tripalda are actually set up as parallels of one another, two characters who are deeply aware of the power of religious superstition to manipulate the masses. Both seek a nebulous form of power, destroying others in the process, and both escape unpunished. Only Beatrice, their mutual victim, pays for their crimes. She dies horribly, from a combination of drugs provided by Mandragola and shock at encountering Tripalda, the "evil genius of her life" (*Valperga*, 283), once more. If the depiction of Mandragola is anti-feminist, it is an antifeminism linked to a broader critique of religious authority and the manipulation of that authority for personal gain.

Through Beatrice, Shelley also criticizes the irrationality associated with too strong religious belief. *Valperga* makes very clear that Beatrice is not actually a prophetess, and that her visions have not come from God. Castruccio refers to her "delusions" (*Valperga*, 156), and this view is reinforced by the narrator, who explains, "the superstitions of her times had obtained credit for, and indeed given birth to her pretentions" (152).[56] Raised in the prophetic tradition, and burdened with the weight of her mother's expectations and the devotion of her followers, she has never learned to differentiate between her own inner voice and God's: "Ever the dupe of her undisciplined thoughts, she cherished her reveries, believing that heavenly and intellectual, which was indebted for its force to earthly mixtures; and she resigned herself entire to her visionary joys, until she finally awoke to truth, fallen, and for ever lost" (153). Later, when she loses her faith, she is tormented by an inner monologue that she now attributes not to God but to Satan and approaching madness. Here again, Beatrice's story echoes Cadière's; as church officials became suspicious, Cadière's visions, once associated with divine inspiration, were reinterpreted as demonic, and she was subjected to a series of exorcisms. Thus in Beatrice, Shelley emphasizes the slippery line between perceived divinity and monstrosity, and the importance of secular logic for understanding the relationship between the two. Piety can always be reinterpreted as its opposite, and to be a true believer is to shut out logic and rationality, the only things that could have saved Beatrice.

It is in Euthanasia, then, that Mary Shelley offers a different path, a more agnostic "alternativ[e] to . . . masculine power."[57] Euthanasia is a believer, insisting that "God is my help, and I fear not" (*Valperga*, 215). Yet unlike Beatrice, she is also an advocate of rationality and what Stuart Curran calls a "liberal democratic alternative" to Castruccio's form of power.[58] While she pities and even loves Beatrice, she never believes her to be divinely inspired. Rather, in her description of the human mind, she suggests that at the very center of human consciousness lies not a deep connection to the divine, but conscience and empathy. She tells Beatrice, "The human soul, dear girl, is a vast cave, in which many powers sit and love. First, Consciousness is as a centinel [sic] at the entrance" (262). Inside the cave sit "Memory," "Judgement," "Reason," "Hope," "Fear," "Joy," and "Religion," along with the negative characteristics of "Hypocrisy, Avarice, and Cruelty" (262). In the further recesses of the mind, we find "Conscience," and beyond Conscience, "an inner cave, difficult of access, rude, strange, and dangerous" (263). Here people justify horrible crimes, yet it is also a space of beauty, of "Poetry and Imagination . . . Heroism and Self-sacrifice, and the highest virtues" (263).[59] The human soul is vast and noble, potentially destructive but also powerfully humane, and all of these characteristics live within the individual, detached from a concept of deity. James Carson writes, "For Shelley, four things may transform a person into a superior being: education, broad cultural forces, compassion, and love."[60] Euthanasia embodies all of these concepts, rejecting enthusiasm for rationality and recognizing that human conscience transcends—and indeed, in many cases exceeds—the goodness promoted by religion and its earthly representatives.

In the end, however, Euthanasia dies as Beatrice dies, and her name is erased from history. "Nothing more was ever known of the Sicilian vessel, which bore Euthanasia. . . . She was never heard of more; even her name perished" (*Valperga*, 322).[61] With Euthanasia, the world loses a kind of agnostic rationality that values people for their humanity, while Castruccio, whose "heart had once been the garden of virtue" (232), succeeds as a tyrant and a torturer. This is not a world in which poetic justice exists and a benevolent deity oversees all according to some master plan. The good characters—Beatrice, Euthanasia, Bondelmonti—die unfairly, while their persecutors survive. At the end of the novel, Castruccio appears in triumph, wearing "a robe of silk richly adorned with gold and jewels; and on the breast were embroidered these words—EGLIE È COME DIO VUOLE. And on the shoulders, È SI SARA QUEL CHE DIO VORRÀ" (324).[62] Castruccio attributes his political and military successes to God's will. He has tortured and murdered his way to power, all the while claiming God's approval and support. He has triumphed because God has permitted him to triumph, and he celebrates his evil acts as a necessary part of God's broader plan.

With Castruccio's victory, *Valperga* develops Shelley's doubts not just of organized religion, the priests and kings of Blake's cosmology, but of deity as a concept. Beatrice's Paterin heresies are treated as antithetical to a Christian worldview, but her beliefs are actually an inversion of Castruccio's normative theology. Castruccio adopts a proto-Calvinist position—because he succeeded, his actions must have divine approval—but Beatrice conversely concludes that a just universe and a divine plan are not guaranteed. Paterinism, the Italian term for the heresy known as Albigensianism in France, "was a Manichean sect so named after the Latin 'pati,' meaning to suffer."[63] Defined by the *Catholic Encyclopedia* as a "neo-Manichæan sect that flourished in southern France in the twelfth and thirteenth centuries,"[64] Paterins adopted a dualist worldview out "of the desire to explain the existence of evil in the world while maintaining a belief in a good deity."[65] Mani, founder of Manichaeism, taught "a cosmogony of a dualistic kind: evil is an eternal cosmic force, not the result of a fall. Two realms or kingdoms, the realm of light and the realm of darkness, good and evil, God and matter, oppose each other implacably."[66] Within this belief system, matter, including the body, was "the inherently and irrevocably corrupt creation of the Evil Principle, designed to sully the pure soul."[67] As we saw in chapter 2 of this volume, Shelley was surrounded by thinkers who flirted with and occasionally adhered to this philosophy, including Byron, Peacock, and Percy Shelley. *Valperga* thus engages with the heretical ideas that so fascinated Shelley's circle. If *Frankenstein* questions what it would mean to live in a world in which God the Father is actively hostile to his creation, *Valperga* goes farther, presenting Beatrice's Paterin heresy as a terrifying but potentially accurate worldview. "Listen to me," she begs Euthanasia, "while I announce to you the eternal and victorious influence of evil, which circulates like air about us, clinging to our flesh like a poisonous garment, eating into us, and destroying us" (*Valperga*, 242). Malevolent forces exist, and God either makes no attempt to stifle them, or He enjoys watching them succeed, a tyrannical father who, like Victor Frankenstein, hates his progeny. According to Beatrice, "Oh! Surely God's hand is the chastening hand of a father, that thus torments his children! His children? his eternal enemies! Look, I am one! He created the seeds of disease, maremma, thirst, want; he created man,- that most wretched of slaves" (243). There is no guarantee of a benevolent deity, nor is there a comforting sense of justice. As Beatrice insists, nothing can "justify an omnipotent deity that . . . permits one particle of pain to subsist in his world" (244).

On July 8, 1822, Shelley's world abruptly changed when Percy and his friend Edward Williams drowned off the coast of the Gulf of Spezia. At the age of twenty-five, Shelley found herself a widow with a young child, and by 1826, she was beginning to feel like the last of her breed. Shelley described her feelings in her journal: "The last man! Yes I may well describe that solitary being's feelings, feeling myself as the last relic of a beloved race, my companions extinct before me."[68] As a result of these powerful words, many critics have read *The Last Man* through the lens of Shelley's biography. For Lisa Hopkins, for instance, "The narrator of the events, Lionel Verney, is a clear portrait of Mary Shelley herself, focusing particularly on her position as sole survivor both of her mother's family and of the Shelley-Byron group."[69] While such readings are undoubtedly perceptive, I want to suggest that the events of Shelley's life did not lead to a profound shift in her religious worldview as it is depicted in *The Last Man*. Rather, the novel's approach to religion represents an intensification of the ideas she was considering in *Frankenstein*, *Mathilda*, and *Valperga*. The world of *Valperga* vacillates between one of randomness—there is no guiding hand to ensure a just conclusion—and a Calvinist-inflected malevolence in which God sees suffering and allows evil to triumph regardless. Through its science-fiction premise, *The Last Man* enables Shelley to confront those possibilities in even starker terms, as divine indifference/malice leads to the end of humanity itself.

*The Last Man* tells the story of the end of the human race via an unstoppable plague. Shelley wrote the novel at the tail end of a vogue for last-man narratives, a fad that began with the 1805 publication of Jean-Baptiste Cousin de Grainville's *Le dernier homme*, and its 1806 bootleg English translation, *The Last Man, or Omegarus and Syderia*. The release of Grainville's novel was followed by the publication of Byron's poem "Darkness" (1816), along with "Last Man" poems by Thomas Campbell (1823) and Thomas Hood (1826). The publication of Campbell's poem led to a minor blowup in the press, as he publicly denounced allegations that his poem plagiarized Byron's.[70] The poem was also met with mixed reviews—*Blackwood's Edinburgh Magazine* proclaimed it "of a very low order . . . the very idea being in itself absurd"—convincing Thomas Lovell Beddoes to abandon a verse play he had planned on the same theme.[71]

When Shelley took up the theme of the last man, therefore, it was by no means original, and she was immediately attacked in the press for publishing a book that was seen alternatively as immoral, derivative, and poorly executed. *The Lady's Monthly Museum*, the kindest of the reviews, praised Shelley's "powers of intellect" but wished she might exercise them on "subjects less removed from nature and probability."[72] More bluntly, *The London Magazine* called the novel "an elaborate piece of gloomy folly—bad enough to read—horrible to write," and advised purchasers of books "to keep their money in their pockets."[73] *The Monthly Review* complained that "this idea of 'The Last Man' has already tempted the genius of more than one of our poets," and it condemned the entire work as "the offspring of a diseased imagination."[74] *The Literary Gazette* expressed horror that a woman would write about a topic that "two of the most successful poets of the day, Byron and Campbell, have dared only just to touch upon."[75] The review concludes with the condescending suggestion that Shelley focus on the last woman instead of the last man, because "she would have known better how to paint her distress at having nobody left to talk to."[76] The author of "The Last Woman" makes a similar joke in *The Literary Lounger*. A satire of the novel written from the first-person perspective of the last living woman, the narrator is annoyed by her husband's death until she thinks to inscribe her own final monument, which hails her as a victor in the battle of the sexes: "A WOMAN HAS THE LAST WORD."[77]

While there were several last-man narratives in circulation at the time of Shelley's novel, they approach the apocalypse in strikingly different ways. Grainville's *Le dernier homme*, written in the aftermath of the French Revolution, is set in a religious cosmology, but it resists the hope of resurrection and final paradise. Initially Grainville, a Catholic priest, believed that the French Revolution promised boundless hope for the future: "The victories of our brothers in arms will change the world. . . . All countries will become fertile; people will unite in a general confederation," he preached in 1792.[78] By 1794, however, he was forced to renounce the priesthood and marry his cousin to avoid execution. The marriage was a sham, and at the conclusion of the revolution he found himself "a pariah in his conservative home town of Amiens."[79] It was during this period of isolation and defeat that Grainville produced *Le dernier homme*. He committed suicide before it saw publication.

Grainville's novel is set in a distant future in which Godwinian evolution has been achieved, but resources have begun to decay and fertility has failed. In this world, Omegarus, the last child born in a generation, has been sent to Brazil to find his prophesied bride, with whom he is destined to reproduce and save the human race. After many travails, Omegarus finally unites with and impregnates Syderia, his appointed bride, but there will be no happy ending to their romance. The biblical Adam announces that it is God's will that Omegarus abandon Syderia and their unborn child, for God has ordained their deaths. According to Adam, "the most accursed of all races will spring from your union," but "if you give up Syderia, your marriage will, on the contrary, be the prelude to the last day of the earth and the resurrection of all mankind."[80] Omegarus can fight to preserve the human race, or he can submit to the apocalypse and welcome death and resurrection. When Omegarus abandons himself to God's will, he and Syderia are treated to separate visions of the end of the world, and the novel ends on an ecstatic note. Syderia "gazed in total ecstasy, for she experienced . . . purest happiness and absolute peace together in the happy union that Heaven reserves for the just."[81] Death is overcome, and the novel ends with a vision of "the dawn of eternity."[82]

Grainville's description of the end of the world is a deeply Christian one, in which the end of all things signals the cessation of suffering for the just. A similarly devout vision underlies Campbell's "The Last Man," as it ends with a sole survivor who "remains constant in his faith" and proclaims his triumph over death:[83]

> This spirit shall return to Him
> That gave its heavenly spark;
> Yet think not, Sun, it shall be dim

When thou thyself art dark!
No! it shall live again, and shine
In bliss unknown to beams of thine,
By Him recalled to breath,
Who captive led captivity.[84]

As R. J. Dingley explains, Campbell's last man is "unshaken in his personal conviction of immortality."[85] For Campbell, as for Grainville, there is triumph in destruction, and "a firm belief in the ever-lasting governance of the Almighty."[86] The promise of resurrection and eternal bliss compensates for the loss of any pleasures to be found in this life.

If Campbell's poem presents an unmitigatedly positive vision of apocalypse, Grainville's novel contains recalcitrant elements that subtly bespeak religious and political doubts. Paley points out, "The theodicy of this novel is, to say the least, problematic: the universe is presided over by a *dieu fainéant*, and Jesus . . . is given no role at all."[87] Omegarus and Syderia both suffer terribly while awaiting their ends, and the typological promise of "Omégare / Adam / Jesus and Syderie / Eve / Mary" does not win out; "Omégare will not regenerate human-kind; the child in Syderie's womb will never be born."[88] Thus if Campbell's last man reflects the comfort of biblical certainty, Grainville's fulsome vision of the end betrays an uncomfortable level of doubt.

In contrast to Grainville and Campbell, Thomas Hood uses the image of the last man for satiric purposes. His poem is narrated by an executioner who is determined to enforce the law despite the mass extinction of humanity. When he comes upon the only other living man, a beggar who has stolen clothing from a deceased nobleman, the executioner insists on trying him for his "crime": "But God forbid that a thief should die / Without his share of the laws! . . . / I was judge, myself, and jury, and all, / And solemnly tried the cause."[89] The poem concludes with the beggar's death by hanging, and the executioner's realization that he is now alone, unable even to risk suicide: "For hang-ing looks sweet,—but, alas! in vain, / My desperate fancy begs . . . / For there is not another man alive, / In the world, to pull my legs!"[90] Hood satirizes the impulse to preserve distinctions of rank, even when the world has ceased to exist. He also implicitly satirizes the last-man genre by constructing a narrator both unaware of the enormity of his situation and uninterested in thinking through the philosophical implications of his lastness. And unlike Grainville or Campbell, Hood offers no biblical explanation of or consolation for the loss of the world. Byron, even more so than Hood, refuses the comfort of biblical timelines; there "is no God and no inherent moral order" in "Darkness."[91] Inspired by the cold, damp summer occasioned by the eruption of Mount Tambora, by the influx of sun spots discovered in the summer of 1816, and by the prediction of a Bolognese astronomer that the sun would burn out on July 18, 1816, Byron describes the experience of the end of the world in a short but powerful poem.[92] After the sun goes out without warning, resources are exhausted, and people become unrecognizable to one another, monstrous in their suffering. When two enemy groups come together, "Each other's aspects—saw, and shriek'd, and died—/ Even of their mutual hideousness they died, / Unknowing who he was upon whose brow / Famine had written Fiend."[93] Finally, there is nothing left, all life extinguished, the natural world a barren wasteland: "The waves were dead; the tides were in their grave, / The moon, their mistress, had expir'd before; / The winds were wither'd in the stagnant air, / And the clouds perish'd."[94] Here is no God, no divine plan, merely senseless and unexplained destruction. In Dingley's words, "Byron nowhere makes any explicit reference to a Divine scheme and the immediate cause of world-ending, the extinction of the Sun, would occur whether mankind has deserved punishment or not."[95]

When Mary Shelley turned to the theme of the last man for her 1826 novel, she drew both on prior works in the genre and the strain of apocalypticism that ran throughout early nineteenth-century British culture. At the same time, her novel engages with advances in scientific knowledge that challenged religious worldviews. In 1794–96, Erasmus Darwin's *Zoonomia* proposed a preliminary version of evolutionary theory, one that was rooted in the religious belief that "God had designed living things to be self-improving," but still implied that the world may have a cycle beyond that articulated by the Bible.[96] Darwin was not himself religious, and references to divine will were likely included in *Zoonomia* to combat accusations of radicalism.[97] Still, according to Darwin, "all warm-blooded animals have arisen from one living filament, which THE GREAT FIRST CAUSE endued with animality, with the power of acquiring new parts . . . and thus possessing the faculty of continuing to improve by its own inherent activity, and of delivering those improvements by generation to its posterity, world without end!"[98] Subsequently, Jean-Baptiste Lamarck's *Philosophie zoologique* (1809) further developed provisional understandings of evolution with a less explicitly religious bent. According to Lamarck, "if it is true that all the living organisms are products of nature, one cannot but believe that [nature] has only been able to produce them in succession and not at all at once in a time without deviation. There is reason to think that it is only with the simplest that she began, having produced only last of all the most complex organisms either of the animal kingdom or of the vegetable kingdom."[99] Larmarck rejected the concept of species extinction, suggesting that species did not disappear but simply evolved into more familiar forms, culminating with humankind. Via this "transformist" theory, he "envisioned evolution without extinction."[100]

In contrast to Lamarck stood Georges Cuvier, who emphasized in his work not transmutation but "catastrophism." Examining the fossils of extinct species, Cuvier came to the conclusion that species extinction was real, and that it was caused by "a series of sudden, violent catastrophes."[101] Melissa Bailes explains, "Following Buffon in claiming that a succession of cataclysmic revolutions divided the history of the earth into six epochs or periods, equated with the 'days' of creation in Genesis, Cuvier viewed these revolutions as geological processes by which dry land emerged from the sea to form new continents while old continents sank beneath sea level. An advocate of species fixity, he asserted that each revolution forced an affected set of the earth's fauna into extinction, only to be replaced by a 'new' group through migration from a different part of the globe."[102] Early nineteenth-century paleontologists were thus divided between "Cuverian catastrophism and Lamarckian anti-catastrophism," in part owing to the religious implications of each work.[103] Although Cuvier remained throughout his life committed "to a firm belief in creationism," and although the epochs he proposed could match up with biblical catastrophes, they also offered the unsettling possibility of a natural world that functions apart from a divine plan.[104] Cuvier's works thus represent "the jettisoning of a theological point of reference" for the study of geology and "an acceptance of historical relativity in the downgrading of the Bible story of the Flood to the position of yet another near-eastern legend."[105] The study of fossils leads to the uncomfortable idea that nature may exist outside of biblical structures and commands.

In 1822, Mary Shelley received a copy of Cuvier's *Recherches*, and several years later, she would invoke his "model for history" in *The Last Man*.[106] Cycles of catastrophe and extinction in the novel do not adhere to any sense of biblical time or divine plan. As Morton Paley writes, "In contrast to the universe of Cousin de Grainville, Mary Shelley's has no sovereign God and no supernatural agency . . . any rational explanation of the destruction of humankind is conspicuously absent."[107] *The Last Man* thus foregrounds a sense of religion's futility, as characters call out to God with prayers that consistently go unanswered. At the beginning of the novel, Adrian is deeply religious, seeing everywhere in nature proof of God's benevolence. "Assuredly," he tells Lionel, "a most benignant power built up the majestic fabric we inhabit, and framed the laws by which it endures."[108] That the world functions so successfully, like an "animal machine," is proof of God's presence: "Why should this be, if HE were not good? (*Last Man*, 62). Adrian concludes this scene with a heartfelt prayer, asking that "death and sickness were banished from our earthly home! that hatred, tyranny, and fear could no longer make their lair in the human heart!" (63). Lionel believes in this moment that God has heard Adrian's prayers, blessing England and its populace for all time. "The spirit of life seemed to linger in his form, as a dying flame on an altar flickers on the embers of an accepted sacrifice" (63). England, Lionel believes with Godwinian faith, is evolving toward perfection, and God himself will oversee its continued happiness.

In actuality, Adrian's prayer has fallen on deaf or nonexistent ears, and Adrian's early confidence in God's blessing gives way by the end of the novel to the recognition that his certainty was only ever in his head. The characters try to personify the horrible events surrounding them and attribute them to a rational plan. Nature the evil mother and God the negligent father are set up as two inexorable forces against which humans must struggle.[109] Lionel also consoles himself with a catastrophist faith that all is not lost, that God will replace humanity with a new, more worthy species. "Will not this world be re-peopled, and the children of a saved pair of lovers, in some to me unknown and unattainable seclusion, wandering to these prodigious relics of the ante-pestilential race, seek to learn how beings so wondrous in their achievements, and imaginations infinite, and powers godlike, had departed from their home to an unknown country?" (*Last Man*, 362). Yet the text offers no outside support for this belief. Lionel may see himself as a second Noah, but the novel provides no proof of God's interest or even his existence. Lionel writes, "A sense of degradation came over me. Did God create man, merely in the end to become dead earth in the midst of healthful vegetating nature?" (309) The fearful current underlying the novel is the possibility that there is no plan, no benevolent divine oversight, that humans have died for nothing. "Death in this virulent form seems *meaningless*," and what remains is shapeless, purposeless entropy.[110]

Lionel is not a second Noah, and the novel consistently rejects biblical symbolism. On the road, Adrian, Lionel, and their followers believe that they are being stalked by death, a figure drawn from the pages of Revelation: "We were haunted for several days by an apparition, to which our people gave the appellation of the Black Spectre. We never saw it except at evening, when his coal black steed, his mourning dress, and plume of black feathers, had a majestic and awe-striking appearance" (*Last Man*, 318). The survivors quickly come to view the "Black Spectre" as a "token of inevitable death" (318), a harbinger of doom. "It was Death himself, they declared, come visibly to seize on subject earth, and quell at once our decreasing numbers" (318). What they soon realize, however, is that the Black Spectre is just a man attempting to survive. "He was a French noble of distinction, who, from the effects of plague, had been left alone in his district" (318). Like Frankenstein's monster, he has lived on the outskirts of humanity (albeit by choice rather than necessity), desperate for any crumbs of human kindness. "He dared not join us, yet he could not resolve to lose sight of us, sole human beings who besides himself existed in wide and fertile France" (319). The Black Spectre later dies amid "the agonies of disease" (318). Biblical truth is reduced to fiction, the horseman of the apocalypse demystified into just another suffering human.

If the Bible proves a fictional text, religion, as in *Valperga*, is revealed as a tool of oppression.[111] When the novel begins, humanity is evolving toward perfection, progressing, as William Godwin promised, beyond the need for monarchs.[112] As the world crumbles, however, the need for centralized control reemerges. Adrian, the rightful heir to the throne, returns to the position he once renounced, but the power vacuum left behind by the plague results in the rise of a pernicious new cult that brainwashes its followers and hastens their deaths. Led by a "self-erected prophet" whose "father had been a methodist preacher" (*Last Man*, 292), the cult embodies the evils of misused religion. The leader is "an imposter in the most determined sense of the term," a man of "vicious propensities" who sees in the outbreak of the plague a means "by which to acquire adherents and power" (292, 293). For the prophet, religion is a convenient avenue for gaining followers, and he creates among his disciples internecine battles that thin further the dwindling human race and hasten humanity's extinction.

In her depiction of the prophet, Shelley employs some of the stereotypes common to anti-Methodist propaganda as detailed in the first chapter of this volume. Eighteenth-century critics of Methodism often complained that for its adherents, "style trumped theology."[113] According to William Warburton, for instance, "precise doctrines . . . are of little consequence, compared with the style and power with which they are enforced."[114] Methodists, their critics argued, care little for doctrine or even God, but instead become devoted to a single preacher whom they endow with an undeserved worldly authority. In such propaganda, believers are viewed as too poor or too uneducated—Alexander Knox calls them the "least cultivated classes of society"[115]—to recognize the truth of the Anglican faith, and they privilege feeling over rationality. Shelley's "self-erected prophet" likewise develops his own cult of personality; he moves his followers until "their obedience to their leader" is "entire" (*Last Man*, 292), leading them to illness and death before killing himself. It is only when the prophet and his cult implode that the remainder of Adrian's followers return with "recovered reason" (292), suggesting that while Methodism may be intensely seductive, it is not rational. It is a tool of earthly control—unnecessary, harmful, imprisoning—cloaked in a dynamic pastoral performance.

While Shelley targets Methodists by name, she implies that all religions may finally be the same, fictional constructs and engines of social power. Indeed, *The Last Man* vacillates between a Calvinist-inflected fear of God's malevolence and an atheist conviction of divine absence. It extends the themes of *Frankenstein*—Victor's hatred for his creature is refracted in the God of *The Last Man*, who views all of humankind with Victor's antipathy—and *Valperga*; Beatrice's fears become terrifyingly real in *The Last Man*, and divine justice becomes ever more elusive. At the same time, it revisits and elaborates on the ideas Shelley first put forth in "Valerius." *The Last Man* concludes in Rome, where Lionel confronts the truth of his situation, that he is the last of all mankind. "I repeated to myself—I am in Rome . . . sovereign mistress of the imagination, majestic and eternal survivor of millions of generations of extinct men" (*The Last Man*, 357). For Lionel as for Valerius, Rome's ruins symbolize both the futility of empire and all he has lost—human companionship, human ingenuity, and human language. Thus as he travels across Europe, Lionel continuously leaves writing behind, hoping to connect with another human consciousness. In France, he writes "in three languages, that 'Verney, the last of the race of Englishmen, had taken up his abode in Rome'" (353). Later, he paints on the walls of a building, "Friend, come! I wait for thee!" (353).[116] But there is no one left to hear him, and thus like Valerius, Lionel heads to the Coliseum, where he mourns the loss of his family, friends, and civilization. "I sat at the foot of these vast columns. The Coliseum, whose naked ruin is robed by nature in a verdurous and glowing veil, lay in the sunlight on my right" (358). Unlike Valerius, however, Lionel has no kindly daughter-figure to console him for his loss. He has nothing and no one, the sole survivor of humanity's extinction and the sole repository of human memory.

Like Valerius, Lionel must come to grips with his loss, and as he does so, *The Last Man* realizes the religious implication of "Valerius," a future world in which Christianity has not only ceased to matter but has functionally ceased to exist. The Rome of "Valerius" is filled with the symbols of Christianity's triumph—crucifixes in the Pantheon, St. Peter's towering over the ruins of the Elysian Fields—reflecting the mutability of religion and hinting at a time in which Christianity will be superseded. That time has arrived in *The Last Man*. Lionel proceeds from the Coliseum, site of the ruins of Roman religion, to the Vatican, which has also begun to decay. "I haunted the Vatican, and stood surrounded by marble forms of divine beauty. . . . They looked on me with unsympathising complacency" (*The Last Man*, 360). As Lionel prowls the halls of St. Peter's, he finds not power and might, but loss and infinite emptiness.[117]

Yet there is hope in *The Last Man*, a turn away from the despair of *Mathilda* and *Valperga* and toward the beauty and wonder of humanity in a godless universe. If God is hostile, disinterested, or fictional, human kindness and ingenuity matter all the more. If initially "the material pressures of disease work to bring out the worst in humanity," the human race finally responds to its extinction with thousands of tiny kindnesses.[118] "In every change goodness and affection can find field for exertion and display. Among some these changes produced a devotion and sacrifice of self at once graceful and heroic" (*Last Man*, 240). As class boundaries and distinctions of rank dissolve, people value in one another their mutual humanity: "A clean hearth and bright fire; the supper ready cooked by beloved hands; gratitude for the provision for tomorrow's meal: strange enjoyments for the high-born English, yet they were now their sole, hard-earned, and dearly prized luxuries" (240). Thus Lionel does not lament the loss of his country, his religion, or his status, as Valerius does, but the loss of love, companionship, and language itself. "Without love, without sympathy, without communion with any, how could I meet the morning sun?" Lionel asks plaintively (359).

Shelley writes a love letter to human creativity in *The Last Man*, to architecture, music, art, and literature, to the products of human minds that transcend God and nature.[119] Power, status, aristocracy, even basic physical comforts are finally worthless, but art still has meaning. As the plague descends, Lionel attends the theatre and notes the popularity of tragedy, even among those seeking escape: "The theatres were kept open; every place of public resort was frequented. . . . Tragedies deep and dire were the chief favourites. Comedy brought with it too great a contrast to the inner despair" (*Last Man*, 217). Later, he visits the theatre for what will be the last time, and mourns the beautiful artistic creations that will be lost when no one is left to perform them. Watching a performance of *Macbeth* in an effort to "forget awhile the protracted scenes of wretchedness" (219), Lionel is drawn into a profound, shared emotional experience with the audience. "A pang of tameless grief wrenched every heart, a burst of despair was echoed from every lip.—I had entered into the universal feeling" (221). Striking back against centuries of antitheatrical propaganda, Lionel elevates the theatre to a site of communal empathy, and mourns a world that no longer has stagecraft in it.[120]

Likewise, Lionel is enchanted by music. As Adrian's band of English refugees wanders across continental Europe, they hear beautiful music coming from a church in Ferney, the first music they have heard in a long time. It is a profound experience for Lionel, who cries out, "O music, in this our desolation, we had forgotten thee!" (*Last Man*, 325). The group approaches the church, where they find an unnamed young woman performing on the organ. Despite Lucy Morrison's claim that "Mary Shelley links music thematically with God,"[121] it is telling that the church itself offers no comfort. Lionel draws no joy from the remnants of his religion. Rather, "we all stood mute; many knelt" to hear the woman play (325). It is a human creation—music—that awes and reminds Lionel of meaning and beauty. Elizabeth Effinger argues that "when music is heard it fails to have an antidotal effect on the surviving listeners,"[122] but when the young woman plays Haydn, at least momentarily the group believes that the world "might still be worthily celebrated by such an hymn of praise" (326). It is not God that inspires, but music composed by human minds and played by human hands.[123]

Religion means little in the face of extinction, and at the end of the novel, what Lionel misses most is human language. *The Last Man* thus flies in the face of Romantic constructions of nature, in which the natural world offers consolation for a disappointing humanity. Traveling to Italy, Lionel climbs to top of "a hill which led to Spoleto" (*Last Man*, 354) and stares down at the natural world. It is a climactic moment, and in many ways, a quintessentially Romantic one, as Lionel experiences the sublime through a sense of his own insignificance. "I sat on a fragment of rock, and looked round. The sun had bathed in gold the western atmosphere, and in the east the clouds caught the radiance, and budded into transient loveliness" (354). Ultimately, however, Lionel turns away from nature. "No, no," he says defiantly, "I will not live among the wild scenes of nature, the enemy of all that lives. I will seek the towns" (356).[124] Lionel's choice recalls that of Wollstonecraft's Mary, for whom isolation in the natural world is also not enough. While Mary's charity is filtered through a religious lens, however, Lionel seeks human connection out of loneliness and a deep need for human connection. The novel concludes not in the natural world, but in Rome, "majestic and eternal survivor of millions of generations of extinct men" (357), and a place in which Lionel can be once more surrounded by language, the proof of human consciousness. True consolation, Shelley suggests, lies with art and literature, with proof of human existence in the face of nature's malevolence and God's vast indifference. Thus when Lionel sets out for the east, he takes with him Homer and Shakespeare, the best of human art: "I have selected a few books; the principal are Homer and Shakespeare.—But the libraries of the world are thrown open to me—and in any port I can renew my stock" (365). He also comforts himself by leaving behind a work of his own, the text of *The Last Man*. There may be no one left to read his memoir, but in writing, he inscribes his own existence and to some extent triumphs over the void. He explains, "I will leave a monument of the existence of Verney, the Last Man" (362). As we saw in chapter 3, multiple critics view Mathilda's decision to write as an expression of self and an act of healing. Something similar might be said of Lionel, who writes to assert his existence in the face of nothingness. Here is not, as Middleton argues, "the futility of existence, the need for resignation";[125] rather, to read and write are in themselves a consolation and, on some level, proof of Lionel's triumph over death.

According to Paul Cantor, "For all her critique of imperialism. . . . Shelley in the end seems to accept a form of aesthetic imperialism. When all else drops out of the lives of her characters, they are left with the pursuit of beauty. For the Last Man, life becomes a kind of perpetual Grand Tour."[126] When read through the lens of the novel's attitude to religion, however, the novel's treatment of art takes on a very different cast, a defiant statement of human value in the face of nothingness. In the absence of God, human minds offer a brilliant contrast to nature's careless destruction. Written during a period of profound personal loss, the novel proclaims the sublime quality of human creation.

Shelley would return explicitly to these themes a final time in her 1826 short story "Roger Dodsworth: The Reanimated Englishman," a story that encapsulates many of the same philosophical musings as "Valerius," *Mathilda*, and *The Last Man*. In 1826, a man named Roger Dodsworth was reportedly thawed from a block of ice and brought back to life following his death in a 1660 avalanche. Dodsworth's story was first reported in France on June 28, 1826, in the *Journal du Commerce de Lyon*, and it was soon after picked up by the British press, appearing in the *New Times* on July 4. According to the *New Times*, Dr. Jason Hotham discovered in Switzerland

> the body of a man, about 30 years of age . . . under a heap of ice, proceeding from an avalanche. As the body seemed to be fresh as if it had been stifled only half an hour before, Dr. Hotham caused it to be taken out, and having had the clothes pulled off, ordered it to be plunged into cold water. . . . Afterwards it was put in a warm bed, and treated as usual in cases of suffocation, but by which means animation was restored. What was the astonishment of every body, when the individual having recovered the use of his faculties, declared that he was Roger Dodsworth, son of the Antiquary of the same name, born in 1629, who, returning from Italy in 1660, a year after the death of his father, was buried under an avalanche.[127]

This story was repeated in a host of British periodicals: the *Morning Chronicle* (July 5), the *London Sun* (July 5), the *Manchester Guardian* (July 8), the *Edinburgh Scotsman* (July 8), and *John Bull* (July 9). Several publications further capitalized on interest in the miraculous resurrection, with Dodsworth himself supposedly writing a series of letters to *John Bull* and *The New Monthly Magazine* recording his observations on modern life, dress, and morals. By November, however, the press had lost interest and Dodsworth faded from sight, leaving Shelley to fictionalize his experience and consider the philosophical implications of his resurrection.[128]

In many ways, Roger Dodsworth's experience mirrors Valerius's. He wakes up in a now-unfamiliar world and is forced to confront the extent to which society has moved on without him. His family and friends are dead, and his understanding of political culture, indeed of the English language itself, has grown obsolete: "Now every human being he had ever seen is 'lapped in lead,' is dust, each voice he ever heard is mute. The very sound of the English language is changed."[129] The property he once called his own is so changed as to be unrecognizable: "His own patrimony . . . sunk into the thirsty gulph that gapes ever greedy to swallow the past" ("Roger Dodsworth," 47). Dodsworth, like Valerius, must confront the reality of the world's mutability; families, governments, and civilizations rise and fall. "His learning, his acquirements, are probably obsolete," and while he slumbered in death, "Empires, religions, races of men, have probably sprung up or faded" (47).

Religions have "sprung up or faded" ("Roger Dodsworth," 47) between Roger Dodsworth's death and reanimation, Shelley posits. Thus as in "Valerius" and The Last Man, "Roger Dodsworth" depicts the impermanence of religious faith. It also disrupts Christian belief systems by focusing on the possibility of reincarnation. Perhaps, Shelley suggests, the skeptical atheists of today were the Christian martyrs of old. Perhaps the devout Roman pagans of the past have become the vehement Christians of the present. "Would not several of our free thinking martyrs wonder to find that they had suffered as Christians under Domitian, while the judge as he passed sentence would suddenly become aware, that formerly he had condemned the saints of the early church to the torture, for not renouncing the religion he now upheld" (49). All of this has happened before, and it will all happen again. Religion is as ephemeral and fleeting as life itself. Stepping outside a Christian understanding of life and death, Shelley implies that there may be no heaven or hell, no biblical cosmology or all-seeing God. One power changes, giving way to the next, and as in The Last Man, only the products of the human mind have meaning.

The narrator of "Roger Dodsworth" does not know what happened to Roger after he dropped out of public view. Perhaps he died, she speculates, or perhaps he assimilated into his new life. All he leaves behind, then, is a written record of his existence (Shelley's story), and an epitaph that will, like Lionel's, transcend the end of the world: "To the Memory of R. Dodsworth, An Englishman, Born April 1, 1617; Died July 16, 1826; Aged 209. An inscription which, if it were preserved during any terrible convulsion that caused the world to begin its life again, would occasion many learned disquisitions and ingenious theories concerning a race which authentic records showed to have secured the privilege of attaining so vast an age" ("Roger Dodsworth," 50). Once again, Shelley positions art as the consolation for death, mutability, and religious uncertainty.[130] "So long lives this, and this gives life to thee," Shakespeare once wrote.[131] At the midpoint of her career, Shelley would concur. In the face of great emptiness, there is beauty in human art.

Multiple critics have treated Shelley's *The Last Man* as a turning point in her career; the savage reviews and poor sales forced her to turn away from the gothic and science fiction elements of her earlier works, taking refuge in historical fiction and the domestic novels popular among readers of her day. *The Last Man* also marks a turning point in Shelley's religious cosmology, as the preoccupations of the first decade of her writing career—absent or malevolent deities—never again take center stage in her texts. Instead, the turn toward human ingenuity and compassion that underlies *The Last Man* becomes the focus of her future works. As we will see, what critics have characterized as the conservative turn in Shelley's writings, the turn toward "utopian domesticity," also represents a new era in her relationship with religious faith.

# 5

# DOMESTICITY

The period following the publication of *The Last Man* was by all measures the most productive of Mary Shelley's career. Between *The Last
Man*'s release in 1826 and her death in 1851, she produced three full-
length novels, a second travel narrative, an edition of her husband's
poetry, numerous short stories, and a series of biographical essays
written for Dionysius Lardner's *Cabinet Cyclopedia*. Despite her substantial output, however, this period remains the least critically studied of Shelley's career. This critical disinterest can be traced in part
to lingering academic sexism (for some critics, Mary Shelley is more
interesting for the insight she provides into the life of Percy Shelley),
in part to the foibles of academic periodization (Romanticists rarely
stray into the Victorian era and vice versa), and in part to backlash
against the perceived conservatism of her later works. Writing in 1984,
Mary Poovey attributed Shelley's seeming rightward turn to a desire to
leave behind her parents' radicalism and the unconventionality of her
younger years to become, finally, a proper lady. The behaviors modeled by her mother and husband were "always at odds with the ideal
of feminine propriety that was endorsed at nearly every level of early

nineteenth-century society," and Shelley progressively "dissociates herself from the more radical position."[1]

In recent years, however, critics have challenged the view of later Shelley as conservative only, viewing in her works a continued interest in European politics and a persistent strain of political radicalism.[2] Still, it is undeniable that something changed for Shelley after the publication of *The Last Man*, as she increasingly foregrounded what Melissa Sites calls "utopian domesticity," a commitment to "realizable social reform centering around a revised model of domesticity."[3] Building on Sites's argument, this chapter argues that Shelley's depiction of the domestic sphere in the latter half of her career represents a logical evolution of her approach to religious belief. Lionel Verney realizes at the end of *The Last Man* that human interaction, human art, and human love are all that matter. For the remainder of Shelley's career, her characters come to similar conclusions, finding faith and happiness in domestic life, and elevating human relations to the point of greatest importance. This shift, I will argue, is indicative of Shelley's awareness of and engagement with Evangelicalism, which by the mid-nineteenth century had become a dominant cultural force. Shelley's later works are not explicitly religious, yet in them she adopts an argument common to many Evangelical texts, that true happiness, value, and meaning for women may be found within the domestic sphere. At the end of her novel-writing career, Shelley abandons her doubts about a distant God, finding Evangelically inflected meaning in family, kindness, and love.

In 1830, Shelley published *The Fortunes of Perkin Warbeck: A Romance*, the longest of her historical fictions, probably in the hopes of capitalizing on the popularity of the genre as promoted by Sir Walter Scott. Despite the change in genre and tone, *Perkin Warbeck* picks up where *The Last Man* left off, with underlying doubts about the veracity of religious faith. Religious belief is never openly questioned in the novel, as it is in *Valperga* and *The Last Man*. The characters are all deeply religious, committed to their individual pursuits of the divine. Yet the novel has not abandoned—although it better conceals—its deep suspicion of organized religion and a just divine plan. As in *Valperga*, religious officials in *Perkin Warbeck* are corrupt or violent. Political machinations frequently take place in churches, and under the watchful eyes of priests and monks: "To modern and protestant England, a cathedral or a church may appear a strange place for private assignations and concealed meetings. It was otherwise in the days of our ancestors."[4] Church officials are all too frequently corrupt and willing to harm others for political gain. Richard Simon, for instance, uses his standing as a priest to "form plans . . . to raise a whirlwind around him" (49). The priests in London, meanwhile, are "impiously permitted to violate the sacrament of confession" (158), while the evil monk Meilar Trangmar uses his standing as a religious figure to infiltrate Richard's circle and justify his evil acts.

Despite the religious fervor of the central characters, God's presence, as in *The Last Man*, is called into doubt. By divine right, Richard is the lawful ruler of Britain, yet God's ostensible favor is never sufficient to overcome Henry's stronger armies. Throughout the novel, Richard's nobility shines through, and he proves himself in every way morally superior to the tyrannical Henry.[5] Richard's "eye beams with nobleness" (*Perkin Warbeck*, 66), and his men "look[ed] on him as a superior being" (107). He possesses a "free and noble spirit" (314), and is "beloved, for he was generous and kind" (315). Henry, in contrast, treats his wife with "studied barbarity" (52), and he respects neither God nor man in his quest for power. But God does not cast down Richard's enemies or pave the way for his restoration. There may be ways to justify God's inaction: perhaps he sought to punish the people with a tyrant, or perhaps he needed to ensure that the Tudor dynasty (and by extension, Anglicanism) would come to pass, but the novel never pursues any such explanation. Lidia Garbin explains, "at the core of *Perkin Warbeck* is a yearning for social and political reforms," but those reforms never materialize.[6] Instead, readers are left with a sense that Richard's religion has proven futile as his political quest has proven futile, the security of religious faith undercut by the uncomfortable possibility of divine indifference or malignity. As Katherine cries out, "God has delivered the innocent into the hands of the cruel" (387).

What emerges from *Perkin Warbeck*, then, as from *The Last Man* and *Valperga*, is a profound sense of the futility of religious and civil warfare. In each of these texts, Shelley focuses on the carnage caused by war, which she understood from a young age, having witnessed firsthand the devastation caused by the Napoleonic Wars, which raged across Europe between 1803 and 1815. Historians often refer to the Napoleonic Wars as the first instance of "total war," that is, "war involving the complete mobilization of a society's resources to achieve the absolute destruction of an enemy, with all distinction erased between combatants and noncombatants."[7] Such behavior, a focus on absolute destruction, broke with eighteenth-century military norms and standards. In the aftermath of the carnage of the Thirty Years' War (1618–48), in which upward of eight million people died,[8] philosophers of the long eighteenth century cautioned moderation in warfare. Colm McKeough explains, "The savagery and atrocities of the Thirty Years War had provoked revulsion and a realization that, unless curbed, war would cease to be a means to any worthwhile ends."[9] According to Emmerich de Vattel, author of *The Law of Nations* (1758), for instance, "If you once open a door for continual accusation of outrageous excess in hostilities, you will only augment the number of complaints, and influence the minds of the contending parties with increasing animosity: fresh injuries will be perpetually springing up; and the sword will never be sheathed till one of the parties be utterly destroyed."[10] De Vattel acknowledges that there are times in which war is necessary—a nation has "a right to prevent . . . intended injury, when she sees herself threatened with it"[11]—but warfare must be selectively practiced, and innocent lives should be spared to the greatest extent possible. "When it is not militarily necessary to kill non-combatants, then it is not honorable to kill them."[12]

In the wake of the French Revolution, however, attitudes toward and practices of military engagement began to change, resulting in the total war of which Bell writes. According to McKeogh, between 1792 and 1815, "there was a broadening of war in all its elements: the combatants, the targets, the victims, the weapons, the aims and the battle plans."[13] The size of armies expanded drastically, leading to bloodier battles and more widespread causalities across Europe. According to David Bell, "before 1790 very few European battles had involved more than 100,000 soldiers. In 1809 the battle of Wagram (the largest yet seen in the gunpowder age) involved 300,000. And in 1813 the battle of Leipzig had 500,000, of whom 150,000 were killed or wounded."[14] By the end of the Napoleonic Wars, upward of 3.5 million people, many of them civilians, were killed, for in this new world, "The aim of Napoleonic warfare became the total annihilation of the enemy," soldiers and civilians alike.[15]

The results of the Napoleonic Wars were therefore death, property loss, and suffering across continental Europe. French (and to a lesser extent British[16]) armies became infamous in Spain for plundering and committing acts of violence during the years of the Peninsular War (1807–14). André François, Comte Miot de Mélito, described in his memoir the carnage left behind in Burgos, Spain in 1808: "Absolutely deserted, almost all the houses had been pillaged and their furniture smashed to pieces and thrown in the mud; part of the city was . . . on fire; a frenzied soldiery was forcing every door and window . . . all the churches had been stripped; and the streets were encumbered with the dead and dying."[17] In Aranjuez, Spain, witnesses reported that "husbands have seen their wives raped, fathers their daughters, sons their aged mothers, and there have even been cases in which the main square was used as the scene of their indescribable lascivities."[18] Another witness reported, "Whenever the French come here . . . they commit the greatest atrocities that Your Excellency can imagine. . . . There is not a statue which they do not burn, nor a woman whom they do not molest. Indeed, at times they kill the women, as they do any man who does not give them what they demand."[19] The French were thus likened to an army of violent locusts, destroying civilians, property, and community as they swept across the country.

Spain was not alone in experiencing the devastation of the Napoleonic Wars. During the Battle of Leipzig, "between 16 and 19 October 1813 a total of more than 171,000 men under Napoleon's supreme command . . . faced 301,500 Coalition forces in Leipzig."[20] Trapped between warring armies, villagers took refuge inside local churches. Dr. Karl August Goldscab, the pastor of Liebertwolkwitz and Großpösna, described the experience as follows: "Dead and dying soldiers lay all about, and the massacre continued, particularly on the market and in the lower reaches of the village, while a large part of our homes appeared to us as smoking ruin. Human misery could scarcely be any worse."[21] Similar scenes were described throughout Europe. According to Leighton James, "Areas of northern Germany, particularly Prussia, were devastated during the 1806 and 1807 campaign."[22] Meanwhile, France, too, bore the scars of carnage. Following a 1793 uprising in the Vendée area of France at the start of the French Revolutionary Wars, civilians were massacred en masse as punishment for disobedience. In a letter supposedly written to the Committee of Public Safety, General François Joseph Westermann celebrated his army's ruthlessness, describing what we would now call genocide: "There is no more Vendée, citizens. . . . I have crushed children under the hooves of horses, and massacred women who, these at least, will give birth to no more brigands. I do not have a single prisoner with which to reproach myself. I have exterminated everything."[23]

Between the outbreak of the French Revolution and the conclusion of the Napoleonic Wars in 1815, then, continental Europe experienced horrific violence and devastating loss of property. By 1816, Jeffrey Veil writes, Europe was "ravaged by crop failures, natural devastation, and social unrest,"[24] and Mary Shelley witnessed this aftermath firsthand in 1817, when she traveled with Percy and Claire to the Continent. She records in *History of a Six Weeks' Tour* (1817) the suffering that she found in France: "The distress of the inhabitants, whose houses had been burned, their cattle killed, and all their wealth destroyed, has given a sting to my detestation of war, which none can feel who have not traveled through a country pillaged and wasted by this plague, which, in his pride, man inflicts upon his fellow."[25] According to Rebecca Domke, the trip "was one of the formative experiences of her life, and she was never afterwards fully persuaded that ideological differences could justify the suffering that an attempt to resolve those differences by force of arms might bring about."[26]

Shelley's horror at the consequences of war finds its way into her fiction, where it is magnified by the lack of a divine plan. In the absence of God's will, warfare is nothing more than a vehicle for power conducted at the expense of innocent lives. Many of Shelley's historical fictions—from *Valperga* and *Perkin Warbeck* to numerous short stories—focus on the consequences of ongoing civil warfare. *Valperga*, for instance, is set during the Ghibelline-Guelph conflict, a war occasioned by a power struggle between the pope and the Holy Roman emperor. As we have seen, Castruccio cares naught for the destruction he leaves in his wake, valuing only his own rise to power. "Accustomed to see men die in battle for his cause, he became callous to blood" (*Valperga*, 183). Factionalism and Castruccio's will to power combine to cause the pointless and painful deaths of millions, and Shelley describes in graphic terms the effect of warfare on the local peasantry. "Some of these poor wretches fled to the open country; others locked themselves up in their houses, and, throwing what they possessed from the windows, strove to save their persons from the brutality of their conquerors" (62). Underlying such representations is a fear that for peace to reign, one party must annihilate the other. Pepi wonders, "Can Ghibellines and Guelphs live within the walls of the same town? . . . If [Castruccio] had meant to establish peace in Italy, he would have assassinated all of one party, to secure the lives of the other" (51–52). Euthanasia tries unsuccessfully to prevent this final brutality, as she understands well the consequences of war. She wants nothing more than "to shew how futile that distinction and enmity were" (78), and she eventually abdicates her authority rather than be the cause of more death.

The theme of war's pointlessness is emphasized even more strongly in *Perkin Warbeck*, which features two different sorts of warfare, the secular battle between the Lancasters and the Yorks in England, and the religious conflict between the Christians and the Muslims in Spain. In both cases, nothing is worth the death and destruction that war leaves in its wake. "The result of the Moorish wars" is "death and misery" (*Perkin Warbeck*, 92), while the War of the Roses takes its toll on the English countryside. Richard and his men come across a village that "had been sacked by the Scotch: it was half burnt and quite deserted; one woman alone remained—she sat on a pile of ashes wailing aloud" (252). These are the real horrors of war, the "woman's cry," the "shrill plaint of infancy," and the "ruins of another village" (253). That Richard understands the suffering his quest for power entails but continues on nonetheless bespeaks his limitations as a potential ruler. As Bennett points out, he is "as guilty of destroying innocent lives as Castruccio was," and while he recognizes fully the "atrocities of war committed in his name," he "does not change his objective."[27] No wonder, then, that he finds so little support for his claim to the throne. The people champion Henry not because they believe in him, but because they are tired of fighting, sick of devastation, and ready to accept any monarch who offers stability and peace. "I love not Tudor," Lord Surrey tells Richard, "but I love my country: and now that I see plenty and peace reign over this fair isle, even though Lancaster be their unworthy viceregent, shall I cast forth these friends of man, to bring back the deadly horrors of unholy civil war? . . . I will not people my country with orphans; nor spread the plague of death from the eastern to the western sea" (195).

Victoria Middleton argues that "after *The Last Man*, the protagonists in Mary Shelley's novels do not quarrel with their makers."[28] *Perkin Warbeck* marks a definitive turning point in Shelley's depiction of religion, a move toward the view that would characterize the rest of her career. If Shelley's prior works contemplated a world in which God is absent or evil, the quiet epilogue to *Perkin Warbeck* downplays those questions in favor of an ethic of domestic harmony and interpersonal care. Set many years after Richard's execution, Katherine, Richard's widow, and Edmund Plantagenet, his cousin and most faithful ally, encounter one another for the last time. Edmund has retreated to the forest, driven by grief to isolate himself, while Katherine has become the beloved companion of Elizabeth of York, Richard's sister and Henry VII's ill-treated queen. Katherine has lost much—her husband, her social standing, her Scottish ancestral home—but she, like the "female survivors" of Shelley's short stories, finds herself content, if not happy.[29] "There was no consolation for Katherine, which could make her for a moment forget her present existence was but the lees of life, the spiritless remnants of a nectareous draught. But Katherine was gentle, good, and resigned; she lived on, dispensing pleasure, adored by all who approached her" (*Perkin Warbeck*, 395). Katherine has abandoned political hatreds and homosocial competition for a life of service to others. Her husband's "last act was to bestow me on his sister" (399), and Katherine will honor her husband by honoring his final wishes. The historical Lady Catherine Gordon went on to marry three more times, but Shelley excises these marriages from the text, focusing instead on Katherine's widowhood and life of service to others.[30] Shelley's Katherine views empathy and service as divine qualities, and she tells Edmund, "He who died on the cross for us, taught us to understand and to appreciate, commanding us to make it the master-law of our lives. Call it love, charity, or sympathy; it is the best, the angelic portion of us. It teaches us to feel pain at others' pain, joy in their joy" (398). As William Brewer explains, for Katherine, "happiness can be found even in the court of her husband's archenemy, as long as she can find people to love and be loved by."[31]

That the historical Katherine remained in Henry VII's court meant that she was "perceived both as a traitor to her husband and to Henry as her supposed lover."[32] Shelley makes clear, however, that such views are narrow-minded and shortsighted. In Richard's lifetime, Katherine "embodies domestic perfection."[33] After his death, the worldly problems of political strife and female rivalries no longer matter, and Katherine's good works become her way of expressing her religious devotion. With her "woman's education . . . which is that of the heart . . . not the head!" (*Perkin Warbeck*, 398), she values humanity, not for what it gives her, but for what she can give others. She is not a mother herself, but she helps raise Elizabeth's children and thus shapes the values of Henry VII's heirs. She is not a nun, but like the women of "The Convent of Chaillot" and "The Trial of Love," she exists in a homosocial world where service brings contentment, if not the ecstasy of her time with Richard; "to love is to exist" (399), she tells Edmund.

In contrast to Katherine, who views human interaction as a mode of religious devotion, Edmund channels his disappointment into misanthropy. He tells Katherine that his "chief labour is to tame my heart to resignation to the will of God" (*Perkin Warbeck*, 397), and he finds God's presence in the natural world, not the domestic sphere. Humankind has failed him politically, morally, and socially, but the sublimity of the natural landscape affords him hope and proof of divinity: "My heart sickens at the evil things that usurp the shape of humanity, and dare deem themselves of the same species: I turn from all, loathing. But here there is no change, no falling off, no loss of beauty and of good: these glades, these copses, the seasons' change and elemental ministrations, are for ever the same—the type of their Maker in glory and in good" (398). Nature, he continues, provides evidence of God's benevolence. Although he will never understand why "God permitted, for some inscrutable purpose, moral evil to be showered so plentifully over us. . . . The loveliness of earth saves me from despair. . . . I drink in the balmy sweetness of the hour, and repose again on the goodness of my Creator" (397, 398). Edmund cannot understand Katherine's preference for society, castigating her for perceived failures: "You need the adulation of the crowd—the luxury of palaces; you purchase these, even by communing with the murderer of him who deserved a dearer recompense at your hands" (398). Katherine, however, defends herself and her right to worship differently from Edmund: "I do not blame you, my Cousin, for seeking repose in solitude after much endurance. But unquiet should I feel in the unreplying loneliness, which forms your peace. I must love and be loved" (400). Katherine argues that devotion can be expressed in multiple ways. The epilogue to *Perkin Warbeck* thus presents two valid modes of worship, one that rejects imperfect mankind for the perfection of nature, another that turns inward to love and interpersonal relationships as the only things of value. It also replicates the endings of *Frankenstein* and *The Last Man*; Edmund's chosen solitude mirrors the monster's choice to isolate himself amidst the arctic ice, while Katherine's found family recalls Lionel's realization that only humanity matters. Here, then, is a logical evolution of the themes of *The Last Man*, a celebration of humanity in the face of divine absence.

After the publication of *Perkin Warbeck*, Shelley turned her attention to a revised edition of *Frankenstein*, which by 1831 had "acquired the status of cultural myth."[34] Her alterations to the novel are reflective both of broader shifts in British religious culture and of her understanding of faith as it developed through *The Last Man* and *Perkin Warbeck*. As we saw in chapter 3, *Frankenstein* questions God's hostility to man, and the 1831 edition, even more so than the 1818 original, emphasizes the importance of human relationships in the face of that divine malevolence. Like *The Last Man* and *Perkin Warbeck*, the 1831 revisions to *Frankenstein* valorize the domestic sphere; if Lionel and Katherine find meaning in human connection, the 1831 *Frankenstein* vests in the love of friends and family a quasi-religious faith. It also affords new power to Elizabeth as an agent of moral goodness. The 1831 *Frankenstein* thus reinforces the growing association of women with the domestic sphere even as it opens up a space in a male-dominated novel for them to exist and to matter.

According to Frankenstein's monster, Victor Frankenstein was his creator and father, and should have been his God and protector: "I remembered Adam's supplication to his Creator. But where was mine? He had abandoned me."[35] The creature chastises Frankenstein for failing to ensure the happiness and safety of the species to which he gave birth. In the 1818 edition of *Frankenstein*, Victor's disgust and fear at his creation are palpable. Read through the lens of *The Last Man*, however, the confrontation between Victor and the creature takes on new resonance. Adrian and Lionel are abandoned by their God and can never know why he has forsaken humanity, or perhaps worse, condemned it to a painful extinction. Their God is always distant, always removed, his very existence uncertain. In *Frankenstein*, however, the creature knows that his creator is real, and Victor, standing in for the God of *The Last Man*, provides the painful and frightening confirmation that he is actively horrified by his creation. We are not perfect creatures made in God's image but grotesque facsimiles from which he flees.

Victor is both a hostile god and a lost soul who, like *Perkin Warbeck*'s Edmund, seeks solace in isolation and nature. *Frankenstein* describes the natural world not as the vindictive mother of *The Last Man* but as sublime and vastly indifferent. According to Victor, the "sublime and magnificent scenes" of nature "afforded me the greatest consolation that I was capable of receiving" (*Frankenstein* [1831], 101). Like Edmund Plantagenet, he comes to prefer "the wondrous works with which Nature adorns her chosen dwelling places" (172), endowing nature with conscious benevolence. Ultimately, however, nature in *Frankenstein*, much like nature in *Perkin Warbeck*, exists beyond human affairs. Victor may believe that "maternal Nature" (99)—a line Shelley added in 1831—cares for him as a benevolent feminine force, but neither he nor the novel offers proof of this claim. Victor may attempt to confer intentionality and meaning on its operations, but nature simply exists, beyond man, beyond conception of God.

If God is hostile and nature indifferent, then human connection, for *Frankenstein* as for *The Last Man* and *Perkin Warbeck*, becomes all the more meaningful. The 1831 edition, even more so than the 1818 original, valorizes the domestic sphere, "lay[ing] even greater stress on the domestic harmony that formed the context of the early education of Elizabeth, Victor, and their friend Clerval."[36] Shelley expands her description of Victor's early life, focusing more fully on his happy childhood. In 1818, Victor's parents are described as loving, but only in passing. "No creature could have more tender parents than mine," he explains briefly (*Frankenstein* [1818], 22). The 1831 edition, by contrast, adds several new paragraphs on Victor's early life, emphasizing the kindness, love, and strong moral instruction of his youth. Victor's father is a doting husband who does everything he can to make his much-younger wife happy. "Everything was made to yield to her wishes and her convenience" (*Frankenstein* [1831], 31). Caroline, in turn, loves her husband and children deeply, creating an Edenic homelife for the family. "My mother's tender caresses and my father's smile of benevolent pleasure while regarding me are my first recollections" (31–32). Alphonse and Caroline treat Victor as a gift and set about to give him the best, most generous upbringing, deeply conscious "of what they owed towards the being to which they had given life" (32).

The alterations to Elizabeth's backstory further emphasize the importance of family. Diana K. Reese attributes these changes to a conservative impulse to "elide the implications of incest between Victor Frankenstein and Elizabeth Lavenza."[37] Nora Crook, by contrast, argues that the change is reflective of Shelley's support for "Italian liberation, one of the great causes of her life."[38] I would suggest instead that the change reflects a revitalized interest in domestic perfection. Rather than a relative foisted on the family by death, the 1831 Elizabeth is a chosen child, described in language that suggests she was fated to join the Frankenstein family and complete their happiness.[39] None "could behold" Elizabeth "without looking on her as of a distant species, a being heaven-sent, and bearing a celestial stamp in all her features" (*Frankenstein* [1831], 32–33). The 1818 *Frankenstein* insists that "every one adored Elizabeth" (*Frankenstein* [1818], 23); she is, in Sylvia Bowerbank's words, the "predictable self-sacrificing female entity which preserves domestic bliss."[40] By 1831, however, she becomes "a child fairer than a pictured cherub" (*Frankenstein* [1831], 33), a veritable angel in the Frankenstein household.

Even more so than in 1818, the women of the Frankenstein family take a central role in determining familial happiness, and as such, they are more active characters than their original counterparts. In the 1818 text, Caroline cannot attend Elizabeth when she is ill with scarlet fever: "During her confinement, many arguments had been urged to persuade my mother to refrain from attending upon her" (*Frankenstein* [1818], 29). It is only once Elizabeth is recovering that Caroline goes to her side, after which she unfortunately becomes ill: "When she heard that her favourite was recovering, she could no longer debar herself from her society, and entered her chamber long before the danger of infection was past. The consequences of this imprudence were fatal" (29). In 1831, by contrast, Caroline deliberately risks her life to save Elizabeth's. "She had at first yielded to our entreaties" not to nurse Elizabeth personally, "but when she heard that the life of her favourite was menaced, she could no longer control her anxiety. She attended her sickbed; her watchful attentions triumphed over the malignity of the distemper—Elizabeth was saved, but the consequences of this imprudence were fatal to her preserver" (*Frankenstein* [1831], 42). Caroline is both Elizabeth's savior and the victim of her own loving impulses, and after her death, Elizabeth takes her place as the guarantor of familial happiness. In a passage new to 1831, Victor emphasizes Elizabeth's centrality to his family's homelife after his mother's passing. "The saintly soul of Elizabeth shone like a shrine-dedicated lamp in our peaceful home. Her sympathy was ours; her smile, her soft voice, the sweet glance of her celestial eyes, were ever there to bless and animate us. She was the living spirit of love to soften and attract us" (37). Elizabeth is rendered quasi-divine in her ability to delight the domestic sphere. Yet she, too, is more active than her 1818 counterpart. In newly added passages, she speaks of her desire to nurse Victor back to health, lamenting that "the task of attending on your sickbed has devolved on some mercenary old nurse, who could never guess your wishes nor minister to them with the care and affection of your poor cousin" (65). Elizabeth is the best nurse possible, and she is well aware of her skill. In Caroline and Elizabeth, Shelley creates stereotypically selfless female characters, but she allows them agency in choosing self-sacrifice.

If the 1831 Elizabeth is more active than her 1818 characterization, she is also afforded more intelligence. The 1818 text implies that Elizabeth cannot or will not understand Victor's studies. Victor writes, "I disclosed my discoveries to Elizabeth . . . under a promise of strict secrecy; but she did not interest herself in the subject, and I was left by her to pursue my studies alone" (*Frankenstein* [1818], 26). In 1831, Shelley excises this passage, along with a passage in which Victor's father teaches him the secrets of electricity. In 1818, Victor's father "made a kite, with a wire and string, which drew down that fluid from the clouds" (27), but the 1831 Victor learns about the "laws of electricity" from "a man of great research in natural philosophy" (*Frankenstein* [1831], 40). As a result, Elizabeth seems more informed and Victor's father less. Shelley also emphasizes her "sensibility and intellect," not merely her "loveliness" (83), suggesting that Victor views her as an intellectual partner as well as a prospective wife.[41] While she is promised to Victor as a "pretty present" (34), a plaything, she is also allowed much more insight into her chosen mate and his family. Thus Shelley's revisions are at once conservative and subversively feminist. She defines women almost solely in relation to the domestic sphere, but she affords them greater importance in the novel.

*Frankenstein* tells the story of men isolated—by circumstance or by choice—from the domestic sphere and the love it represents. Read through the lens of *The Last Man* and *Perkin Warbeck*, it is all the more significant that the novel concludes with a turn away from science and imperialism and back to the world of humanity. In passages new to the 1831 edition, Walton becomes a double for Victor, an imperialist in the realm of science who values abstract knowledge over humankind. "One man's life or death," he explains, "were but a small price to pay for the acquirement of the knowledge which I sought, for the dominion I should acquire and transmit over the elemental foes of our race" (*Frankenstein* [1831], 24–25). He leaves his sister and proceeds to the arctic, a place in which human contact is rare, and human contact of the right sort class-wise is nearly impossible. "I shall certainly find no friend on the wide ocean, nor even here in Archangel, among merchants and seamen," he writes (15). After hearing Victor's story, however, he realizes that human relationships matter more than abstract findings.

On the request of his sailors, he turns his boat around, abandoning his pursuit in favor of safety. "I have consented to return if we are not destroyed. Thus are my hopes blasted by cowardice and indecision; I come back ignorant and disappointed" (233). Walton is disappointed, weighed down by the seeming "injustice" of the failure of his enterprise (233), yet he turns back all the same, and against Victor's objections. As the monster sets out alone across the frozen waste—an involuntary Edmund Plantagenet—Walton is left behind with his men, suggesting that there is more righteousness in humanity than in religion of the traditional sort.

In rejecting humanity, *Frankenstein*'s monster echoes not only *Perkin Warbeck*'s Edmund Plantagenet but Byron's Childe Harold, who concludes, "I have not loved the world, nor the world me,—/ But let us part fair foes."[42] Elizabeth's embrace of domestic duty, by contrast, reflects the increasing influence of Evangelical domestic ideals on Shelley's fictions. Amid the political and economic instability described in the first chapter of this volume, British culture took a rightward turn as the nineteenth century progressed. Central to the growing dominance of Evangelicalism was the cultural force of the so-called Clapham Sect, "a wealthy, influential group of upper-middle-class laymen, politically active and socially reforming in disposition," which centered around William Wilberforce in the late eighteenth and early nineteenth centuries.[43] Wilberforce is most famous today for the role he played in abolishing the British slave trade, but from the 1790s on, he viewed the reformation of manners as his primary goal. In his *A Practical View of the Prevailing Religious System* (1797), Wilberforce criticizes a culture that has become too permissive of vice. He writes, "the generality of professed Christians among the higher classes, either altogether overlook or deny, or at least greatly extenuate the corruption and weakness here in question."[44] Too many Christians, Wilberforce continues, view sin as the product of overwhelming temptation, an involuntary reflex, rather than a conscious choice. "Vice with them is rather an accidental and temporary, than a constitutional and habitual distemper; a noxious plant, which, though found to live and even to thrive in the human mind, is not the natural growth and production of the soil."[45] Instead, he argues, man is "prone to vice, it is natural and easy to him; disinclined to virtue, it is difficult and laborious."[46] It thus falls to individual Christians to be ever vigilant, to police their own behaviors and those of society, and to root out vice wherever it may grow.

As the members of the Clapham Sect were neither a sect nor exclusively from Clapham, their name is somewhat misleading.[47] A "group of friends who shared a particular religious outlook," members of the sect were "powerfully bound together by shared moral and spiritual values, by religious mission and social activism, by love for each other, and by marriage."[48] Central to their values was a commitment to improving the poor and reforming the rich. They sought to facilitate social improvement among the lower classes, "founding schools, orphanages, and medical dispensaries."[49] They were equally concerned with reshaping the morality of the aristocracy, which was meant to set an example for the country. Hannah More, an influential Evangelical author associated with the Clapham circle, explained in 1788 that "reformation must begin with the GREAT, or it will never be effectual. . . . To expect to reform the poor while the opulent are corrupt is to throw odours into the stream while the springs are poisoned."[50] The Clapham circle "fostered new concepts of public probity and national honour, based on ideals of oeconomy [sic], frugality, professionalism, and financial rectitude,"[51] and their influence became apparent as early as June 1787, when, with Wilberforce's encouragement, George III issued his Royal Proclamation for the Encouragement of Piety and Virtue, and for the Preventing and Punishing of Vice, Profaneness, and Immorality. Later that year, Wilberforce established the "Society for Carrying into Effect His Majesty's Proclamation against Vice and Immorality," which he hoped would help "purify the nation's morals."[52] Thus members of the Clapham Sect positioned themselves—and middle-class Evangelicals more broadly—as the arbiters of social virtue.

In the wake of the French Revolution, British political culture became increasingly conservative. "In 1794, Pitt suspended habeas corpus, allowing the state to imprison suspected revolutionaries without trial for the sake of wartime security."[53] Wilberforce firmly supported Pitt's measures, and Anglican Evangelicals sought to distance themselves from the radicalism of the Jacobins and the perceived disloyalty of dissenting denominations.[54] As Bebbington explains, "in the wake of the French Revolution, submission to the existing order was given a divine sanction."[55] Changes in the political realm thus accompanied an increasingly conservative approach to religious life, which in turn led to fundamental shifts in middle-class culture. Thus began a backlash against early feminism, which was increasingly dismissed as the product of radical Jacobinism. That Mary Wollstonecraft's reputation was largely destroyed by the 1798 publication of Godwin's *Memoirs* only served to confirm the belief that the concept of women's rights was too French, too dangerous, and too disruptive to the natural order.

The writings of Hannah More are instructive for understanding Anglican Evangelical attitudes toward womanhood. More, as we have seen, fervently rejected the works of Mary Wollstonecraft, refusing on general principle to read material she considered immoral, but her arguments about female education are strongly reminiscent of Wollstonecraft's.[56] Early in *Coelebs in Search of a Wife* (1809), the protagonist's mother impresses on him the necessity of finding an educated wife, and she disdains popular forms of female education. "The education of the present race of females is not very favourable to domestic happiness," she tells her son.[57] The best sort of education, she insists, "tends to form a friend, a companion, and a wife. I call education not that which is made up of the shreds and patches of useless arts, but that which inculcates principles, polishes taste, regulates temper, cultivates reason, subdues the passions, directs the feelings, habituates to reflections, trains to self-denial, and, more especially, that which refers all actions, feelings, sentiments, tastes, and passions, to the love and fear of God."[58] Only a woman inculcated with deep religious sentiments can be an appropriate companionate mate, for such a woman will recognize that "obedience is woman's highest honour and her praise."[59] Female happiness may be found in a form of education that promotes piety and contentment within the domestic sphere.

More returned to the theme of female education in her 1819 *Moral Sketches*, praising "ladies, whose own education not having been limited to the harp and the sketch-book, though not unskilled in either, are competent to teach others what themselves have been taught; who disdain not to be employed in the humble offices of Christian charity . . . whose houses are houses of prayer, whose closets are the scene of devout meditation."[60] Women should commit themselves to acts of charity, piety, and humility. They should not call attention to themselves with superficial skills such as music, drawing, or dancing but focus instead on private acts of devotion that transform the home into a religious sanctuary. Similar ideas would be circulated throughout the nineteenth century. According to one late-century publication, "Submission, love, tenderness, self-sacrifice, devotement, sympathy, are characteristic features of the piety of women. . . . Without preaching, without descending to the lecture-room or the arena of controversy, the Christian woman may go about doing good and to an extent that a seraph would envy."[61] Women should not usurp male authority through the act of preaching, but they should set an example within the household, demonstrating piety through acts of love and submission.

Evangelicals sanctified the domestic sphere, elevating care of the home to a woman's highest duty and feminizing the practices of religion and the domestic arts. All women, More writes, must "study household good," which, she insists, "involves a large and comprehensive scheme of excellence. . . . Without it, however she may inspire admiration abroad, she will never excite esteem, nor of course, durable affection, at home."[62] As the doctrine of separate spheres became more entrenched, the home was increasingly seen both as woman's rightful sphere and as man's refuge from the rougher worlds of business and politics. It fell to women to "make of the home a holy sanctum where, under the influence of their purity and piety, men's moral nature would be refreshed and refurbished."[63] A wife ruled under her husband's benevolent guidance, overseeing a world considered at once beneath male notice and more important to society than any other: "Men could be presidents, but only women could do society's most important work—rearing good children."[64]

As woman's inherently religious character was praised, religious instruction was increasingly left to the province of mothers, a trend evidenced by the deluge of religious instructional books published by and for women. According to one Sunday school handbook, "It is the mother who instructs the children, to her they look up for all they want and in general as she is, so are they."[65] Implicit in women's duty to instruct the young was a belief that they were moral agents capable of reason. Women were also supposed to use gentle guidance to steer men away from sin. A woman must "'promote good works' in her husband," writes More. To do so "raises her condition, and restores her to all the dignity of equality; it makes her not only the associate but the inspirer of his virtues."[66] Similarly, the author of the *Report of the Debates at Cork* writes, "upon the virtues of women much of that of man depended, and the religious habits of the sex could not fail to exercise a salutary influence."[67] Women thus gained power over the home, even as they were confined within the domestic sphere.

Mary Shelley both recognizes and reflects this trend in her later writings, in which women increasingly reign over the domestic sphere as angelic creators of Edenic happiness. If her late works do not become explicitly religious in nature, they are marked by an Evangelical world-view in which the domestic sphere—and female submission within that sphere—becomes a space for, and form of, devotion. Just as *Perkin Warbeck*'s Katherine finds religious meaning in service to family and children, Shelley's last novels feature female characters who sanctify the home, who find meaning and purpose in creating domestic para-dises. Her late works both reflect and contribute to the dominance of Evangelical ideals permeating the culture.

Toward the end of Mary Shelley's 1833 novel *Lodore*, Cornelia, Lady Lodore, laments that she has not been a better wife and mother, and she wishes for a Protestant alternative to a nunnery. "She often regret-ted that there were no convents, to which she might retire with safety and dignity."[68] Like Louise de la Vallière of "The Convent of Chaillot" or Angeline of "The Trial of Love," Cornelia hopes to withdraw from the world—she wants to be content, if not happy—and the convent seems an ideal location for quiet reflection, homosocial bonding, and retreat from aristocratic artificiality. As Cornelia is Protestant, the convent is not available to her, and she dreads a future in which "friendless, unknown, and therefore despised, she must shift for herself, and rely on her own resources for prudence to ensure safety" (*Lodore*, 264). Even-tually, however, she finds happiness not in isolation but in returning to the world, reconciling with her daughter, and entering into a second, more successful marriage. When the convent is impossible, a revitalized domestic sphere provides a quasi-religious form of happiness.

*Lodore*, Shelley's penultimate novel, represents in many ways a profound departure from her oeuvre to date. Lacking the historical interest of works like *Valperga* and *The Fortunes of Perkin Warbeck*, or the science fiction elements of *The Last Man* and *Frankenstein*, the novel instead focuses on the domestic struggles of the Lodore family and is closer in tone to the Silver Fork novels of the 1820s and '30s.[69] The characters are driven not by apocalyptic events or monumental historical movements but by much more mundane concerns: unhappy marriages, familial estrangements, and financial need. On the surface, the novel discusses faith only in passing, yet the novel is profoundly marked by Evangelical ideas about the home and woman's place within it. In keeping with the tone of *Perkin Warbeck* and the 1831 *Frankenstein*, *Lodore* locates happiness—and by extension, religion and godliness—in the domestic sphere. Unlike in those works, however, God reemerges as a comforting presence, his love evident in the bliss of marital felicity. That love is joined by a restored view of nature as a loving mother, underscoring the novel's emphasis on maternity.

*Lodore* tells the story of a broken marriage and its effects on the next generation. Upon publication, the novel was a modest success, and it received largely positive reviews. *The Literary Gazette* praised the novel for being "full of talent and feeling, and, we must add, of knowledge."[70] According to *The Athenaeum*, "It will be easy for our readers to perceive, that we have been well pleased with 'Lodore,' and we think, that all who can appreciate what is refined, and breathes of the affections rather than the passions, will share our pleasure."[71] *Leigh Hunt's London Journal* named the novel Shelley's "most agreeable work," praising her "decided ear for the musical in writing."[72] Modern critics have been less convinced, criticizing the novel for its gender conservatism. According to Nicholas Williams, for instance, literary critics have tended to dismiss the novel for its "fairly quotidian" subject matter and for the fact that it is "less daring politically than its predecessors . . . representative of Shelley's retreat into the safety of propriety in the face of social and financial pressure."[73] Such readings are understandable; despite Lodore's obvious flaws as a husband (he is repeatedly described as tyrannical and he continuously rushes to judgment, condemning his wife's behavior unjustly and refusing to treat her as a person with her own thoughts and desires[74]) and as a father (he privileges honor over his duty to his daughter and dies in an entirely preventable duel), Cornelia must finally repent of her obstinacy as a wife. At the end of the novel, "She is humble, knowing how much she was deceived in herself" (*Lodore*, 312). While she never fully absolves her husband of blame for his treatment of her—even after her repentance, she insists, "surely I was not guilty towards him" (269)—Cornelia does blame herself for her part in the breakdown of her marriage. Like the women against whom both Wollstonecraft and More warn, she has been poorly educated and thus has grown into a silly, vapid woman who has parlor skills but no deep moral values, beauty but no substance. Convinced at the age of thirty-four that "the name of beauty was a mockery as applied to her" (245), she castigates herself for her willfulness and her preference for society, and she sacrifices her fortune in an attempt to make amends. In a scene reflecting the Evangelical focus on philanthropy and self-renunciation, she retreats to the countryside, no longer Lady Lodore, but content in a life of service. Like so many of Shelley's other female characters, she finds herself content, if not happy, in a world of same-sex companions.

Cornelia abandons selfhood for domestic service, and her generosity both wins her the long-withheld admiration of her son-in-law, Edward Villiers, and enables her to repair her relationship with Ethel. Where Ethel used to see a "semi-gorgon, hiding behind a deceptive mask," she now perceives a "soft-voiced, angelic-looking woman" (*Lodore*, 179). Her admission of wrongdoing in her marriage also enables her reconciliation with her former sister-in-law, Elizabeth Fitzhenry. Elizabeth is shocked that "the grand, the exclusive Lady Lodore—the haughty, fashionable, worldly, heartless wife thus metamorphosed into a tender-hearted mother" (303). Cornelia's rejection of what Julie Carson calls "the 'flimsy web' of appearance that constitutes the world of high society,"[75] and her new seriousness of purpose, also win the affections of Horatio Saville, allowing her to end the novel safely ensconced in domestic felicity. When he learns that she has sacrificed her fortune for her child, Saville "paid a warm tribute of admiration to her virtues, and acknowledged to himself his own passionate love" (287). As Katherine C. Hill-Miller explains, the ending of the novel "endorses and celebrates her formerly defiant heroine's redemption into conventional femininity—a domesticity that elevates the self-sacrifice and self-abnegation of motherhood."[76] No longer the willful wife who will not accept a husband's abuse, Cornelia's "pride is gone, or rather, her pride is now placed in redeeming her faults" (312).

The Evangelical undercurrent that pervades *Lodore*'s privileging of feminine domestic engagement and submission also extends to its depiction of nature as a model for appropriate female gender roles. According to the narrator, "A river pursues forever its course, accomplishing the task its Creator has imposed" (*Lodore*, 150); that is to say, God the Father sets the course for Mother Nature, and she carries out his will to the betterment of mankind. Later, Villiers describes nature as "a type of heaven," praising "the glory of the sky—the green expanse variegated by streams, teeming with life, and prolific to sustain that life," and the God who "set forth our table" with such beauty and "magnificence" (185). God impregnates Mother Nature, who "teems" with nourishment for her young. At the end of the novel, Cornelia learns to value the beauty of nature over the artificiality of the social world. Nature becomes to Cornelia "the mother of life—the temple of God" (308), nature and God united as parents that bless Cornelia's role as mother and wife. "Nature," she says, "is the refuge and home for women: they have no public career—no aim nor end beyond their domestic circle; but they can extend that, and make all the creations of nature their own, to foster and do good to" (309). Cornelia has learned to put family first, to be an appropriately submissive wife and mother. As a result, she finds absolution: "God blesses all things . . . and he will also bless me" (310). Her own marital felicity mirrors in microcosm God's happy union with Mother Nature.

If Lady Lodore must learn to appreciate the domestic sphere, Ethel is raised not to consider other options. When they wed, Lodore assumes Cornelia is "white paper to be written upon at will" (*Lodore*, 41), and she is horrified to realize that Cornelia has thoughts and opinions of her own. As a result, he takes pains to ensure that his daughter will have no independent will. According to Sharon Jowell, he seeks to "infantilize his child,"[77] and in this, he is successful. He educates her in such a way as "to render her ever pliant to his will" (18) and to "know herself dependent" (19) until she "leant on her father as a prop that could not fail" (19), fearing nothing "except his disapprobation" (15). She is educated only in the female graces, taught not to think for herself or to question Lodore's will. "To love her father was the first law of nature, the chief duty of a child" (83), and *Lodore* naturalizes the need for obedience: "There is something so awful in a father. His words are laws, and to obey them happiness" (83).

At least initially, the novel seems to critique the limitations placed on Ethel's education. She is utterly dependent on the men in her life, and when Lodore dies, she is left to fend for herself in a world she has not been taught to navigate. In different authorial hands, Ethel's future would have been very bleak, indeed. However, she is never in any physical danger, as she passes from daughter to wife, and her central defining characteristic is her devotion to the domestic sphere, to her father, her husband, and eventually, her son. "The first and only wish of [Ethel's] heart was to conduce to [Edward's] happiness" (*Lodore*, 190), Shelley explains. Unlike Fanny Derham, who seeks a single life of the mind—she says that she has "never been attached to any thing but" her "dear books" (225)—Ethel has no wishes apart from her family, and the narrator finds religious significance in that devotion. She approaches her husband with "sacred tenderness" (196) and disobeys him only when doing so will make him more comfortable, as when she insists on sharing his prison cell over his objections.

Ethel "serves as a contrastive model of angelic behavior for those other female characters, Lady Lodore and Clorinda, who refuse to compromise their independence."[78] As a result of her insistent domesticity, she is praised throughout the novel, likened to an angel and protected by all who meet her. Lodore finds comfort for his broken marriage in his daughter, whom he describes as "his angelic child" (*Lodore*, 25) and an "earthly angel of peace" (70). Despite the seeming problems with Lodore's education of Ethel, their home in Illinois is paradisiacal. Like Hannah More, whose Coeleb praises Milton's submissive prelapsarian Eve as a model of feminine perfection, Lodore draws "his chief ideas" of child-raising "from Milton's Eve," convinced that Ethel would then become "the embodied ideal of all that is adorable and estimable in her sex" (18). Because they are so far from society, a deliberate act of self-isolation on Lodore's part that mirrors Edmund Plantagenet's, they can exist in an Edenic paradise of their own, in which the harmony of the domestic sphere is never breached and the patriarch's will is absolute. Ethel becomes the perfect patriarchal subject.[79]

Eventually, Ethel and Lodore must leave their Eden, and their domestic happiness is destroyed with Lodore's death. In Edward, however, Ethel finds again the happiness she lost, and she re-creates a world in which patriarch, God, and nature are all united. Edward, like Lodore, has his failings. He is unable to handle money effectively, he is extremely proud to the point of masculine fragility,[80] and he is very quick to judge Lady Lodore unfairly. Yet he shares with Edmund Plantagenet and Lodore an understanding of nature as the sanctified alternative to the dissipations of society: "The more barriers we place between ourselves and nature, the more completely we cut ourselves off from her generous but simple munificence" (*Lodore*, 186), he says. Ethel has, from the early stages of the novel, been "associated with redemptive Nature," and she will, like *Perkin Warbeck*'s Katherine, practice devotion through service in the domestic sphere.[81] When the couple visits Rome, "the heartfelt and innocent caress of two united in the sight of Heaven, wedded together for the endurance of the good and ills of life, hallowed the spot" (175). It is likely no coincidence that this scene of domestic harmony occurs at the Coliseum, the site of great loss in Shelley's earlier fictions. The uncertainty and misery of "Valerius" and *The Last Man* are here replaced by the sacred harmony of marital love.

In 1829, the United Kingdom passed the Roman Catholic Relief Act, enabling British Catholics to participate fully in civic life for the first time in several hundred years. The Act of Union with Ireland in 1800 had incorporated millions of Catholic citizens into the United Kingdom, but it did not lessen preexisting restrictions on those citizens, despite promises made by Prime Minister William Pitt the Younger. The passage of the act—ultimately over the objections of George IV—thus brought to a close several decades of agitation on behalf of Catholics.[82] In 1823, Daniel O'Connell, an Irish leader and politician, founded the

Catholic Association, a political organization aimed at fighting for Irish Catholic rights. Charging only a penny for membership—an amount accessible to all but the very poorest—the association gave O'Connell consistent financial backing for his campaigns and created a sense of political unity and purpose in Ireland. In 1828, O'Connell was elected by a landslide to a seat in the House of Commons, a seat his religion prevented him from taking.[83] The controversy placed new pressure on the British government to act, culminating in the 1829 passage of the Relief Act. O'Connell took up his seat in 1829, following a second election in which he ran unopposed.

Throughout the 1820s, many periodicals unsurprisingly agitated against rights for Catholics. An 1829 essay printed in *The Imperial Magazine* dismissed the concept of emancipation in its entirety, suggesting that Catholics already had all the rights they needed. "Are they hindered from making a public profession of Popery? Are they forbidden the public celebration of mass? Are they not allowed to make secret confession to their priests? Are they excluded from the advantages of trade and commerce? May they not plead in our courts of justice, and rise to stations of honour in our armies and fleets? Why then all this feminine 'quailing?' Why! Because, forsooth, they are not eligible to become either our legislators or our kings. And this is persecution! And this is the Egyptian bondage from which they must be emancipated!"[84] Catholics do not need to be emancipated, the author explains, because they are already free; the inability to serve in government, he suggests, is not the same as oppression.

More frequently, opponents of emancipation circulated stories of Catholic treachery in an attempt at fear-mongering. "I am no enemy to papists personally," wrote one author in the *Christian Remembrancer*, but he does not trust their priests, who "are essentially schismatics" and "look to the Roman see as the only jurisdiction to which they owe submission and respect."[85] This sentiment was echoed in a letter to the editor printed by *The Imperial Magazine* in 1821: "It would not be sound policy in our government to grant the Catholics their claims, until they are first emancipated from their Priests. What can we think of those men who can commit the blackest crimes with impunity, and think they have done no harm, because they have only injured heretics, presuming their priests will forgive them?"[86] An 1827 essay printed in *Blackwood's Edinburgh Magazine* was even harsher, conflating Catholics with their clergy as twin enemies of the state: "Looking at the United Kingdom, five or six millions of its population are inveterately hostile to the Established Church, and are clamouring for the destruction of this church . . . nearly one third of its inhabitants are inflamed with religious and political fury against the remainder, are practically under the control of the Pope of Rome . . . in a word are dangerously disaffected, and are holding principles flatly opposed to the Constitution and civil and religious liberty, and tending to the dismemberment of the empire."[87]

For many, then, the fear was that Catholic emancipation was the first step toward Catholic tyranny. "When the door is once thrown open, it is impossible to say what abuses may enter," the *Gentleman's Magazine* wrote in 1825.[88] Catholics are wolves, and Protestants are sheep who have forgotten that they are in danger, John Graham writes in "Catholic Emancipation: A Fable" (1826). The wolves begin to ·

> petition,
> To pity their forlorn condition;
> Of their primeval rights denuded,
> And from the pasturage excluded;
> They vow'd, they swore, their alter'd mind
> To sheep had long become so kind,
> They would not put a tooth or foot on
> The choicest, fattest leg of mutton.[89]

The sheep relent, and the poem ends with a bloody attack: "Destruction rages through the fold; / The sheep are slaughtered, young and old,"[90] proof that Catholics want nothing more than to kill Protestants and destroy the country from within. Thus the *Examiner* reported in 1829 that the Earl of Winchilsea was "confident that our gracious Sovereign, true to the sacred oath which he has taken upon the altars of our country, to defend our Constitution and our religion from that Church, which is bent upon their destruction, will not turn a deaf ear to the prayers and supplications of his loyal Protestant subjects."[91]

Fear-mongering aside, the Roman Catholic Relief Act passed because public opinion increasingly turned in its favor. "The conduct of the Catholic is repulsive," an 1827 article in the *Monthly Magazine* comments, but "the question is, whether we are withholding from the Catholic—no matter how his *manners* seem to us—that which is his *due*."[92] Catholics have rights, and "if we withhold from the Catholic even the slightest privilege . . . we are doing him injustice, and he is entitled to relief."[93] In 1829, the *New Monthly Magazine* offered tepid praise for both the Catholic Association and the act: "While we acknowledged the dangerous power of the Catholic Association, we never condemned its formation, for it was the only medium through which subjects so oppressed could make a call for the redress of their grievances effective."[94] That same year, the *Examiner* quoted Irish politician Richard Lalor Sheil as saying that perceived Catholic treachery was the result, not the cause, of oppressive legislation. "Individuals who would, under other circumstances, be disposed to adopt a different course, will be driven by the Government itself into the receptacles of intolerance."[95]

Thus some publications not only defended the Irish but condemned the English for their treatment of Catholics. *Cobbett's Weekly Register*, for instance, criticized the British government for forcing Catholics to support the Church of England against their consciences: "There is something so unnatural; something so monstrous; something so insulting to the common understanding of all mankind, in compelling the people of a country to maintain, at prodigious expense, an establishment called religious, and which that people in all sincerity and from the bottom of their souls regard as a damnable heresy."[96] The *Dublin and London Magazine* was even more openly condemnatory of Britain's treatment of the Irish: "Towards Ireland you have been cruel, vindictive, and unjust; you have heaped wrongs upon wrongs. . . . The tales of English cruelty and injustice are yet warm in Ireland."[97] The *Dublin and London Magazine* thus countered tales of Irish atrocities with a reminder of English cruelties committed in Ireland.

Although Mary Shelley does not respond directly to the Roman Catholic Relief Act in any of her late works, *Falkner*, her final novel, offers an indirect response to Catholic emancipation. Published in 1837 but set earlier, *Falkner* engages directly with Catholicism in the character of Oswi Raby, father to Edwin Raby, and grandfather to the novel's heroine. The Rabys, Shelley explains, are a "wealthy Catholic family, proud of their ancestry, and devoted to their faith."[98] They are also extremely bigoted in their devotion, to the point that they disown their son for marrying outside the faith. "Edwin Raby had apostasized from the Catholic faith; he had married a portionless girl of inferior birth, and entered the profession of the law. His parents looked with indignation on the dishonor entailed on their name through his falling off; but his death relieved their terrors" (*Falkner*, 139). Oswi in particular has become ossified in his beliefs, viewing all Protestants as other and refusing to accept Elizabeth into his home because she has been reared in the wrong religion. He curses Edwin for being "rebellious and apostate," and he says of Elizabeth, "We cannot look with favour on the child of an apostate; educated in a faith which we consider pernicious" (142). His Catholicism is cold and uncaring, and it destroys the natural bonds between family members.

Despite the anti-Catholicism of this portrayal, *Falkner* does evince some sympathy for individual families suffering from the effects of anti-Catholic prejudice. Because of the Raby family's faith, they have had few options for social and cultural advancement, in part by choice. "Surrounded by Protestants, and consequently, as they believed, by enemies, it was the aim of their existence to keep their honour unsullied" (*Falkner*, 227), the narrator reveals, yet Shelley acknowledges that their prejudice is as much the result of circumstance as disposition. "This indeed was not to be attributed entirely to the family failing—a few years ago, English Catholics were barred out from every road to emolument and distinction in their native country" (227). As a result, daughters of the Raby family are "doomed, for the most part, to the cloister"—there are not enough Catholic men to go around and marriage to a Protestant is unacceptable—while sons are consigned to "foreign service," prevented by their religion from entering into English civic life or serving in their own country's military (227). Despite the clearly prejudiced depiction of Catholics, then, *Falkner* suggests that sectarian tensions are both harmful and pointless. The Raby family's relationships have been damaged by forces outside their control, by ongoing religious tensions that ultimately serve no one.

By the end of *Falkner*, Elizabeth succeeds in reconciling with her aunt, Mrs. Raby, if not her grandfather. Unlike Oswi, Mrs. Raby is able to step outside her religious prejudices and recognize Elizabeth's good qualities in a way that her grandfather cannot, coming to admire her as a "young Christian martyr" (*Falkner*, 235). With that reconciliation, Shelley turns away from Catholicism to the Evangelically inflected themes of *Lodore*, the idea that true divinity is found not in impersonal forms of organized religion but in familial love. In *Falkner*, as in *Lodore*, the domestic sphere (when it is functional) is a space of perfect harmony and happiness. In practically every scene, Elizabeth is described as an angel, her greatest talent her ability to create a happy home life for the men around her. Early in Elizabeth's life, Mrs. Baker calls her "expression of face . . . angelic" (7), and similar descriptors follow her throughout the novel. Elizabeth's mother writes of her, "if ever angel assumed an earthy vesture, it took a form like my darling" (11). Later, she becomes Falkner's "angel of innocence" (32), who nurses him with "almost unnatural perfection" (55). Neville, her future husband, too, thinks that "she looked beautiful as an angel" (259). Those who would try to destroy the domestic sphere are linked in contrast with the demonic. When Sir Boyvill's pursuit of justice would drive a wedge between Neville and his future bride, Neville condemns his "demoniacal hope of revenge" (257) and castigates his "foul appetite for evil" (258).[99] Falkner himself becomes satanic, an "arch fiend" (88), in his pursuit of the married Alithea. To create homelife and community, in *Falkner* as in *Lodore*, is to live a life of true godliness.

According to Melissa Sites, "Mary Shelley creates in Elizabeth a heroine who could not be faulted by traditional critics for any lack of 'womanly' skills."[100] Neville loves Elizabeth for "her generosity—her total abnegation of self—her understanding so just and true, yet tempered with feminine aptitude to adapt itself to the situation and sentiments of others" (*Falkner*, 209). Elizabeth's entire identity is to be an angelic helpmate, both to Gerard and to Falkner. "She never thought of herself. This was Elizabeth's peculiarity. She could be so engrossed by sympathy for others, that she could forget herself wholly" (195).[101] Elizabeth is daughter to Falkner and wife to Neville, but slippages in language suggest that she is always playing multiple roles. "They did not take the usual position of father and child" (59), the narrator says of Elizabeth and Falkner. Falkner tells her that when she marries, she must "leave father, mother, all, and follow the fortunes of" her husband, but Elizabeth responds that she cannot abandon Falkner for Neville: "Our position is different from that of any other parent and child. . . . I cannot leave you" (278). Falkner is "sacred in her eyes" (42), and Elizabeth "watched him as a mother may a child" (223). She is wife-daughter-mother all at once to both men.[102]

Elizabeth's blurred roles create a parallel between herself and Alithea. Falkner confuses the two women in a dream. "He had been dreaming—and he asked himself what had been the subject of his dreams. Was it Greece—or the dreary waste shores of Cumberland? And why did that fair lingering shape beckon him? Was it Alithea or Elizabeth?" (Falkner, 280). The potentially incestuous undertones of these relationships, however, are softened by the fact that Alithea is consistently desexualized; as Bryn J. Gravitt explains, "Alithea can only be a mother to her children to the exclusion of sexual desire."[103] She is described as mother only, her existence as a sexual being downplayed to the point that her maternity is likened to the Virgin Birth. She is "angelic" in her love for her son, and Falkner describes her "modest earnest manner, a manner which spoke of the maternal nature, such as Catholics imagine it, without a tincture of the wife, a girlish, yet enthusiastic rapture at the very thought of her child" (181). Alithea herself admits that she is "more maternal than wife-like" (182), willing to tolerate her obnoxious husband for love of her child. We "do not live to be happy," she tells Falkner, "but to perform our duties" (180). Later, after her death, Falkner laments that "to the last she was all mother; her heart filled with that deep yearning, which a young mother feels to be the very essence of her life" (195). Maternity and woman's place in the domestic sphere are therefore apotheosized; motherhood is the novel's new religion.

In its sanctification of maternity, Falkner may be read as a rejection of Wollstonecraftian feminism, promoting the safety and security of patriarchal marriage over women's education and independence. At the same time, however, there are several ways in which to read a more feminist politics into the text. As Julia Saunders argues, "female duties, such as sacrifice and obedience, can be configured into strengths,"[104] and throughout the novel, women gain power through their command over the domestic. Mrs. Raby, for instance, controls the Raby household. Although she has been "bred to submission" (*Falkner*, 228), her status as a widow allows her to exercise power over Oswi Raby; "her authority became paramount" (228). More subtly, Elizabeth gains power through strict adherence to her domestic duties; as Jowell points out, she becomes her father's "primary caretaker," giving her an implicit authority over him, even as she remains dependent on him emotionally.[105] She commands her father in all things and decides for herself the limits and boundaries of her conduct. Despite being encouraged by all to abandon Falkner in prison, Elizabeth chooses to join him in jail. Even when Neville attempts to stop her, she obeys the voice of her conscience over the demands of her future husband. Elizabeth's choices are justified by domestic duty, but she chooses that duty all the same. Hempton and Hill have argued that "Evangelical religion was more important than feminism in enlarging women's sphere of action during the nineteenth century," an argument sustained by *Falkner*'s treatment of Elizabeth's simultaneous authority and submission.[106]

Additionally, as in *Valperga*, the novel's events and central tragic death are precipitated by men's persistent failure to listen to and believe women. Like Lodore, Sir Boyvill is unwilling to accept his wife's fidelity. No matter how often she demonstrates her chastity, no proof is enough. Much like Lodore, he embarks on a campaign of isolation and abuse because he can never be convinced; no woman's word—nor even the word of his son—suffices. On the surface, Sir Boyvill and Falkner appear vastly different characters, as Falkner adheres to the old ways of chivalric masculinity, while Sir Boyvill prefers the modern rule of law.[107] Yet Falkner ultimately makes the same mistake as Sir Boyvill, insofar as he is unwilling to listen to Alithea and accept her gentle rejection, admitting only in retrospect that she "did not feel the passion that ruled my bosom" (*Falkner*, 171). When she "implore[d] me not again to seek her in this way," he "decreed to see her again" (183). Like Sir Boyvill, Falkner does not accept the reality of Alithea's fidelity to her husband, preferring instead the narrative of unrequited love and yearning that he has concocted to justify his feelings. Sir Boÿvill abuses Alithea because he does not believe her. Falkner abducts Alithea and precipitates her death because he, too, does not accept her word. He "'elevates' women to a 'shrine' and 'altar' and thinks them a 'better species'" while simultaneously allowing them "no agency of their own."[108] In the process, he "disregards [Alithea's] right to determine her own future."[109] The novel therefore contains an implicit criticism of the ways in which men disbelieve and by extension destroy women. It falls to Neville, a new kind of man described as an "angel" in his own right (95), to take his mother's word over his father's, Elizabeth's word over his family's, and thereby create the harmonious, Edenic domestic sphere for which Evangelicals—and finally Shelley—advocated. Through her femininity and maternal capacity, Elizabeth restores Eden on earth and creates a space of sanctified familial love.

At the end of her novel-writing career, Shelley emphasizes the power and divinity not of God but of maternity and the domestic sphere. As in *Lodore*, the divine is found in domestic harmony, mutual love, and familial compassion. Even more so than in *Lodore*, *Falkner* suggests that it is woman's power to create holiness, a view reflective of mid-nineteenth-century conceptions of religious devotion. Women are apotheosized for their divine maternity even as they are relegated to the domestic sphere. It is at once a conservative vision and a more forceful statement of feminine power than any other Shelley would offer.

# CONCLUSION

## ON GHOSTS

In a climactic moment at the end of *Rambles in Germany and Italy* (1844), Mary Shelley's final published work, she visits Rome for the first time since the death of her husband. As she gazes out over the "Temple of Venus, the Palatine Mount, and the ruins of the Forum" from the vantage point of the Coliseum, Shelley experiences her trip as a religious journey: "I revisit it as the bourne of pious pilgrimage. The treasures of my youth lie buried here."[1] At the Coliseum, Shelley is surrounded by ghosts—of lost friends and family, of the people and stories that once inspired her pen, and of the person she was herself so many years ago. She also merges imaginatively with her own characters, becoming Valerius and Lionel Verney as she thinks back to what is lost and forward to what remains.

*Rambles in Germany and Italy* is many things: an homage to Wollstonecraft's *Letters Written During a Short Residence in Sweden, Norway, and Denmark*, a travel narrative, and a political manifesto.[2] At base, however, it is a retrospective on Shelley's life and career, a culminating statement on religious faith, and an elegy to ghosts. Throughout the text, Shelley muses on spirits, wondering whether the dead continue to surround us, unseen. From Como, she writes, "It has seemed to me—and on such an evening, I have felt it,—that this world, endowed as it is outwardly with endless shapes and influences of beauty and enjoyment, is peopled also in its spiritual life by myriads of loving spirits; from whom, unawares, we catch impressions, which mould our thoughts to good, and thus they guide beneficially the course of events, and minister to the destiny of man. Whether the beloved dead make a portion of this holy company, I dare not guess; but that such exists, I feel" (*Rambles*, 123). She speaks of these spirits again amidst the grandeur of the Alps, writing, "There was a majestic simplicity that inspired awe; the naked bones of a gigantic world were here: the elemental substance of fair mother Earth, an abode for mighty spirits who need not the ministrations of food and shelter that keep man alive, but whose vast shapes could only find, in these giant crags, a home proportionate to their power" (145). And from Gmuden, she writes, "If the earthly scales fell from our eyes, should we not perceive that 'all the regions of nature swarm with spirits,' and affirm, with Milton, that—'Millions of spiritual creatures walk the Earth / Unseen, both when we wake and when we sleep'" (241).[3]

In each instance, Shelley links these spirits with memory, with the husband, children, and friends she has lost, and with her younger self as yet unmarked by sorrow. Visiting the Villa Diodati again for the first time in many years, she writes,

> Was I the same person who had lived there, the companion of the dead? For all were gone: even my young child, whom I had looked upon as the joy of future years, had died in infancy—not one hope, then in fair bud, had opened into maturity; storm, and blight, and death, had passed over, and destroyed all. While yet very young, I had reached the position of an aged person, driven back on memory for companionship with the beloved; and now I looked on the inanimate objects that had surrounded me, which survived, the same in aspect as then, to feel that all my life since was but an unreal phantasmagoria—the shades that gathered round that scene were the realities—the

substance and truth of the soul's life, which I shall, I trust, hereafter rejoin. (*Rambles*, 148)

Shelley has become, she explains, a living ghost, surrounded by memories that she finds almost more real than reality. That she refers obliquely to her mother's work in describing the "naked bones of a gigantic world" suggests that Wollstonecraft, too, is one of the ghosts that peoples her imaginative world.[4]

In returning to Rome, Shelley finds herself existing in both the past and the present, in the memory of the world she knew as a young woman and in the life she currently lives. As such, she depicts herself following in the footsteps of Lionel Verney and Valerius, her own literary creations, two men displaced in time and condemned to live largely in their memories of the past. In describing the 1837 cholera epidemic that decimated Rome, Shelley reports that "people fell down in the streets, convulsed by the frightful spasms of the terrible disease" (*Rambles*, 356), recalling the starker passages of devastation in *The Last Man*. When she ascends to the top of the Capitoline Hill, she, like Valerius, imagines ancient Rome, past and present temporarily blending together. "We looked round, and fancied how, from this height, the patricians and consuls of Old Rome watched the advance of marauding parties that wound out from the ravines of the hills" (349). As she wanders the "deserted part of Rome," she imagines a time when that area "was the centre of [Roman] magnificence" (350). And as she observes the rituals of Holy Week, with the remnants of the pagan past still visible in contemporary forms of worship, she considers, like Valerius, the replacement of one religious tradition by another. "It is curious to see all these solemnities—many of them doubtless of Pagan origin—dear to the people, and therefore preserved and christianised by the Popes—and to reflect, that such, for many, many centuries, was the chief link fostered by religion between man and the Divinity" (353). As in Shelley's earlier works, nothing is eternal, not religion, not empire, not human relationships or human love.

I want to suggest, however, that at the end of her career, Shelley revisits her earlier works and earlier selves to reach a much more hopeful conclusion. Unlike the people of *The Last Man*, the people of Rome survive the cholera epidemic, and Shelley emphasizes the thousand acts of kindness performed by and among them. Eschewing anti-Catholicism, Shelley writes approvingly of the church's conduct during the outbreak: "Yet there was not absent many redeeming touches in the dark picture of the times. The regular clergy fulfilled their duties unshrinkingly; and the conduct of the Jesuits was particularly admirable. They visited every corner of the city, watching by death-beds with unwearied zeal. They were seen taking, with gentle care, babes from the sides of their mothers, who lay dead in the streets, wrapping them tenderly in their black gowns, and carrying them to places appointed for their refuge" (*Rambles*, 356).[5] Laypeople, too, behaved heroically. "A Roman told me he was one of three brothers; they removed their aged father to a safe place, at a distance from contagion, and remained themselves: they were employed at different quarters of the city. 'I never felt happier,' said my informant; 'our father was in safety; we had no fears for ourselves. All day we were busied among the sick, and when we met in the evening, it was with light heart . . . the dangers we might be supposed to run, endeared us to each other'" (356). This is not the world of *The Last Man* but a world in which kindness persists, and even disease can be defeated by human compassion and human ingenuity. It is also a world in which God and nature have resumed their positions of love and compassion for humankind. Writing from France, Shelley says, "The season setting in so genially in early spring, joined to the refreshing rains which have since succeeded, have caused rich promise of abundance to appear everywhere. I never remember feeling so intimately how bounteous a mother is this fair earth, yielding such plenteous store of food to her children, and this food in its growth so beautiful to look on. How full of gratitude and love for the Creator does the beauty of the creation make us!" (81). The love of God for his creation is reaffirmed by Shelley's hopeful experiences of the natural world.[6]

*Rambles in Germany and Italy* ends with an image of sublimity in nature. "The Cocumella has become our home," Shelley writes. "It is a joy to return to our terrace, to breathe the fragrance of the orange-flowers—to see the calm sea spread out at our feet, as we look over the bay to Naples—while above us bends a sky—in whose pure depths ship-like clouds glide—and the moon hangs luminous, a pendant sphere of silver fire" (*Rambles*, 386). Shelley lives among ghosts, but there is peace in the natural world and in the idea of divine will. At the end of her career, then, Shelley revisits her former literary and biographical selves, experiencing at last the contentment, if not happiness, that so long eluded her. She died on February 1, 1851, following a protracted battle with a brain tumor.

# NOTES

## INTRODUCTION

1. Shelley, *Journals*, 506.
2. Ibid., 549.
3. Shelley, *Letters of Mary Shelley*, 1:331.
4. Godwin, "Of Religion," 76.
5. Shelley, *Letters of Mary Shelley*, 2:215.
6. Shelley, *Frankenstein* (1831), 176.
7. Mary Shelley at least initially seemed to encourage Hogg's attentions. In January 1815, she wrote to him, "we have known each other for so short a time and I did not think about love—so that I think that that also will come in time & then we shall be happier I do think than the angels who sing for ever" (Shelley, *Letters of Mary Shelley*, 1:6).
8. Ibid., 1:45.
9. Godwin, reprinted in Paul, *William Godwin*, 269.
10. Shelley, *Journals*, 473.
11. Ibid., 554.
12. Spark, *Informed Air*, 139.
13. See Charlotte Gordon, *Romantic Outlaws*, and Mellor, *Mary Shelley*, along with Sunstein, *Mary Shelley*; Nitchie, *Mary Shelley*; Walling, *Mary Shelley*; and Gerson, *Daughter of Earth and Water*.
14. Allen, "Beyond Biographism," 170.
15. Since the 1990s, critics have made a concerted effort to examine Shelley's later works, but even now, studies of *Frankenstein* are vastly more common. For foundational works on Shelley's broader career, see Conger, Frank, and O'Dea, *Iconoclastic Departures*; Bennett and Curran, *Mary Shelley in Her Times*; and Fisch, Mellor, and Schor, *Other Mary Shelley*.

## CHAPTER 1

1. Blake, "Urizen," 1:1, 2, in *Complete Poetry and Prose*, 70. Further references to this poem will be cited parenthetically in the text by stanza and line number.
2. Cooper, "Freedom," 191.

3. Mellor, "Human Form," 595.

4. Kozlowski, "Resonating Resins," 411.

5. According to Roderick Tweedy, Urizen represents "the emergence of a Power within the human psyche which [Blake] calls the 'Reasoning Power'" (Tweedy, *God of the Left Hemisphere*, 3).

6. Blake, "Milton," 19:6–14, in *Complete Poetry and Prose of William Blake*, 112.

7. Milton's red clay, by contrast, "is one of Blake's symbols of creative power" (Frye, *Fearful Symmetry*, 229).

8. J. Jones, "Self-Annihilation," 4.

9. Blake, "Europe," 10:23, in *Complete Poetry and Prose of William Blake*, 63.

10. According to Anderson, "Between twelve and twenty-four thousand people came to hear Whitefield on Kensington Common in August of 1739 . . . and by September, he commanded crowds of thirty thousand" (Anderson, *Imagining Methodism*, 134). Thompson describes these gatherings as follows: "The methods of the revivalist preachers were noted for their emotional violence. . . . And the open-air crowds and early congregations of Methodism were also noted for the violence of their 'enthusiasm'—swooning, groaning, crying out, weeping and falling into paroxysms" (Thompson, *Making of the English Working Class*, 380).

11. Bebbington, *Evangelicalism*, 2. In contrast to Bebbington, George Marsden describes five main characteristics of Evangelical belief: "(1) the Reformation doctrine of the final authority of the Bible, (2) the real historical character of God's saving work recorded in Scripture, (3) salvation to eternal life based on the redemptive work of Christ, (4) the importance of evangelism and missions, and (5) the importance of a spiritually transformed life" (Marsden, *Understanding Fundamentalism*, 4–5). For other discussions of the rise of Evangelicalism, see also Hilton, *Age of Atonement*; Noll, *Rise of Evangelicalism*; Bebbington and Rawlyk, *Evangelicalism*; Haykin and Stewart, *Emergence of Evangelicalism*; Ward, *Early Evangelicalism*; and M. Watts, *Dissenters*.

12. Bebbington, *Evangelicalism*, 15.

13. Venn, *Complete Duty*, vii.

14. Early accounts of the growth of Methodism tended to view the religion as a "socially regressive movement, either at odds with good modernizing forces or an agent of bad modernizing forces" (Hempton, *Methodism*, 11). For one such reading, see E. P. Thompson, who writes, "It is difficult to conceive of a more essential disorganization of human life, a pollution of the sources of spontaneity bound to reflect itself in every aspect of personality" (Thompson, *Making of the English Working Class*, 372).

15. Bebbington, *Evangelicalism*, 63.

16. Ibid., 2.

17. Anderson, *Imagining Methodism*, 3.

18. Ibid., 4.

19. Staniforth, "Sampson Staniforth," 74–75.

20. Wesley, *Journal*, 2:333.

21. Bebbington, *Evangelicalism*, 7.

22. Edwards, *Works*, 424.

23. Bebbington, *Evangelicalism*, 11.

24. Anderson, *Imagining Methodism*, 133.

25. Cragwall, *Lake Methodism*, 37.

26. Hempton, *Religion of the People*, 7.

27. Walpole, *Yale Edition of Horace Walpole's Correspondence*, 35:118.

28. L. Hunt, "Attempt to Shew the Folly," 335.

29. Lackington, *Memoirs*, 134.

30. Anderson, *Imagining Methodism*, 172.

31. Hempton, *Methodism*, 5.

32. Anderson, *Imagining Methodism*, 38.

33. Ibid., 6.

34. Foote, *Letter from Mr. Foote*, 2.

35. Anderson, *Imagining Methodism*, 139.

36. S. Johnson, *Dictionary of the English Language*, 1:740.

37. Bebbington, *Evangelicalism*, 22.

38. Gibson, *Observations*, 13.

39. Mee, *Romanticism, Enthusiasm, and Regulation*, 24.

40. An Anti-Empiric, "Remarks on the Enthusiasm," 216.

41. Anonymous, cited in Tyerman, *Life and Times*, 1:249.

42. Anderson, *Imagining Methodism*, 43.

43. Lavington, *Enthusiasm*, 1:i.

44. Ibid., 1:ii.

45. Hazlitt, "On the Causes of Methodism," 1:58.

46. For further discussion of outbreaks of violence against Methodists, see Hempton, *Methodism*.

47. Jonathan Sheehan has argued that modern critics too often treat secularization as "shorthand for the inevitable . . . slide of the pre-modern religious past into the modern secular future" (Sheehan, "Enlightenment, Religion," 1076–77). The irrational aspects of religion coexisted with and overlapped with more seemingly rational expressions of religious devotion.

48. Mack, *Heart Religion*, 13–14.

49. Wesley, *Letters*, 5:364. It is this blend of rationality and faith that led historian Henry Rack to title his book on Wesley *Reasonable Enthusiast*.

50. B. Taylor, "Religious Foundations of Mary Wollstonecraft's Feminism," 108. As Franklin explains, Price in particular insisted that "the individual should by the rigorous exercise of his reason determine for himself what was moral law and thus practise virtue" (Franklin, *Mary Wollstonecraft*, 15).

51. R. Watts, "Rational Religion," 40–41.

52. Priestley, *Reflections on Death*, 23.

53. R. Watts, *Gender, Power and the Unitarians*, 36.

54. Tapper, "Priestley on Politics," 273.

55. Nicholls, *God and Government*, 45. Arians rejected the Trinity but accepted the divinity of Christ as a lesser being than God; Socinians, by contrast, believed that Jesus was fully human. Materialists privileged bodily reality

over a conception of soul, while necessarians held that "all human actions could be traced to motives and intentions which themselves originated in upbringing and environment. No-one could be termed a 'free agent,' since all acted according to the strongest impulse affecting their will at any one time" (Claeys, *Citizens and Saints*, 115).

56. Gordon, *Mary Wollstonecraft*, 52.
57. Priestley, *History of the Corruptions of Christianity*, 302.
58. Ibid., 302.
59. Priestley, *Memoirs of Dr. Joseph Priestley*, 80.
60. Anonymous, *Essay on the Immateriality*, 66.
61. Benson, *Remarks on Dr. Priestley's system*, v.
62. Franklin, *Mary Wollstonecraft*, 16.
63. Price, *Additional Observations*, 28.
64. Price, *Discourse*, 50.
65. Burke, *Reflections on the Revolution*, 11.
66. Sheps, "Sedition, Vice, and Atheism," 51.
67. George III, cited in Sheps, "Sedition, Vice, and Atheism," 51. E. P. Thompson describes "the undoubted complicity of several prominent Tory magistrates and clergy, who encouraged the rioters at their commencement, directed them to the meeting-houses, intervened only half-heartedly, [and] refused to prosecute offenders" (Thompson, *Making of the English Working Class*, 73–74).
68. Fulford, "Millenarianism and the Study of Romanticism," 1–2. Throughout the period, believers continuously debated the relationship between apocalypse and millennium (a thousand years of peace culminating in the Last Judgment). For millenarians (also known as premillennialists), the millennium would necessarily commence with a series of apocalyptic events that would fundamentally reshape the world's political and social landscapes. Millennialists (or postmillennialists), by contrast, believed that the Last Judgment would follow a "smooth, gradual and peaceable transition," a process of evolution toward perfection (Oliver, *Prophets and Millenialists*, 21). For further discussion of the differences between pre- and postmillennialism, see also Paley, *Apocalypse and Millennium*.
69. Brothers, *Revealed Knowledge*, 18.
70. Goodwin, *French Revolution Foreseen*, 54.
71. Pirie, *French Revolution Exhibited*, 1.
72. See Snodgrass, *Commentary*, especially 515–20. For similar prophetic materials, see also J. L. Towers's *Illustrations of Prophecy*.
73. Paley, *Apocalypse and Millennium*, 21.
74. Priestley, *Present State of Europe*, 25–26. For further discussion of Priestley's millenarianism, see C. Garrett, *Respectable Folly*, and Fruchtman, *Apocalyptic Politics*.
75. Fulford, "Millenarianism and the Study of Romanticism," 5.
76. Beer, "Romantic Apocalypses," 56.
77. Frere, *Combined View*, 308.

78. Irving, *Discourse on the Prophecies*, 114–15.

79. For discussion of Irving's life, see Stewart Brown, "Irving, Edward."

80. Fulford, "Millenarianism and the Study of Romanticism," 10.

81. Riggs, *World of Christopher Marlowe*, 30.

82. Broughton, *Bibliotheca*, 1:97.

83. Anonymous, "Universal Spectator."

84. Berman, *History of Atheism in Britain*, 2.

85. Balguy, "extreme Folly and Wretchedness," 1.

86. Ibid., 2.

87. Hammon, *Answer to Dr Priestley's Letters*, xvii.

88. Ibid., vi.

89. Ibid., v–vi.

90. Priestman, *Romantic Atheism*, 9.

91. Buckley, *At the Origins of Modern Atheism*, 249.

92. Diderot, *Skeptic's Walk*, location 223.

93. Hyman, "Atheism in Modern History," 30.

94. Priestman, *Romantic Atheism*, 9.

95. D'Holbach, *System of Nature*, xii.

96. Ibid., xii.

97. Ibid., xi.

98. Gay, *Enlightenment*, 526. For further discussion of atheism among French Enlightenment philosophes, see also M. Curran, *Atheism, Religion and Enlightenment*.

99. Hammon, *Answer to Dr Priestley's Letters*, xxiv.

100. Ibid., xxiv.

101. Priestman, *Romantic Atheism*, 19. The subject of Hume's atheism has occasioned a long-standing critical debate. See, for instance, Andre, "Was Hume an Atheist?"; Bailey and O'Brien, *Continuum Companion to Hume*; Berman, "David Hume," Penelhum, *Themes in Hume*; and Russell, *Riddle of Hume's* Treatise.

102. Priestman, *Romantic Atheism*, 19.

103. Gibbon, *Decline and Fall*, 1:452.

104. Watson, *Apology for Christianity*, 3–4.

105. Gibbon, *Decline and Fall*, 1:348.

106. Watson, *Apology for Christianity*, 7.

107. Ibid., 203.

108. Ibid., 204–5. Gibbon for his part hit back against his critics in *A Vindication of Some Passages in the Fifteenth and Sixteenth Chapters of the History of the Decline and Fall of the Roman Empire*, whose objections, he argued, "were founded on misrepresentation or mistake" (Gibbon, *Vindication of Some Passages*, 4).

109. Anonymous, "essay Against atheism," 9.

110. Priestman, *Romantic Atheism*, 26.

111. Burke, *Reflections on the Revolution*, 91.

112. Pappin, *Metaphysics of Edmund Burke*, 119. For further discussion of Burke's attitude to atheism, see E. Jones, *Edmund Burke*, and O'Neill, *Edmund Burke*.

113. More, *Remarks on the Speech*, 7.
114. Paine, *Age of Reason*, 3. According to Robert M. Ryan, Paine "identified organized Christianity as the chief abettor of repressive government" (Ryan, *Romantic Reformation*, 17).
115. Hernon, *Riot*, 13.
116. Glen, *Urban Workers*, 144.
117. Hernon, *Riot*, 22.
118. Hilton, *Mad, Bad, and Dangerous People*, 264.
119. Pickering and Tyrrell, *People's Bread*, 10.
120. Glen, *Urban Workers*, 194.
121. Gilmartin, *Writing Against Revolution*, 115.
122. Hernon, *Riot*, 10.
123. Glen, *Urban Workers*, 206.
124. Poole, "French Revolution," 6.
125. Gardner, *Poetry and Popular Protest*, 15.
126. Ibid., 17. The precise number of the wounded has been long disputed. For further discussion of the casualties of Peterloo, see Bush, *Casualties of Peterloo*. For debate about the extent of the government's responsibility in precipitating the events at Peterloo, see Gash, *Aristocracy and the People*, and Poole, "By the Law or the Sword."
127. Poole, "By the Law or the Sword," 254.
128. Ibid., 254.
129. Ibid., 255.
130. Bush, "Women at Peterloo," 209.
131. Ibid., 211.
132. Hall, *White, Male and Middle-Class*, 76.
133. Davidoff and Hall, *Family Fortunes*, 76.
134. Ibid., 93.
135. Robert Owen (1771–1858) was a Welsh philanthropist and social reformer who attempted to form a utopian socialist community in New Harmony, Indiana.
136. Bebbington, *Evangelicalism*, 60.
137. Barbauld, "Wilberforce," 98–99, 104–5, in *Selected Letters and Prose*, 126.
138. For further discussion of the role of Dissenters in the fight for abolition, see Clapp and Jeffrey, *Women, Dissent, and Anti-Slavery*.
139. Davidoff and Hall, *Family Fortunes*, 82. Davidoff and Hall's groundbreaking work has been complicated by critics such as Vickery, Hall, and Nair, but its overarching thesis has been generally upheld. For a discussion of recent historiography on women and religion in nineteenth-century Britain, see Sarah C. Williams, "Is There a Bible."
140. Davidoff and Hall, *Family Fortunes*, 88.
141. Wilberforce, *Practical View*, 298.
142. Davidoff and Hall, *Family Fortunes*, 89.
143. Gail Malmgreen cautions, "It is surely neither possible nor necessary to weigh up, once and for all, the gains and losses for women of religious commitment" (Malmgreen, *Religion*, 7).

144. Prochaska, *Women and Philanthropy*, 12.

145. Brown, *Death*, 58, 59.

146. Wilberforce, *Practical View*, 453.

147. Malmgreen, *Religion*, 5. For discussion of women as writers of hymns, see Maison, "Thine, Only Thine."

148. Foxe's *Acts and Monuments* was "no less influential than the Bible and the Prayer Book in constructing a new, Protestant identity for the English people as an elect nation, if not the elect nation, in God's esteem and design" (Collinson, Hunt, and Walsham, "Religious Publishing," 36).

149. Anonymous, *Bloody Tragedie*, sig. b3r.

150. Anonymous, *Kings Majesties Speech*, sig. a24.

151. Colley, *Britons*, 337.

152. Ibid., 339.

153. Ibid., 333–34.

154. Pionke, *Plots of Opportunity*, 54.

155. Ryan, *Romantic Reformation*, 18–19.

156. Southey, *Book of the Church*, 2.

157. Southey, *Vindiciae Ecclesiae Anglicanae*, xv.

158. Bostrom, "Novel and Catholic Emancipation," 157.

159. Colley, *Britons*, 340. For further discussion of reactions to Catholic Emancipation, see also Burstein, *Victorian Reformations*; J. C. D. Clark, *English Society*; and Tomko, *British Romanticism and the Catholic Question*.

160. Colley, *Britons*, 339.

## CHAPTER 2

1. Conger, "Multivocality in Mary Shelley's Unfinished Memoirs," 318.

2. St. Clair, *Godwins and the Shelleys*, 10.

3. P. Marshall, *William Godwin*, 22.

4. Ibid., 22–23.

5. Godwin, *Autobiography*, 30.

6. Ibid., 29.

7. St .Clair, *Godwins and the Shelleys*, 15. Godwin's transition from minister to unbeliever did not happen instantaneously. As Kathleen Bell points out, he "continued to use the title 'Reverend' for some years after his hopes of a congregation had perished," and it was only at the age of thirty-five that he fully abandoned his religious aspirations (Bell, "Family Man" 52).

8. St. Clair, *Godwins and the Shelleys*, 15.

9. P. Marshall, *William Godwin*, 39.

10. Godwin, *Autobiographical Fragments and Reflections*, 53.

11. White, *Early Romanticism and Religious Dissent*, 93.

12. Godwin, *Enquiry Concerning Political Justice*, 16.

13. Tichelear, *Gothic Wanderer*, 63.

14. Godwin, *Enquiry Concerning Political Justice*, 16.

15. Hindle, introduction, xxxii.
16. Godwin, "Of Religion," 76.
17. Weston, "Politics, Passion, and the 'Puritan Temper,'" 446.
18. White, *Early Romanticism and Religious Dissent*, 94. For further analysis of the impact of Godwin's religion on *Political Justice*, see Trott, "Coleridge Circle." Trott argues that Godwin's "'system of disinterested benevolence' secularized the Calvinist doctrine of election" (215).
19. Godwin, *Autobiographical Fragments and Reflections*, 54.
20. Weston, "Politics, Passion, and the 'Puritan Temper,'" 459.
21. Godwin, *Enquiry Concerning Political Justice*, 446.
22. Godwin, *St. Leon*, 282.
23. Weston, "Politics, Passion, and the 'Puritan Temper,'" 460.
24. Godwin, *Enquiry Concerning Political Justice*, 458.
25. Sterrenberg, "Last Man," 334. For discussion of Godwin's public arguments with Malthus, see R. Anderson, "Misery Made Me a Fiend"; Tuite, "Frankenstein's Monster and Malthus' 'Jaundiced Eye'"; and Wright, *British Women Writers and Race*.
26. Labbe, "Family Romance," 220.
27. Faubert, introduction, 12.
28. Godwin, *Memoirs*, 215.
29. Ibid.
30. Ibid.
31. Ibid., 236.
32. Godwin, *Memoirs*, 270.
33. Anonymous, "MEMOIRS of Mrs Mary Wollstonecraft Godwin," 301.
34. J. Moore, introduction, xiv.
35. Cited in J. Moore, introduction, xxi.
36. Anonymous, "Memoirs of the Author," 414.
37. Walker, *Memoirs*, 480.
38. Hays, *Annual Necrology*, 490.
39. Ibid.
40. Ibid., 531.
41. Ibid.
42. Wollstonecraft, *Collected Letters*, 404.
43. Lokke, "Radical Spirituality and Reason," 52.
44. Hays, *Annual Necrology*, 489–90.
45. Kelly, "Subject of Mary Versus Mary," 10.
46. Wollstonecraft, *Vindication of the Rights of Woman*, 81.
47. Ibid., 282–83.
48. Wollstonecraft, *Short Residence*, 147.
49. Ibid.
50. Ibid.
51. Ibid.
52. Franklin, *Mary Wollstonecraft*, 15.
53. B. Taylor, "Religious Foundations of Mary Wollstonecraft's Feminism," 109.
54. Franklin, *Mary Wollstonecraft*, 15.

55. As Watt explains, she "was much influenced by Price's views on the perfect-ibility of humankind, by the general Unitarian emphasis on reason and the need for all to develop their mental and moral abilities through education, and by their respect for women's intellectual powers" (R. Watts, *Gender, Power and the Unitarians*, 92).

56. Melissa Butler, "Wollstonecraft versus Rousseau," 66; Taylor, "Religious Foundations of Mary Wollstonecraft's Feminism," 108.

57. Wollstonecraft, *Vindication of the Rights of Woman*, 71.

58. As such, Sharon Lynne Joffe reads the novella as Wollstonecraft's investiga-tion into "the ramifications of ineffective maternal bonding and . . . maternal cruelty" (Joffe, *Kinship Coterie*, 35).

59. Wollstonecraft, *Mary*, 7.

60. Ibid., 8.

61. Ibid., 11.

62. Ibid.

63. Byron, *Childe Harold's Pilgrimage, Canto III*, lines 681–84.

64. Wollstonecraft, *Mary*, 11.

65. Ibid.

66. Ibid.

67. Ibid.

68. Ibid.

69. For some critics, Mary is a sentimental heroine, and a "pro-Patmorian 'angel in the house' who is so morally above debasing sensual needs that she is almost bodiless" (Faubert, introduction, 39). According to Faubert, "Wollstonecraft lays on the sensibility so thickly that she appears to be writing a manifesto of the form" (Faubert, introduction, 38). Likewise, Janet Todd writes that "*Mary* has considerable interest as a late work of sensibility" (Todd, introduction, x).

70. Wollstonecraft, *Mary*, 53.

71. Shelley, "Convent of Chaillot," 283. Although the authorship of "Convent of Chaillot" has not been conclusively established, its tone and content are in keeping with Shelley's known corpus, and I will therefore treat it as a part of her canon.

72. P. Shelley, *Necessity of Atheism*, 35.

73. Ibid., 32, 33, 34.

74. Ibid., 58.

75. Wroe, *Being Shelley*, 101.

76. Gavin Hopps points out that "Byron discreetly erased the entry, commenting, according to Hobhouse's *Recollections*, 'Do you not think I shall do Shelley a service by scratching this out?'" (Hopps, "Religion and Ethics," 117).

77. Shelley, cited in Freeman, "Shelley's Early Letters," 121.

78. Trelawny, *Recollections of the Last Days*, 60.

79. Shelley, *Letters of Mary Shelley*, 1:143.

80. P. Shelley, "Queen Mab," 80, 104–7. "Queen Mab" became, in Richard Holmes's words, "the most widely read, the most notorious, and the most influential" of Percy's poems (Holmes, *Shelley*, 208).

81. Baker, *Shelley's Major Poetry*, 29; Hopps, "Religion," 130. As John Freeman points out, even as Percy was composing *The Necessity of Atheism* with Hogg, he "had not given up a belief in the afterlife" (Freeman, "Shelley's Early Letters," 121). For other readings disputing the label of atheist for Percy, see McGrath, *Twilight of Modern Atheism*; and D. Clark, *Shelley's Prose.*

82. P. Shelley, "Queen Mab," lines 6.197, 199–200. In his final essay on religion, "Essay on Christianity" (ca. 1817), Percy takes a much more measured approach to religion. He writes, "We die, says Jesus Christ; and, when we awaken from the lang[uo]r of disease, the glories and the happiness of Paradise are around us. All evil and pain have ceased for ever. . . . How delightful a picture, even if it be not true!" (P. Shelley, "On Christianity," 236). He thus finds some beauty in the tenets of the Christian faith, even as he distances himself from belief. Such commentary later led Robert Browning to "surmise that Shelley would have ended up, had he lived, converted to the faith he attacked so energetically" (M. O'Neill, *Percy Bysshe Shelley*, 39).

83. P. Shelley, "Queen Mab," lines 7.84–85.

84. Ibid., lines 7.107–14. Hopps points out that in "Queen Mab," "Shelley seems to want to have his cake and eat it, by suggesting that God is malicious *and* doesn't exist" (Hopps, "Religion and Ethics," 119).

85. P. Shelley, *Refutation*, 36. Eusebes eventually convinces Theosophus to reject "cold and dreary Atheism" in favor of Christianity, but Theosophus's conversion is deliberately unsatisfying (P. Shelley, *Refutation*, 42, 57). As Hopps explains, "Theosophus' speech has already vitiated Eusebes' position to an 'irrational' fideism. Thus, the latter's effective refutation of Deism means that the two arguments appear to cancel each other out, and the most plausible position at the end of their dispute turns out ironically to be atheism" (Hopps, "Religion and Ethics," 121). For further exploration of *A Refutation of Deism*, see Wasserman, *Shelley.*

86. According to Baker, Ahasuerus is a "type of the eternal rebel . . . closely modeled on the most famous example of Christian poetry, Milton's Satan" (Baker, *Shelley's Major Poetry*, 277).

87. Paterson-Morgan, "Bloodless Church," 97.

88. Ibid., 97.

89. Rieger, *Mutiny Within*, 112.

90. Byron, *Cain*, lines 436–40.

91. Heber, "Review," 243.

92. Byron, *Byron's Letters and Journals*, 188.

93. P. Shelley, "Essay on the Devil and Devils," 265.

94. Barnard, *Shelley's Religion*, 153.

95. Hopps, "Religion and Ethics," 128.

96. Wallace, "Copying Shelley's Letters," 407. For further analysis of the role of reading in the Shelleys' romance, see T. Webb, "Reading Aloud in the Shelley Circle."

97. After his death, the tables would turn, and she would do the same for Percy. If Mary Shelley's early works were guided by Percy's hand, his poetry as we

know it today was shaped by her intellectual guidance. For discussions of Mary Shelley as the creator of her husband's legacy, see Gladden, "Mary Shelley's Editions," North, "Shelley Revitalized," and Favret, "Mary Shelley's Sympathy."

98. Indeed, according to Noel Gerson, she insisted on having her children baptized, apparently over Percy's objections (Gerson, *Daughter of Earth and Water*, 111).

99. Bresadola, "Medicine and Science," 371.

100. Ibid.

101. Ibid., 372.

102. Galvani, translated in Bresadola, "Medicine and Science," 372.

103. Galvani, translated in Montillo, *Lady and Her Monsters*, 6.

104. Montillo, *Lady and Her Monsters*, 51.

105. Ibid., 55.

106. Sha, "Volta's Battery," 21.

107. For further discussion of the founding of the Royal Humane Society, see C. Williams, "Inhumanly Brought Back to Life and Misery.'"

108. Montillo, *Lad and Her Monsters y*, 76.

109. Wordsworth, "Tables Turned," line 28. For discussion of grave robbing and distrust of the medical profession in relation to *Frankenstein*, see T. Marshall, *Murdering to Dissect*.

110. Sleigh, "Judgments of Regency Literature," 3.

111. Knapp, *New Newgate Calendar*, 189.

112. Montillo, *Lady and Her Monsters*, 87.

113. Knapp, *New Newgate Calendar*, 189.

114. Aldini, cited in Montillo, *Lady and Her Monsters*, 88.

115. Hogg, *Life of Percy Bysshe Shelley*, 92.

116. Wolfson, "This Is My Lightning," 773.

117. Shelley, *Journals*, 56.

118. R. Hunt, "Crosse, Andrew," n.p.

119. Ulf Houe points out that "in Mary Shelley's novel there is no mention of electricity at the moment of creation. There are 'instruments of life' and there is a 'spark of being,' but no lightning, no Galvanic fluid, and certainly no robotic slave. Nonetheless, scholars assert the electric animation with surprising confidence" (Houe, "*Frankenstein* Without Electricity," 95). In contast, Sha argues that the creature was "born from a voltaic battery designed to prove the existence of Galvanism" (Sha, "Volta's Battery," 36).

120. Hunt, "Crosse, Andrew," n.p.

121. Anonymous, "Memoirs of Crosse," 665.

122. Hawes, Untitled, MS. ADD c. 229. 104b.

123. Historicus, "Letter," 422.

124. Davy, *Consolations in Travel*, 219.

125. Ruston, "Resurrecting *Frankenstein*," 99.

126. Knight, *Humphry Davy*, 75.

127. Davy, *Elements of Chemical Philosophy*, 4:127.

128. Caldwell, *Literature and Medicine*, 26.
129. Abernethy, *Enquiry into the Probability*, 41.
130. Hindle, "Vital Matters," 33.
131. Lawrence, *Introduction to Comparative Anatomy and Physiology*, 120–21.
132. Caldwell, *Literature and Medicine*, 26. For further discussion of criticisms of Lawrence, see Vernon, "*Frankenstein*: Science and Electricity."
133. Lawrence, "Mr. Lawrence's Retraction," 450.
134. Mellor, "*Frankenstein*, Racial Science," 180, 178.
135. Ibid., 178.
136. Hogsette, "Metaphysical Intersections in *Frankenstein*," 550, 552. For a contrasting reading, see Marilyn Butler's "Introduction to *Frankenstein*," where she argues that *Frankenstein* takes Lawrence's side in the debate.
137. Winn, *When Beauty Fires the Blood*, 225.
138. Crawford, "Milton's Heirs," 442.
139. Ryan, *Romantic Reformation*, 5.
140. Blake, "Marriage," in *Complete Poetry and Prose of William Blake*, 35.
141. P. Shelley, "Defence of Poetry," 1044.
142. Milton, *Paradise Lost*, 1.224–25, 1.258–59.
143. Thorslev, "Romantic Mind Is Its Own Place," 251.
144. Ibid., 252.
145. S. Curran, "Political Prometheus," 431.
146. Ibid. For discussion of uses of the Prometheus myth in the long eighteenth century, see Gillespie, "Prometheus in the Romantic Age"; and Givens and Russell, "Romantic Agonies."
147. Byron, "Prometheus," lines 35, 36–37, 6, 23.
148. 1 Cor 15:55.
149. Byron, "Prometheus," lines 55–59.
150. Thorslev, "Romantic Mind Is Its Own Place," 252.
151. Hatlen, "Milton, Mary Shelley, and Patriarchy," 19.
152. Much has been written about Milton's impact on Mary Shelley and on Romanticism more broadly. For key studies, see Acosta, *Reading Genesis*; Beshero-Bondar, *Women, Epic, and Transition*; Gilbert and Gubar, *Madwoman in the Attic*; Gillespie, "Prometheus in the Romantic Age"; Lamb, "Mary Shelley's *Frankenstein*"; Low and Harding, *Milton, the Metaphysicals, and Romanticism*; and Wade, "Shelley and the Miltonic Element."
153. Volney's *Ruins* was extremely popular in England; there were "at least eleven different editions of Volney between 1792 and 1822" (G. Williams, "Romanticism in Wales," 15).
154. Volney, *Ruins*, 1.
155. Ibid., 2.
156. Ibid., 10.
157. Ibid., 14.
158. Ibid., 18.
159. Duffy, *Shelley and the Revolutionary Sublime*, 44.
160. Volney, *Ruins*, 36.

161. Ibid., 221.
162. Schlereth, *Age of Infidels*, 66.
163. Volney, *Ruins*, 189.
164. Ibid., 178–79.
165. Ibid., 224.
166. They were also influential on Percy Shelley's work. Arthur Bradley calls "Queen Mab" "both a Volneyan *memento mori* and a Holbachian symbol" (Bradley, "Until Death Tramples It to Fragments," 197).
167. Shelley, *Frankenstein* (1831), 89.


CHAPTER 3

1. For discussion of gender roles in *Frankenstein*, see Dickerson, "Ghost of a Self"; Ellis, "Monsters"; Gilbert, "Horror's Twin"; Gilbert and Gubar, *Madwoman in the Attic*; B. Johnson, *Life with Mary Shelley*; Liggins, "Medical Gaze and the Female Corpse"; Moers, "Female Gothic"; Rubenstein, "My Accursed Origin"; and Schoene-Harwood, *Writing Men*. For politics, see Botting, *Making Monstrous*; Brewster, "From Albion to Frankenstein's Creature"; Randel, "Political Geography of Horror"; and Sterrenberg, "Mary Shelley's Monster." Sources for discussion of science and nature include Banerjee, "Home Is Where Mamma Is"; Bewell, "Issue of Monstrous Desire"; Feder, "Blot upon the Earth"; and Hadley, "Mary Shelley's Literary Laboratory." For treatments of the legal system, see Grossman, *Art of Alibi*; Bridget M. Marshall, *Transatlantic Gothic Novel*; and Vincent, "This Wretched Mockery of Justice." For discussion of the treatment of women in the Romantic ethos, see Behrendt, "Mary Shelley"; and Bump, "Mary Shelley's Subversion." For discussion of Shelley's relationship to male Romantic ideology more broadly, see Lau, "*Rime of the Ancient Mariner*." For discussion of the novel's engagement with debates over race and imperial expansion, see Bugg, "Master of Their language"; Mellor, "*Frankenstein*, Racial Science"; and A. L. Smith, "This Thing of Darkness." For analysis of the text's depiction of the arctic as a site of imperial expansion, see Carroll, *Empire of Air*; Craciun, "Writing the Disaster"; Garrison, "Imperial Vision in the Arctic"; Hill, *White Horizon*; and Lanone, "Monsters on the Ice."
2. Shelley, *Frankenstein* (1818), 160. Subsequent references to this text will be made parenthetically as (*Frankenstein* [1818], page number).
3. Robinson, "Percy Bysshe Shelley's Text(s)," 117. The extent of Percy's editorial contributions has led Robinson, problematically in my opinion, to call *Frankenstein* "one of the most 'neglected' or, more precisely, most 'overlooked' of Percy Bysshe Shelley's texts" (117).
4. Mellor, *Mary Shelley*, 59.
5. P. Shelley, cited in Robinson, "Percy Bysshe Shelley's Text(s)," 133.
6. For further discussion of Percy Shelley's alterations and emendations to the text, see Robinson, "Percy Bysshe Shelley's Text(s)," and Mellor, *Mary Shelley*.

7. Castellano, "Legacy of Gilbert and Gubar's Readings," 88.

8. Shelley, *Selected Letters*, 12.

9. Byron, "Darkness," line 6.

10. See also Phillips, "*Frankenstein*," which links Frankenstein's creature with the weather.

11. For discussion of the novel's interaction with early evolutionary theory, see Aldiss with Wingrove, "On the Origin of Species."

12. Goodall, "*Frankenstein* and the Reprobate's Conscience," 23.

13. Perkins, *Treatise*, 111.

14. Calvin, *Institutes of the Christian Religion*, 146.

15. Goodall, "*Frankenstein* and the Reprobate's Conscience," 34.

16. Ibid., 25.

17. Ibid., 26.

18. Tannenbaum, "From Filthy Type to Truth," 106.

19. Multiple critics have written about the place of Milton and the creature's reading in the novel. See, for instance, Acosta, *Reading Genesis*; Hatlen, "Milton, Mary Shelley, and Patriarchy"; Lamb, "Mary Shelley's *Frankenstein*"; Punter, "Mary Shelley"; and Soyka, "*Frankenstein* and the Miltonic Creation." As many critics point out, both Victor and the creature are also likened to Prometheus, in John Beer's words, "the greatest saint in the Romantic calendar" (Beer, *Romantic Consciousness*, 172). For further discussion of the Prometheus myth's place in *Frankenstein*, see Small, *Mary Shelley's Frankenstein*.

20. Levine, "Ambiguous Heritage of *Frankenstein*," 27.

21. See, for instance, Homans, "Bearing Demons."

22. That Victor dreams of Elizabeth's body transforming into his mother's corpse underscores the extent to which he mentally merges the two women. As Debra Best points out, such doublings are inherently problematic. "Victor's domestic relationships create confusion concerning one's proper role in the family, while also leading one towards social and familial taboos, such as incest and gender transgression" (Best, "Monster in the Family," 370).

23. Bowerbank, "Social Order vs. The Wretch," 421.

24. Hawley, "Bride and Her Afterlife," 221.

25. Ryan, "Mary Shelley's Christian Monster," 152.

26. L. Hopkins, *Hall of Mirrors*, 5.

27. LeCussan, "*Frankenstein*," 111.

28. Shelley, "Valerius," 332, in *Mary Shelley: Collected Tales and Stories*. Subsequent citations of this work will occur parenthetically as ("Valerius," page number).

29. Halmi, "Ruins Without a Past," 8. Later authors concurred. "Lo! the resistless theme, imperial Rome," John Dyer wrote in an 1740 poem; "Fall 'n, fall'n, a silent heap; her heroes all / Sunk in their urns; behold the pride of pomp, / The throne of nations fall'n; obscur'd in dust" (Dyer, "Ruins of Rome," 19).

30. Schildgen, "Cardinal Paleotti and the *Discorso*," 8.

31. Vatican, "History of the Vatican Museum."

32. De Sanctis, translated in Springer, *Marble Wilderness*, 50.

33. Anonymous, cited in ibid., 51.
34. Ibid., 44.
35. As Springer explains, it is the "elegiac mode of archeological representation that we have come to regard as 'romantic'" (ibid., 2).
36. Keach, "Ruins of Empire," n.p.
37. Bridges, "Ruining History," 107.
38. P. Shelley, "Ozymandias," lines 12–13, 14.
39. Byron, *Childe Harold's Pilgrimage, Canto IV*, lines 703, 967.
40. Sandy, "Colossal Fabric's Form," n.p.
41. Byron, *Childe Harold's Pilgrimage, Canto IV*, lines 1294–96.
42. Ibid., 4.1296.
43. C. Middleton, *History of the Life*, 2:102–3.
44. Keach, "Ruins of Empire," n.p.
45. Barbauld, "Eighteen Hundred," lines 1–2, in *Selected Poetry and Prose*.
46. Ibid., line 158.
47. Ibid., lines 177–80.
48. Halmi, "Ruins Without a Past," 24. In Penny Bradshaw's words, "These relics function not only as reminders of earlier civilisations gone before but as symbols of Britain's own corruption" (P. Bradshaw, "Dystopian Futures," n.p.).
49. According to Bridges, Valerius's narrative "emphasizes the degree of decay evident in almost all aspects of modern Rome" (Bridges, "Ruining History," 117), while in Graham Allen's words, "the ancient, ruined Rome . . . bespeaks in part an Imperialism which for him is a betrayal of the Republican values to which he still holds" (Allen, "Reanimation," 26). Those values, his narrative makes clear, however, were always to some extent a fiction.
50. For discussion of Isabell, see Bridges, "Ruining History," which reads her as a stand-in for Percy Shelley, or Seymour, *Mary Shelley*, which links her with Shelley's friend Isabella Baxter Booth.
51. Here, then, I implicitly disagree with Graham Allen and Elisabetta Marino. For Allen, "the lesson Mary Shelley's reanimated Roman must learn is that the spirit of Republican Rome can be reanimated, that an apparent historical decline of that spirit can be reversed" (Allen, "Reanimated," 29). Marino likewise suggests that "the invention of the 'reanimated Roman' . . . turns into a political tool that enables Mary Shelley to shake the conscience of the enfeebled Italians. The resurrected consul seems to be entrusted with a vitalizing mission: by remembering the lost glories of Rome, by uncovering its dormant values" (Marino, "Themes of Reanimation and Immortality," 26). I would suggest in contrast that the story finally posits that all states are temporary. A republic may rise again, but it, too, will fall, as Rome has fallen, as Christianity will one day fall.
52. Biographical criticism of *Mathilda* abounds. In her introduction to *Mathilda*, then a newly discovered text, Elizabeth Nitchie writes, "The biographical elements are clear: Mathilda is certainly Mary herself; Mathilda's father is Godwin; Woodville is an idealized Shelley" (Nitchie, introduction, xii). More

recent critics have followed suit. Janet Todd writes, "If Mathilda can be seen to echo Mary Shelley's half-sister and her mother, it is more in open dialogue and even contest with the men in her life, Godwin and Shelley" (Todd, introduction, xxi). For other biographical readings, see Koyanagi, "Mary Shelley's *Mathilda*"; Hill-Miller, *"My Hideous Progeny"*; and Polhemus, *Lot's Daughters*.

53. Clery, *Women's Gothic*, 135. Mark Boren and Katherine Montwieler also treat the creature and Mathilda as parallel figures, insofar as both "yearn for a transcendent reunion not with an equal companion but with a parent" (Boren and Montwieler, "Pathology of the Romantic Subject," n.p.).

54. Shelley, *Mathilda*, 13. Subsequent citations of this work will occur parenthetically as (*Mathilda*, page number).

55. Rousseau, *Emile*, 393.

56. Ibid. Shelley was no fan of Rousseau. According to Zoe Beenstock, "her encyclopedia entry is more focused on Rousseau's parental neglect than on his social philosophy" (Beenstock, "Lyrical Sociability," 408). Rousseau becomes, like Victor Frankenstein, another failed patriarch who abandons the creations he should have loved. For further discussion of Shelley's life of Rousseau, see O'Rourke, "Nothing More Unnatural."

57. Fuchs and Thompson, *Women in Nineteenth-Century Europe*, 87.

58. Wollstonecraft, *Vindication of the Rights of Woman*, 71.

59. Stott, "Singular Injustice Towards Women," 24.

60. More, *Strictures on the Modern System*, ix.

61. More, *Coelebs in Search of a Wife*, 7.

62. Fordyce, *Sermons to Young Women*, 1:209.

63. Ibid., 1:216.

64. Ibid., 1:222–23.

65. Ibid., 1:216, 217. Here, Fordyce is participating in a long tradition of antinovel discourse, which feared the effect of novel reading on young, especially female, minds. By the time of Shelley's *Mathilda*, such rhetoric was outdated: "Some would still oppose all novel reading, but it was an extreme position, usually held by members of the religious right" (Warner, *Licensing Entertainment*, 14).

66. M. Hilton, *Women and the Shaping*, 2.

67. Anonymous, "DANGER and INUTILITY of ATHEISM," 301.

68. Ibid., 302.

69. Some critics attribute Mathilda's withdrawal from the world to her sense of guilt over her father's incestuous desire. According to Susan Allen Ford, "Mathilda's guilt—that she is responsible for her father's desire as well as for his death—drives the last half of the novel" (Ford, "Name More Dear," 53–54). Diane Long Hoeveler, by contrast, argues that Mathilda punishes herself for her anger at her father. "The illness from which she truly suffers and has suffered throughout the novella, however, is hatred towards her father and 'guilt for her hatred'" (Hoeveler, "Screen Memories and Fictionalized Autobiography," 85–86). More problematically, Melina Moore argues that Mathilda enjoys playing the role of the violated daughter; Shelley "leaves open the possibility that the heroine knows her real crime is the deliberate

entrapment and disposal of the father" (Moore, "Mary Shelley's 'Mathilda' and the Struggle," 212). Christa Schönfelder raises a similar question: "Issues of guilt and shame lead me to a textual crux of the novella, namely, the question of whether the incestuous passion represented here is one-sided or reciprocal" (Schönfelder, *Wounds and Words*, 179). Charles Robinson goes so far as to suggest that Mathilda has deliberately seduced her father: "It is possible to argue that she, rather than her father, initiates the incest or that she at least misrepresents her own sexual desire for her father" (Robinson, "Mathilda as Dramatic Actress," 83). I am inclined to accept Mathilda at her word; Mathilda does enjoy playacting in her youth, but there is no textual evidence to support the claim that she has deliberately seduced her father, the one man in her life who should be above sexual approach.

70. Bennet, *Mary Wollstonecraft Shelley*, 54.

71. As such, several critics have argued that Shelley uses *Mathilda* to criticize Romanticism as it was defined by male poets like her husband. Mark Boren and Katherine Montwieler, for instance, describe the novel as "Shelley's critique of the Romantic ego" (Boren and Montwieler, "Pathology of the Romantic Subject," n.p.).

72. P. Shelley, "Defence of Poetry," 1055.

73. See Airey, "Mary Shelley's *Mathilda*."

74. Brewer, "Mary Shelley on the Therapeutic Value," 387.


CHAPTER 4

1. T. Webb, "Reading Aloud in the Shelley Circle," 120.

2. Shelley, *Journals*, 2:476–77.

3. Montagu, *Turkish Embassy Letters*, 28.

4. Acosta, "Hotbeds of Popery," 617.

5. Ibid., 621. As Fran Dolan points out, Catholic women were frequently attacked for "withholding themselves from marriage and overvaluing their own virginity," a species of attack that Percy Shelley implicitly invokes in proclaiming the virtues of free love (Dolan, *Whores of Babylon*, 62).

6. Mangion, "Women, Religious Ministry," 79.

7. P. Shelley, "Epipsychidion," 373, 374; Shelley, *Letters of Mary Shelley*, 1:172.

8. Shelley, "Convent of Chaillot," 283. Further references will be cited parenthetically in the text as ("Convent of Chaillot," page number).

9. Shelley, "Trial of Love," 243, in *Mary Shelley: Collected Tales and Stories*. Subsequent citations of this work will occur parenthetically as ("Trial of Love," page number).

10. Shelley, *Valperga*, 265. Further references will be cited parenthetically in the text as (*Valperga*, page number).

11. Mekler, "Broken Mirrors," 478.

12. Euthanasia's interactions with the "mad" imprisoned Beatrice also recall Jemima's interactions with Maria in Wollstonecraft's *Maria, or the Wrongs of*

*Woman*, albeit with the social class hierarchies inverted. Shelley creates an imaginative homosocial union with her mother's work through the depiction of female religious communion.

13. Choudhury, *Wanton Jesuit*, location 449.
14. Ibid., location 857.
15. For discussion of women's prophetic activity in the seventeenth century, see Mack, "Women as Prophets."
16. Valenze, *Prophetic Sons and Daughters*, 140.
17. Juster, *Doomsayers*, 53. Lower-class male visionaries were subject to similar class-based attacks.
18. Ibid., 7.
19. For further discussion of Gott's influence on Blake, see Cho and Worrall, "William Blake's Meeting."
20. Gott, *Christ the Standard of Truth*, 10.
21. Ibid., 37–38.
22. We know for certain that Byron was familiar with Southcott; he mocked her "spiritual impregnation" and joked about the man who had "gotten her with prophet" in his letters to Murray (Byron, *Byron's Letters and Journals*, 4:164, 167).
23. For Southcott's biography, see J. Hopkins, *Woman to Deliver Her People*; and F. Brown, *Joanna Southcott*.
24. Mellor, "Blake, the Apocalypse," 145.
25. Cragwall, *Lake Methodism*, 159.
26. Southcott writes of her sister, "she began to blame me, and offered to assist me in any thing in this world, if I would give up my prophecies" (Southcott, *Warning to the World*, 20).
27. Binfield, "French, the 'Long-Wished for Revolution,'" 140.
28. Southcott, *Warning to the World*, 18.
29. J. Hopkins, *Woman to Deliver Her People*, 85.
30. Southcott, *Long-Wished for Revolution*, 8.
31. O. Smith, *Romantic Women Writers, Revolution, and Prophecy*, 66.
32. Thomas, *Romanticism and Slave Narratives*, 55.
33. Ibid., 53.
34. O. Smith, *Romantic Women Writers, Revolution, and Prophecy*, 201. Barbara Jane O'Sullivan agrees that in Wilhelmina, Shelley "invents a cult of female messianism reminiscent of the life of Joanna Southcott" (O'Sullivan, "Beatrice in *Valperga*," 144).
35. Frank Wake, "Women in the Active Voice," 252.
36. Lew, "God's Sister," 169.
37. O. Smith, *Romantic Women Writers, Revolution, and Prophecy*, 210. Smith views Beatrice and Euthanasia as two different types of female prophets: if Beatrice is the figurative daughter of Southcott and the Civil War prophetesses, Euthanasia is the figurative daughter of the self-styled prophetesses of the French Revolution, including Shelley's own mother, Wollstonecraft.
38. Frank Wake, "Women in the Active Voice," 252.

39. Shelley, "Mourner," 88.
40. Lutz, *Relics of Death*, 4, 2, 1.
41. Rovee, "Monsters, Marbles, and Miniatures," 151.
42. Maunu, "Connecting Threads of War," 463.
43. Cox, *Romanticism in the Shadow of War*, 154. Beatrice's experiences form an interesting contrast with Euthanasia's. Toward the end of volume 2, Castruccio besieges Euthanasia's castle, determined to overtake Valperga by force. He announces that "he is commanded by the ruling powers of his country, to compel the submission of the castle and rock of Valperga" (201). There is, of course, a long history of authors using besieged castles as a metaphor for the female body; as far back to the *Roman de la Rose*, the image of the castle taken by force stood in for the act of rape. Given this long-standing subtext, it is all the more surprising that Euthanasia's body is never actually in peril in *Valperga*. Euthanasia's castle is never treated as a metaphor, but as an actual political reality, and while Beatrice's body suffers from acts of violence, Euthanasia's is never threatened. Indeed, Castruccio is a curiously asexual villain. He does not insist on Euthanasia's sexual submission, nor does he replace her with another woman in a quest for heirs. Instead, he dies childless, as Euthanasia dies childless, his reputation his only legacy.
44. Euthanasia also serves as a foil to Beatrice, insofar as she refuses to become a spectacle in her suffering, as Beatrice does. Unlike Beatrice, Euthansia refuses Castruccio the satisfaction of seeing her mourn. When forced to vacate Valperga for the last time, she "folded her veil close to her face, that no rudely curious eye might read in its expression the sorrow that she felt in her heart. 'My grief is my own,' she thought; 'the only treasure that remains to me; and I will hoard it with more jealousy from the sight and knowledge of others, than a miser does his gold'" (218). Euthanasia is not willing to become a spectacle. Her reactions are not for public consumption.
45. See Kuznicki, "Sorcery and Publicity."
46. See, for instance, Choudhury, *Wanton Jesuit*; Lamotte, "P. Girard et la cadière"; and Darmon, "Mystiques Chrétiennes ou Simulatrices?"
47. Anonymous, *Memoirs of Miss Mary-Catherine Cadiere*, 12.
48. Wagner, "Pornographer in the Courtroom," 120.
49. Anonymous, *Case of Mrs. Mary Catherine Cadière*, i.
50. See Simpson, "'Blackmail Myth' and the Prosecution of Rape.'"
51. Choudhury, *Wanton Jesuit*, location 1078.
52. Hoeveler, "Anti-Catholicism," 12–13.
53. Ibid., 12.
54. Shelley writes, Mandragola "knew how powerless she was" (269), whereas Beatrice "had sanctified and obeyed every impulse as of divine origin" (270).
55. Lokke, "Sibylline Leaves," 161.
56. Thus for Tilottama Rajan, the novel "trivialize[s]" Beatrice's "powers" (Rajan, "Poetry of Philology," 114).
57. White, "Mary Shelley's *Valperga*," 75.

58. S. Curran, introduction, xxiii. For other readings of the political content of *Valperga*, see also Kasmer, who argues that the novel "reveals the political demise of the republican state, which for many Romantic writers represents the zenith of political progress" (Kasmer, *Novel Histories*, 126); Kelley, for whom the story of Castruccio reflects "the failure of the revolutionary project" (Kelley, "Romantic Temporality," 643); Maunu, for whom the figure of Castruccio is used to "critique the legacy of the Napoleonic wars" (Maunu, "Connecting Threads of War," 450); and Suzuki, for whom Castruccio recalls "Napoleon who betrayed the liberal cause despite the high hopes invested in him" (Suzuki, "Romantic Truth of History," 62).

59. Euthanasia's view of the arts contrasts powerfully with Beatrice's, as Beatrice can view imagination only as "a tyrant, armed with fire, and venomed darts, to drive me to despair" (263).

60. Carson, *Populism, Gender, and Sympathy*, 174.

61. It is somewhat surprising that Syndy M. Conger writes that Euthanasia "drowns in a shipwreck, and her heroic example lives on in the minds of her faithful subjects" (Conger, "Mary Shelley's Women in Prison," 93). I concur with Anne K. Mellor's more pessimistic reading that Shelley "emphasizes the inability of women, whether as adoring worshippers (like Beatrice) or active leads (like Euthanasia), to influence political events or to translate an ethic of care . . . into historical reality" (Mellor, *Mary Shelley*, 210).

62. Crook translates the Italian as follows: "What is, is as God wills"; "What God shall will shall be" (Crook in Shelley, *Valperga*, 324).

63. Rajan, introduction, 461.

64. Herbermann, *Catholic Encyclopedia*, 267.

65. Paterson-Morgan, "Bloodless Church," 97.

66. van Oort, "Manichaeism," 45.

67. Paterson-Morgan, "Bloodless Church," 97.

68. Shelley, *Journals*, 476–77.

69. L. Hopkins, "Memory at the End of History," n.p. For other biographical readings, see Mellor, *Mary Shelley*; Poovey, *Proper Lady and the Woman Writer*; and Kilgour, "One Immortality."

70. For discussion of Byron's debt to Campbell, see Yu, "Byron's Reworking of Thomas Campbell."

71. Anonymous, "Hood's Whims," *Blackwood's Edinburgh Magazine*, 21, 57. For discussion of Beddoes, see Paley, "Envisioning Lastness."

72. Anonymous, "Book Review," *Lady's Monthly Museum*, 169.

73. Anonymous, "Monthly Advice," *London Magazine*, 422.

74. Anonymous, "Book Review," *Monthly Review*, 334, 335.

75. Anonymous, "Last Man," *Literary Gazette*, 103, 102.

76. Ibid., 103.

77. Anonymous, "Last Woman," *Literary Lounger*, 411.

78. Grainville, cited in Paley, "Envisioning Lastness," 68.

79. Ransom, "First Last," 322.

80. Grainville, *Last Man*, 93.

81. Ibid., 122.
82. Ibid., 135.
83. Paley, "Envisioning Lastness," 7.
84. T. Campbell, "Last Man," 132.
85. Dingley, "I Had a Dream," 20.
86. Yu, "Byron's Reworking of Thomas Campbell," 383.
87. Paley, "Envisioning Lastness," 4.
88. Paley, "Le dernier homme," 72. Alkon and Gillet both attribute the moral complexity of Syderia's suffering to Grainville's own conflicted attitude toward his faith.
89. Hood, "Last Man," 29.
90. Ibid., 32.
91. Schroeder, "Byron's 'Darkness,'" 114. Paley thus views the poem as a "satirical response to the millennial vision" (Paley, *Apocalypse and Millennium*, 108).
92. For discussion of contemporary fears of the sun's extinction, see Veil, "Bright Sun Was Extinguish'd."
93. Byron, "Darkness," lines 66–69.
94. Ibid., lines 78–82.
95. Dingley, "I Had a Dream," 29. For further discussion of religious imagery in Byron's poem, see also M. Bradshaw, "Mary Shelley's *The Last Man*."
96. Bowler, *Evolution*, 86.
97. Desmond King-Hele explains, "He escaped early from his vague belief in a benevolent God and he was psychologically free to go against the Church's dogma that species were created and altered by God for his own inscrutable purposes" (King-Hele, "Shelley and Erasmus Darwin," 132).
98. Darwin, *Zoonomia*, XXIX.4.8.
99. Lamarck, translated in G. Simpson, "Extinction," 409.
100. Ibid., 410.
101. Mathias, "Sand, Flaubert, Cuvier," 520.
102. Bailes, "Psychologization of Geological Catastrophe," 675.
103. Somerset, "Transformism, Evolution, and Romanticism," 2.
104. Jeffrey, "Cuvierian Catastrophism," 149.
105. Outram, *Georges Cuvier*, 148–49.
106. Cameron, "Questioning Agency," 263. Robert Lance Snyder concurs: "She probably incorporated shadings of cataclysmic theory in her depiction of plague" (Snyder, "Apocalpyse and Indeterminacy," 442).
107. Paley, "*Last Man*," 110. See also Michael R. Page, who calls the novel's central disaster a "secular apocalypse" (Page, *Literary Imagination*, 98).
108. Shelley, *Last Man*, 62. Further references will be cited parenthetically in the text as (*Last Man*, page number).
109. Lionel complains that "Nature, our mother, and our friend, had turned on us a brow of menace" (183), reflecting the extent to which, as Sandra Gilbert points out, the plague itself is "characterized as female" (Gilbert, "Horror's Twin," 59). Ranita Chatterjee concurs that "the Plague is depicted as an insidious feminine sovereign" (Chatterjee, "Our Bodies," 37). Eve Tavor

Bannett links the plague to "the Furies who take their revenge on men" (Bannet, "Abyss of the Present," 364).

110. V. Middleton, "Exile, Isolation, and Accommodation," 174.

111. Forms of oppression in the novel are linked with Shelley's treatment of imperialism and the slave trade. The plague originates in Greece and spreads as a direct result of Raymond's hypermasculine colonialist goals, which destroy Raymond along with the rest of the world. He dies amidst the remnants of Constantinople, as the city literally collapses around him. According to some critics, Shelley "participates in the demonization of Islam by Christian Europeans that goes back to the Crusades," and constructs a nightmare of reverse colonization, the plague returning from the East to destroy the West (McWhir, introduction, xxviii). In contrast, Humberto Garcia argues that Shelley used images of Islamic Republicanism not to demonize Muslims but to offer "a renovated constitutional idiom for reclaiming political subjectivity and national identity, reworking the universal ideals of liberty, equality, and fraternity into a new vocabulary for redefining the power struggle among state sovereignty, church authority, and the people" (Garcia, *Islam and the English Enlightenment*, 11). Meanwhile, as several critics have pointed out, Verney contracts the plague from a black man, representing for some period typical racism, for others the contaminating effects of slavery on the British public. According to Kevin Hutchings, "it would be tempting—and perhaps not entirely inaccurate—to suggest that Shelley has herself succumbed to the racism so common in her era by representing the novel's only African as an object of physical horror, an abject source of deathly contamination" (Hutchings, "Dark Image in a Phantasmagoria," 39). To Young-Ok An, in contrast, he represents "a symptom of uneasiness towards the African colonial subject" (An, "Read Your Fall," 598). For further discussion of Shelley's treatment of race, see also Carroll, "Global Atmosphere," and Lew, "Plague of Imperial Desire." For discussion of early nineteenth-century theories about the transmission of disease, see McKusick, *Green Writing*; McWhir, "Mary Shelley's Anti-Contagionism"; and Melville, "Problem of Immunity."

112. At least to an extent; the parliament finally prefers Raymond's brand of brash imperialism to Adrian's protosocialism. In the failure of the dream of political evolution, Shelley rejects at least partially her father's philosophy, adopting a Malthusian perspective that "humankind cannot be perfected—there is a brutish part of human nature that cannot be eliminated and that overpowers benevolence, particularly in a crisis situation" (Cameron, "Mary Shelley's Malthusian Objections," 184). For further discussion of Shelley's reaction to the public conflict between Godwin and Malthus, see Sheridan, "Tragedy Called 'The Last Man'"; and Sterrenberg, "Last Man."

113. Cragwall, *Lake Methodism*, 35.

114. Warburton, *Doctrine of Grace*, 131.

115. Knox, "Remarks on the Life," 335.

116. Lionel's trail of writing also recalls the writing that the creature leaves behind for Victor to follow. Both are isolated and alone, reaching out to others through the medium of the written word.

117. Here, then, I disagree with Paul Cantor, who argues that Lionel's final moments invoke the "emerging language of European tourism and museum going," and thereby replicate the same imperial impulse that brought disease to British shores (Cantor, "Apocalypse of Empire," 205).

118. Ibid., 194.

119. I strongly disagree with Paley's contention that "art takes on a sinister aspect" in the novel (Paley, "Last Man," 114).

120. David Taylor reads Lionel's theatre more pessimistically, as a "stage of destruction and death" (D. Taylor, "Vacant Space," 26, 25). For further discussion of the theater scene, see Jennifer Wagner-Lawlor, who writes, "The theatrical space, including stage and audience, becomes universal as reality itself seems to become actual tragedy" (Wagner-Lawlor, "Performing History," 763). I also disagree with Elizabeth Effinger, who argues that "literature proves to be no balm, no salve against the vacuous horror of their dis-eased existence" (Effinger, "Clandestine Catastrophe," 21).

121. Morrison, "Listen While You Read," 157.

122. Effinger, "Clandestine Catastrophe," 54.

123. It is worth noting that the libretto to Haydn's *Creation* "moves from God's foundation of the physical universe, to the materialization of plants and animals, and finally, the creation of Adam and Eve, accompanied in each instance with angelic praise" (Adams, "Discourse Excellent Music," 106). The libretto describes a religiously ordered worldview that has become increasingly irrelevant.

124. In this, Lionel represents the inversion of Byron's Childe Harold, who calls "the hum / Of human cities torture," and finds "Nothing to loathe in nature, save to be / A link reluctant in a fleshly chain" (Byron, *Childe Harold's Pilgrimage, Canto III*, lines 682–83, 684–85).

125. V. Middleton, "Exile, Isolation, and Accommodation," 179. Middleton acknowledges that Lionel finds consolation in writing, but argues that the consolation is fleeting and false.

126. Cantor, "Apocalypse of Empire," 206.

127. Anonymous, "Roger Dodsworth," *New Times*, 3.

128. For a full discussion of the historical Roger Dodsworth hoax and the periodical war it occasioned, see Robinson, "Shelley and the Roger Dodsworth Hoax."

129. Shelley, "Roger Dodsworth," 47. Further references will be cited parenthetically in the text as ("Roger Dodsworth," page number).

130. Of course, this text is much lighter in tone than *The Last Man*, *Valerius*, or *Valperga*, leading A. A. Markley to describe it as "political satire in so far as Mary Shelley exposes the circular nature of history and the ephemeral quality

of all political developments" (Markley, "Laughing That I May Not Weep,"
124). Despite the humorous tone, however, she comes to the same religious
conclusions as in her earlier works.
131. Shakespeare, "Sonnet 18," 18.


## CHAPTER 5

1. Poovey, *Proper Lady and the Woman Writer*, xvi. Anne Mellor agrees that
   Shelley idealizes the bourgeois family in her later writings, but she views
   that idealization as much more potentially radical: her "writings support a
   feminist position which argues that female culture is morally superior to
   male culture, that men should become more like women, more 'feminine' in
   their behavior" (Mellor, *Mary Shelley*, 216).
2. See, for instance, Marino, "Italian Risorgimento."
3. Sites, "Chivalry and Utopian Domesticity," 525.
4. Shelley, *Fortunes of Perkin Warbeck*, 44. Further references will be cited
   parenthetically in the text as (*Perkin Warbeck*, page number).
5. Bennett, "Political Philosophy of Mary Shelley's Novels," 365.
6. Garbin, "Mary Shelley and Walter Scott," 153.
7. Bell, *First Total War*, 6.
8. Historians differ on their estimates of the death toll during the Thirty Years'
   War. For discussion of the war's impact on Europe, see Fuller, *Conduct of War*;
   and Davies, *Europe*.
9. McKeogh, *Innocent Civilians*, 100.
10. De Vattel, *Law of Nations*, 369.
11. Ibid., 302.
12. McKeogh, *Innocent Civilians*, 117.
13. Ibid., 123.
14. Bell, "Limits of Conflict in Napoleonic Europe," 202.
15. McKeogh, *Innocent Civilians*, 124.
16. According to Gavin Daly, "Redcoats plundered as they marched . . . they
    plundered from the rich and the poor, and from the living and the dead"
    (Daly, "Plunder on the Peninsula," 213). British soldiers often justified their
    behavior by referring to "the anti-Catholic traditions of the Black Legend,"
    stories of Spanish atrocity committed against Protestants in Europe and
    indigenous peoples in the Americas (211).
17. Miot, translated in Esdaile, *Peninsular War*, 242.
18. S. Andrés de Embite, cited in ibid., 243.
19. M. de la Ceda, cited in ibid., 244.
20. Hagemann, "Unimaginable Horror and Misery," 157.
21. Goldschab, translated in ibid., 165.
22. James, "Invasion and Occupation," 227.
23. Westermann, cited in Bell, *First Total War*, 173.
24. Veil, "Bright Sun Was Extinguish'd," 185.

25. Shelley, *History of a Six Weeks' Tour*, 21.
26. Domke, "Feminizing the Historical Novel," 242.
27. Bennett, "Political Philosophy of Mary Shelley's Novels," 364, 365. For further discussion of Richard's failings as a potential ruler, see also Garbin, "Fortunes of Perkin Warbeck."
28. V. Middleton, "Exile, Isolation, and Accommodation," 166.
29. Frank Wake, "Women in the Active Voice," 245.
30. Shelley's choice to alter Katherine's biography has led several critics to position Katherine "as a spokeswoman for her author" giving voice to "Shelley's own response to those who blamed her for being able to live and even to love after her husband's death (Berton, "Fortunes of Perkin Warbeck," 285–86). See also Domke, who argues that Shelley "is interested not in vindicating the reputation of the husband but that of the wife," possibly to "justify her concessions to her father-in-law's demands" (Domke, "Feminizing the Historical Novel," 244, 245).
31. Brewer, "William Godwin," 201.
32. Frank Wake, "Women in the Active Voice," 247.
33. Sites, "Chivalry and Utopian Domesticity," 527.
34. Linley, "*Frankenstein* Revisited," 259.
35. Shelley, *Frankenstein* (1831), 141. Subsequent references to this text will be made parenthetically as (*Frankenstein* [1831], page number).
36. Ellis, "Monsters in the Garden," 133.
37. Reese, *Reproducing Enlightenment*, 24.
38. Crook, "In Defence of the 1831 *Frankenstein*," 5. James O'Rourke also refutes this reading: "The 1831 revised edition of the novel, far from being a recantation of Shelley's iconoclasm in 1818, extends and elaborates her critique of the erotic hierarchies that simultaneously bind together the social order and turn Victor Frankenstein's creature into a monster" (O'Rourke, *Sex, Lies, and Autobiography*, 96).
39. As several critics have commented, the 1831 edition of *Frankenstein* emphasizes fate; according to Jane Goodall, for instance, Victor's "consistent assumption that his course is predestined . . . is amplified in the revisions made for the 1831 edition" (Goodall, "*Frankenstein* and the Reprobate's Conscience," 31. For further discussion of fate in the 1831 *Frankenstein*, see also David S. Hogsette, who argues that "Victor expresses (in the 1831 edition) what appears to be religious fatalism" (Hogsette, "Metaphysical Intersections in *Frankenstein*," 549).
40. Bowerbank, "Social Order vs. The Wretch," 421. For further discussion of Elizabeth as an embodiment of perfect womanhood, see Mary Lowe-Evans, who writes, "Justine's mandate for Elizabeth to behave like a saint and martyr was added for the 1831 edition of *Frankenstein* during the period when, as we have seen, the woman's role as angel in the home was being loudly debated" (Lowe-Evans, *Frankenstein*, 65).
41. It is interesting, therefore, that, as William Crissman points out, "Victor's murderous antagonism toward Elizabeth becomes more prominent in the

1831 edition" (Crisman, "Now Misery Has Come Home," 37). As Elizabeth's agency increases, so does the violence of Victor's language towards her.

42. Byron, *Childe Harold's Pilgrimage, Canto III*, lines 1058–59.

43. Jay, *Religion of the Heart*, 23.

44. Wilberforce, *Practical View*, 24–25.

45. Ibid., 26.

46. Ibid., 26.

47. The name was in fact coined in error by Sir James Stephen, a member of the group who publicly misquoted a mocking article in the *Edinburgh Review*.

48. Tomkins, *Clapham Sect*, 11.

49. Ibid., 19.

50. More, *Thoughts on the Importance of Manners*, 116.

51. Hilton, *Age of Atonement*, 7.

52. Susan Brown, "Policing and Privilege," 116.

53. Tomkins, *Clapham Sect*, 155.

54. According to Elisabeth Jay, "The French Revolution heightened the anxiety of the Evangelicals to stress their separateness from Dissent, which frequently bore the taint of Radicalism" (Jay, *Religion of the Heart*, 17–18). James Bean, for instance, suggests in his popular Evangelical treatise, *Zeal Without Innovation*, that declines in church attendance preface political unrest: "The desertion of the temples has ever been held as a threatening omen, not only by the pious, but by all who have studied human nature" (Bean, *Zeal Without Innovation*, 13).

55. Bebbington, *Evangelicalism in Modern Britain*, 68. For further discussion of Evangelical reactions to the French Revolution, see also Spring, who argues that Wilberforce "offered Evangelical Christianity as the best antidote to atheistical Jacobinism" (Spring, "Clapham Sect," 47).

56. More is an interesting, often problematic figure, insofar as she encouraged women to confine themselves to the domestic sphere while remaining a stubbornly public writer herself. As Tomkins points out, "She repeatedly urged women to keep to their natural stations," even as she "made a fortune as a playwright, novelist, poet, and essayist, and established and managed eleven schools" (Tomkins, *Clapham Sect*, 61).

57. More, *Coelebs in Search of a Wife*, 47.

58. Ibid., 47–48.

59. Ibid., 42. More here quotes Milton's *Paradise Lost*.

60. More, *Moral Sketches*, 200–201.

61. Anonymous, *Report of the Female Association*, cited in Hempton, *Religion of the People*, 193.

62. More, *Coelebs in Search of a Wife*, 41–42.

63. Jordan, *Women's Movement*, 95.

64. Boylan, "Evangelical Womanhood in the Nineteenth Century," 66.

65. Anonymous, "Hints for Conducting Sunday Schools," n.p.

66. More, *Coelebs in Search of a Wife*, 43.

67. Anonymous, *Report of the Debates at Cork*, cited in Hempton, *Religion of the People*, 194.

68. Shelley, *Lodore*, 44. Further references will be cited parenthetically in the text as (*Lodore*, page number).

69. For discussion of the Silver Fork genre, see Copeland, *Silver Fork Novel*.

70. Anonymous, "Lodore," *Literary Gazette*, 195.

71. Anonymous, "Lodore," *Athenaeum*, 239.

72. Anonymous, "Lodore," *Leigh Hunt's London Journal*, 138.

73. N. Williams, "Angelic Realism," 397.

74. Cornelia initially justifies her refusal to "bend to her husband's will, or to submit to his tyranny" (*Lodore*, 116) and feels "she was justified before God and her conscience for refusing to submit to the most insulting tyranny" (255). While Cornelia will later repent for this disobedience, the text never fully absolves Lodore for his unfair treatment of her. She is not, nor did she intend to be, unfaithful to him, suggesting that his desire to restrict her movements may in fact be evidence of husbandly overreach. Shelley's use of the word tyrant for Lodore—obviously a loaded political term—suggests her deep suspicion of his character, even as she ultimately champions Cornelia's final submission to her second husband.

75. Carlson, *England's First Family of Writers*, 122.

76. Hill-Miller, "*My Hideous Progeny*," 161.

77. Jowell, "Mary Shelley's Mothers," 309.

78. Williams, "Angelic Realism," 399.

79. Fanny Derham, in contrast, is subject to unnamed future tragedies, perhaps as punishment for rejecting traditional femininity. Fanny serves as a foil to Ethel, educated and self-possessed in a way that Ethel is not. For discussions of Fanny Derham, see Vargo, "Aikins and the Godwins"; Gonda, "*Lodore* and Fanny Derham's Story"; and Allen, "Beyond Biographism."

80. He will not ask for financial help, even at the expense of Ethel's life and his own.

81. E. Garrett, "White Papers and Black Figures," 195.

82. For historical background on the long fight for Catholic Emancipation, see, for instance, Hinde, *Catholic Emancipation*; Jenkins, *Era of Emancipation*; and Reynolds, *Catholic Emancipation Crisis in Ireland*.

83. For historical discussions of O'Connell, see MacDonagh, *O'Connell*; and O'Ferrall, *Catholic Emancipation*.

84. Nehemiah, "Observations Occasioned By Hamilton's Letter," 222.

85. Bene, "Roman Catholic Emancipation," 628.

86. Anonymous, "Catholic Emancipation." *Imperial Magazine*, 560.

87. Anonymous, "Catholic Question," *Blackwood's Edinburgh Magazine*, 575–76.

88. P.A.N., "On Catholic Emancipation," 211.

89. Graham, "Catholic Emancipation," 356.

90. Ibid., 356.

91. Anonymous, "Untitled Item," 108. George William Finch-Hatton, Earl of Winchilsea, was a staunch opponent of Catholic emancipation and even went so far as to fight a duel with the Duke of Wellington over his support for the act.

92. Anonymous, "Catholics of Ireland," 6.

93. Ibid.

94. Anonymous, "Wellington and Emancipation," 201.

95. Anonymous, "Catholic Emancipation," *Examiner*, 697.

96. Anonymous, "Ireland," 210.

97. Anonymous, "Ought England to Emancipate the Irish?" 20.

98. Shelley, *Falkner*, 139. Further references will be cited parenthetically in the text as (*Falkner*, page number).

99. Sir Boyville, like Lodore, is also described in the political language of tyranny. He believes that his station entitles him to obedience, and he is described as a "soulless niggard tyrant" (*Falkner*, 94), who treats his son like a "galley-slave" (123), possibly an invocation of and reference to Godwinian political theory. That Falkner hides his papers in a box much like the iron chest of *Caleb Williams*'s Falkland (whose name Falkner recalls) bespeaks Shelley's desire later in life to engage with her father's works.

100. Sites, "Utopian Domesticity as Social Reform," 154. For Jonas Cope, Elizabeth's perfections are unnatural. "Put bluntly, Elizabeth is an ethical automaton whose passivity and devotion are perpetually obscured and romanticized by organic tropes" (Cope, "Passive and Dynamic Sincerity," 131). She is, he claims, a "half-Platonic, half-Christian demigoddess come to earth" (131).

101. Elizabeth's mother displays similarly self-negating tendencies. Her love for her husband was her "divine joy," and upon his death, it is only love for her child that keeps her alive (*Falkner*, 10).

102. For discussion of the similarities between *Falkner* and *Mathilda*, see also Bennett, who writes, "The John Falkner-Elizabeth Raby relationship revisits the guilty father—innocent daughter relationship in *Matilda* and again poses the recurrent Romantic conflict between self-interest and social need" (Bennett, *Mary Wollstonecraft Shelley*, 101).

103. Gravitt, "Feminist Utopia," n.p.

104. Saunders, "Rehabilitating the Family in Shelley's *Falkner*," 221.

105. Jowell, "Mary Shelley's Mothers," 315.

106. Hempton and Hill, *Evangelical Protestantism*, 129.

107. The novel's good characters are horrified by the specter of the legal system. Gerard is disgusted by his father's choice to involve the authorities in his dispute with Falkner, rather than seeking honorable satisfaction in a duel. Elizabeth meanwhile claims that it is better for the criminal to be "treated with the indulgence of a correcting father" than by "the cruel vengeance of the law" (*Falkner*, 237).

108. Sites, "Utopian Domesticity as Social Reform," 162.

109. Ibid., 163.

## CONCLUSION

1. Shelley, *Rambles in Germany and Italy*, 348. Further references will be cited parenthetically in the text as (*Rambles*, page number).

2. For analysis of the text as an example of travel writing by a celebrity author, see Campbell Orr, "Mary Shelley's *Rambles*." For discussion of the text's political content, see Bennet, *Mary Wollstonecraft Shelley*; Crook, "Meek and Bold"; Marino, "Italian Risorgimento in Mary Shelley's *Rambles*"; and Moskal, "Gender and Italian Nationalism in *Rambles*." For discussion of Shelley's strategies for overcoming the limits of gender in the text, see Schoina, *Romantic 'Anglo-Italians'*.

3. Shelley here quotes Addison's *Spectator* no. 12 and Milton's *Paradise Lost* 4.677–78.

4. Wollstonecraft's description of nature as "the bones of the world waiting to be clothed with everything necessary to give life and beauty" was one of Shelley's favorite lines from her mother's works (Wollstonecraft, *Short Residence*, 88).

5. Elisabetta Marino links Shelley's positive treatment of the Roman Catholic clergy with her desire to support Italian liberation: "When a cholera epidemics [*sic*] spread across the Capital of the world in 1837, the Pope encouraged processions and public prayers which, far from dispelling the disease, increased the opportunity for contagion. Since Mary Shelley wished to advocate the Italian cause, however, she could not insist on the portrayal of religion as an insurmountable hindrance to the people's emancipation, otherwise she would have strengthened the already mentioned, deeply ingrained stereotype" (Marino, "Italian Risorgimento in Mary Shelley's *Rambles*," 58).

6. For Beth Dolan Katz, the landscape has a positive effect on Shelley's physical health. Writing of Shelley's experience with the various spas she visits, Katz explains that she "links their healing capacity with their geographical location, and implies that the landscape may have a more positive effect on her health than does the spa regimen" (Katz, "Spas and Salutary Landscapes," 172).

# WORKS CITED

Abernethy, John. *An Enquiry into the Probability and Rationality of Mr. Hunter's Theory of Life.* London: Longman, Hurst, Rees, Orne, and Brown, 1814.

Acosta, Ana M. "Hotbeds of Popery: Convents in the English Literary Imagination." *Eighteenth-Century Fiction* 15, no. 3–4 (2003): 615–42.

———. *Reading Genesis in the Long Eighteenth Century: From Milton to Mary Shelley.* Burlington: Ashgate, 2007.

Adams, Vicky L. "'Discourse Excellent Music': Romantic Rhetoric and Ecofeminism in Mary Shelley's *The Last Man.*" In *Feminist Ecocriticism: Environment, Women, and Literature,* edited by Douglas A. Vakoch, 105–21. Lanham: Lexington Books, 2012.

Addison, Joseph, and Richard Steele. *The Spectator.* The Spectator Project. http://www2.scc.rutgers.edu/spectator/complete.html.

Airey, Jennifer L. "Mary Shelley's *Mathilda*: Gender and the Limits of Authorial Leadership." In *Cultural Icons and Cultural Leadership,* edited by Peter Iver Kaufman and Kristin M. S. Bezio, 54–68. Northampton: Edward Elgar Publishing, 2017.

Aldiss, Brian W., with David Wingrove. "On the Origin of Species: Mary Shelley." In *Speculations on Speculation: Theories of Science Fiction,* edited by James Gunn and Matthew Candelaria, 163–203. Lanham: Scarecrow Press, 2005.

Alkon, Paul K. *Origins of Futuristic Fiction.* Athens: University of Georgia Press, 1987.

Allen, Graham. "Beyond Biographism: Mary Shelley's *Mathilda*, Intertextuality, and the Wandering Subject." *Romanticism* 3, no. 2 (1997): 170–84.

———. "Reanimation or Reversibility in 'Valerius: The Reanimated Roman': A Response to Elena Anastasaki." *Connotations* 19, nos. 1–3 (2009–10): 21–33.

———. "The Gift and the Return: Deconstructing Mary Shelley's *Lodore.*" *Derrida Today* 4, no. 1 (2011): 44–58.

An, Young-Ok———. "'Read Your Fall': The Signs of Plague in *The Last Man.*" *Studies in Romanticism* 44, no. 4 (2005): 581–604.

Anderson, Misty G. *Imagining Methodism in Eighteenth-Century Britain: Enthusiasm, Belief, and the Borders of the Self.* Baltimore: Johns Hopkins University Press, 2012.

Anderson, Robert. "'Misery Made Me a Fiend': Social Reproduction in Mary
  Shelley's *Frankenstein* and Robert Owen's Early Writings." *Nineteenth
  Century Contexts* 24, no. 2 (2002): 417–38.
Andre, Shane. "Was Hume an Atheist?" *Hume Studies* 19, no. 1 (1993): 141–66.
Anonymous. "ART. V. Frankenstein, Or the Modern Prometheus." *Quarterly Review*
  18, no. 36 (1818): 379–85.
———. "Art. XII. Frankenstein; Or the Modern Prometheus." *British Critic,*
  *1793–1826* 9 (1818): 432–38.
———. *A Bloody Tragedie, Or Romish Maske: Acted by five Iesuites, and sixteene young*
  *German Maides.* London: E. E., 1607.
———. "Book Review." *Lady's Monthly Museum* 23 (1826): 169.
———. "Book Review." *Monthly Review* 1, no. 3 (1826): 334–35.
———. *The Case of Mrs. Mary Catherine Cadière, Against the Jesuit Father John Baptist*
  *Girard.* London: J. Roberts, 1732.
———. "Catholic Emancipation." *Examiner* 1135 (1829): 697–98.
———. "Catholic Emancipation." *Imperial Magazine* 3, no. 28 (1821): 559–61.
———. "The Catholic Question." *Blackwood's Edinburgh Magazine* 21, no. 125 (1827):
  575–96.
———. "The Catholics of Ireland." *Monthly Magazine; or, British Regster, Feb. 1800–*
  *June 1836* 3, no. 13 (1827): 5–19.
———. "The DANGER and INUTILITY of ATHEISM." *Universal Magazine* 19, no. 113 (1813):
  301–4.
———. "An ESSAY Against ATHEISM." *Weekly Magazine; or, Edinburgh Amusement,*
  *1768–1779* 20 (1773): 9–10.
———. *An Essay on the Immateriality and Immortality of the Soul.* London, 1778.
———. *Hints for Conducting Sunday Schools, Useful also for Day Schools and Families.*
  Dublin, 1819.
———. "Hood's Whims and Oddities." *Blackwood's Edinburgh Magazine* 21, no. 121
  (1827): 45–60.
———. "Ireland." *Cobbett's Weekly Register, July 21, 1821–Sept.12, 1835* 71, no. 4 (1831):
  209–11.
———. *The Kings Majesties Speech On the 2. Day of December, 1641.* London: John
  Greensmith, 1641.
———. "The Last Man." *Literary Gazette* (1826): 102–3.
———. "The Last Woman." *Literary Lounger* (1826): 404–11.
———. "Lodore." *Athenaeum* 387 (1835): 238–39.
———. "Lodore." *Leigh Hunt's London Journal* 58 (1835): 138–39.
———. "Lodore." *Literary Gazette: A Weekly Journal of Literature, Science, and the Fine*
  *Arts* 949 (1835): 194–95.
———. "Memoirs of Crosse the Electrician." *Leader and Saturday Analyst, Jan. 7–*
  *June 30, 1860* 8, no. 381 (1857): 665–66.
———. *Memoirs of Miss Mary-Catherine Cadiere and Father Girard, Jesuit.* London:
  J. Isted, 1731.
———. "MEMOIRS of Mrs Mary Wollstonecraft Godwin, Author of A Vindication of the
  Rights of Woman, &c." *Scots Magazine, 1739–1803* 60 (1798): 295–301.

———. "Memoirs of the Author of a Vindication of the Rights of Woman." *Critical Review; or, Annals of Literature* 22 (1798): 414–19.

———. "Monthly Advice to Purchasers of Books." *London Magazine* 4, no. 15 (1826): 422.

———. "Ought England to Emancipate the Irish Catholics?" *Dublin and London Magazine, Mar. 1825–Dec. 1826* 1, no. 1 (1825): 16–22.

———. "Remarks on Frankenstein, or the Modern Prometheus; A Novel." *Blackwood's Edinburgh Magazine* 2, no. 12 (1818): 613–20.

———. "Roger Dodsworth." *New Times* (1826): 3.

———. "Universal Spectator." *London Magazine; or, Gentleman's Monthly Intelligencer* (June 1734): 309.

———. "Untitled Item." *Examiner* 1098 (1829): 108.

———. "Wellington and Emancipation." *New Monthly Magazine and Literary Journal, Jan. 1821–Dec. 1836* 25, no. 97 (1829): 201–10.

An Anti-Empiric. "Remarks on the Enthusiasm of the Public in Favour of Quackery." *New London Magazine* 5 (1793): 216.

Bailes, Melissa. "The Psychologization of Geological Catastrophe in Mary Shelley's *The Last Man*." *English Literary History* 82, no. 2 (2015): 671–99.

Bailey, Alan, and Dan O'Brien. *The Continuum Companion to Hume*. London: Continuum, 2012.

Baker, Carlos. *Shelley's Major Poetry: The Fabric of a Vision*. New York: Russell & Russell, 1961.

Balguy, John. "The extreme Folly and Wretchedness of an Atheistic Inclination." In *Five Sermons*. London: J and J. Pemberton, 1738.

Banerjee, Suparna. "Home Is Where Mamma Is: Reframing the Science Question in *Frankenstein*." *Women's Studies* 40, no. 1 (2010): 1–22.

Bannet, Eve Tavor. "The 'Abyss of the Present' and Women's Time in Mary Shelley's *The Last Man*." *Eighteenth-Century Novel* 2 (2002): 353–81.

Barbauld, Anna Letitia. *Selected Poetry and Prose*. Edited by William McCarthy and Elizabeth Kraft. Peterborough: Broadview Press, 2002.

Barnard, Ellsworth. *Shelley's Religion*. Minneapolis: University of Minnesota Press, 1937.

Bean, James. *Zeal Without Innovation*. London: F. C. and J. Rivington, 1808.

Bebbington, David W. *Evangelicalism in Modern Britain: A History from the 1730s to the 1980s*. London: Routledge, 1989.

Bebbington, David W., and George A. Rawlyk, eds. *Evangelicalism: Comparative Studies of Popular Protestantism in North America, The British Isles, and Beyond, 1700–1900*. Oxford: Oxford University Press, 1994.

Beenstock, Zoe. "Lyrical Sociability: The Social Contract and Mary Shelley's *Frankenstein*." *Philosophy and Literature* 39, no. 2 (2015): 406–21.

Beer, John. "Romantic Apocalypses." In *Romanticism and Millenarianism*, edited by Tim Fulford, 53–70. New York: Palgrave, 2002.

———. *Romantic Consciousness: Blake to Mary Shelley*. New York: Palgrave Macmillan, 2003.

Behrendt, Stephen. "Mary Shelley, *Frankenstein*, and the Woman Writer's Fate."
In *Romantic Women Writers: Voices and Countervoices*, edited by Paula R.
Feldman and Theresa M. Kelley, 69–87. Hanover: University Press of
New England, 1995.

Bell, David A. *The First Total War: Napoleon's Europe and the Birth of Warfare as We
Know It*. Boston: Houghton Mifflin, 2007.

———. "The Limits of Conflict in Napoleonic Europe—And Their Transgression."
In *Civilians and War in Europe, 1618–1815*, edited by Erica Charters, Eve
Rosenhaft, and Hannah Smith, 201–8. Liverpool: Liverpool University
Press, 2012.

Bell, Kathleen. "A Family Man: The Godwin and Shelley Circles." *Critical Survey* 4,
no. 1 (1992): 52–61.

Bene, Nota. "Roman Catholic Emancipation." *Christian Remembrancer; or, The
Churchman's Biblical, Ecclesiastical & Literary Miscellany, 1819–1840* 9, no.
10 (1827): 626–30.

Bennett, Betty T. *Mary Wollstonecraft Shelley: An Introduction*. Baltimore: Johns
Hopkins University Press, 1996.

———. "The Political Philosophy of Mary Shelley's Historical Novels: *Valperga* and
*Perkin Warbeck*." In *The Evidence of the Imagination: Studies of Interactions
Between Life and Art in English Romantic Literature*, edited by Donald H.
Reiman, Michael C. Jaye, and Betty T. Bennett, 354–71. New York: New
York University Press, 1978.

Bennett, Betty T., and Stuart Curran, eds. *Mary Shelley in Her Times*. Baltimore:
Johns Hopkins University Press, 2000.

Benson, Joseph. *Remarks on Dr. Priestley's system of materialism, mechanism, and
necessity*. London, 1788.

Berman, David. "David Hume and the Suppression of 'Atheism.'" *Journal of the
History of Philosophy* 21, no. 3 (1983): 375–87.

———. *A History of Atheism in Britain: From Hobbes to Russell*. London: Croom Helm, 1988.

Berton, Anne. "*The Fortunes of Perkin Warbeck, a Romance*: Mary Shelley's Elegy
for a Lost (K)night." In *The Enlightenment by Night: Essays on After-Dark
Culture in the Long Eighteenth Century*, edited by Serge Soupel, Kevin L.
Cope, and Alexander Pettit, 277–88. New York: AMS Press, 2010.

Beshero-Bondar, Elisa. *Women, Epic, and Transition in British Romanticism*. Newark: University of Delaware Press, 2011.

Best, Debra E. "The Monster in the Family: A Reconsideration of *Frankenstein*'s
Domestic Relationships." *Women's Writing* 6, no. 3 (1999): 365–84.

Bewell, Alan. "'An Issue of Monstrous Desire': *Frankenstein* and Obstetrics." *Yale
Journal of Criticism* 2, no. 1 (1988): 105–28.

Binfield, Kevin. "The French, the 'Long-Wished for Revolution,' and the Just War
in Joanna Southcott." In *Rebellious Hearts: British Women Writers and the
French Revolution*, edited by Adriana Craciun and Kari E. Lokke, 135–59.
Albany: State University of New York Press, 2001.

Blake, William. *The Complete Poetry and Prose of William Blake*. Edited by David V.
Erdman. New York: Anchor Books, 1988.

Boren, Mark E., and Katherine Montwieler, "The Pathology of the Romantic Subject and Mary Shelley's Cure for Melancholia in *Frankenstein* and *Matilda*." *PsyArt* (2012): n.p.

Bostrom, Irene. "The Novel and Catholic Emancipation." *Studies in Romanticism* 2, no. 3 (1963): 155–76.

Botting, Fred. *Making Monstrous: Frankenstein, Criticism, Theory*. Manchester: Manchester University Press, 1991.

Bowerbank, Sylvia. "The Social Order vs. The Wretch: Mary Shelley's Contradictory-Mindedness in *Frankenstein*." *English Literary History* 46, no. 3 (1979): 418–31.

Bowler, Peter. *Evolution: The History of an Idea*. Berkeley: University of California Press, 2003.

Boylan, Anne M. "Evangelical Womanhood in the Nineteenth Century: The Role of Women in Sunday Schools." *Feminist Studies* 4, no. 3 (1978): 62–80.

Bradley, Arthur. "'Until Death Tramples It to Fragments': Percy Bysshe Shelley After Postmodern Theology." In *Romanticism and Religion from William Cowper to Wallace Stevens*, edited by Gavin Hopps and Jane Stabler, 191–206. Burlington: Ashgate, 2006.

Bradshaw, Michael. "Mary Shelley's *The Last Man* (The End of the World as We Know It)." In *Impossibility Fiction: Alternativity—Extrapolation—Speculation*, edited by Derek Littlewood and Peter Stockwell, 163–75. Amsterdam: Rodopi, 1996.

Bradshaw, Penny. "Dystopian Futures: Time-Travel and Millenarian Visions in the Poetry of Anna Barbauld and Charlotte Smith." *Romanticism on the Net* 21 (2001): n.p. https://doi.org/10.7202/005959ar.

Bresadola, Marco. "Medicine and Science in the Life of Luigi Galvani (1737–1798)." *Brain Research Bulletin* 46, no. 5 (1998): 367–80.

Brewer, William D. "Mary Shelley on the Therapeutic Value of Language." *Papers on Language and Literature* 30, no. 4 (1994): 387–407.

———. "William Godwin, Chivalry, and Mary Shelley's *The Fortunes of Perkin Warbeck*." *Papers on Language and Literature* 35, no. 2 (1999): 187–205.

Brewster, Glen. "From Albion to Frankenstein's Creature: The Disintegration of the Social Body in Blake and Mary Shelley." In *Romantic Generations: Essays in Honor of Robert F. Gleckner*, edited by Ghislaine McDayter, Guinn Batten, and Barry Milligan, 64–82. London: Associated University Press, 2001.

Bridges, Meilee D. "Ruining History: The Shelleys' Fragments of Rome." In *Mary Shelley: Her Circle and Her Contemporaries*, edited by L. Adam Mekler and Lucy Morrison, 105–30. Newcastle upon Tyne: Cambridge Scholars Publishing, 2010.

Brothers, Richard. *A Revealed Knowledge of the Prophecies and Times, Book the Second*. London, 1794.

Broughton, Thomas. *Bibliotheca Historico-sacra*. Vol. 1. London: R. Reily, 1737.

Brown, Callum G. *The Death of Christian Britain: Understanding Secularisation, 1800–2000*. London: Routledge, 2001.

Brown, Frances. *Joanna Southcott: The Woman Clothed with the Sun*. Cambridge: The Lutterworth Press, 2002.

Brown, Stewart J. "Irving, Edward (1792–1834)." *Oxford Dictionary of National Biography*. Oxford: Oxford University Press, 2004. Online ed., Jan 2014. http://0-www.oxforddnb.com.library.utulsa.edu/view/article/14473/.

Brown, Susan E. "Policing and Privilege: The Resistance to Penal Reform in Eighteenth-Century London." In *Institutional Culture in Early Modern Society*, edited by Anne Goldgar and Robert I. Frost, 103–32. Boston: Brill, 2004.

Buckley, Michael J. *At the Origins of Modern Atheism*. New Haven: Yale University Press, 1990.

Bugg, John. "'Master of Their language': Education and Exile in Mary Shelley's *Frankenstein*." *Huntington Library Quarterly* 68, no. 4 (2005): 655–66.

Bump, Jerome. "Mary Shelley's Subversion of Male Myths of Creativity in *Frankenstein*." In *The Ethics of Popular Culture: From Frankenstein to Cyberculture*, edited by Ingo R. Stoehr, 18–42. Kilgore, Tex.: The Second Dimension Press, 1995.

Burke, Edmund. *Reflections on the Revolution in France*. Oxford: Oxford University Press, 1993.

Burstein, Miriam Elizabeth. *Victorian Reformations: Historical Fiction and Religious Controversy, 1820–1904*. Notre Dame: University of Notre Dame Press, 2013.

Bush, Michael. *The Casualties of Peterloo*. Manchester: Carnegie Publishing, 2005.

———. "The Women at Peterloo: The Impact of Female Reform on the Manchester Meeting of 16 August 1819." *History* 89, no. 294 (2004): 209–32.

Butler, Marilyn. Introduction to *Frankenstein*, by Mary Shelley, ix–li. Oxford: Oxford University Press, 1993.

Butler, Melissa. "Wollstonecraft versus Rousseau: Natural Religion and the Sex of Virtue and Reason." In *Man, God, and Nature in the Enlightenment*, edited by Donald C. Mell Jr., Theodore E. D. Braun, and Lucia M. Palmer, 65–73. East Lansing, Mich.: Colleagues Press, 1988.

Byron, George Gordon, Lord. *Byron's Letters and Journals*. Edited by Leslie A. Marchand. Cambridge: Harvard University Press, 1973.

———. *Cain*. In *The Major Works*. 881–938. Oxford: Oxford University Press, 1986.

———. *Childe Harold's Pilgrimage, Canto III*. In *Selected Poems*, edited by Peter J. Manning, 415–62. London: Penguin Books, 1996.

———. *Childe Harold's Pilgrimage, Canto IV*. In *Selected Poems*, edited by Peter J. Manning, 508–69. London: Penguin Books, 1996.

———. "Darkness." In *Selected Poems*, edited by Peter J. Manning, 412–14. London: Penguin Books, 1996.

Cafarelli, Annette Wheeler. "How Theories of Romanticism Exclude Women: Radcliffe, Milton, and the Legitimation of the Gothic Novel." In *Milton, the Metaphysicals, and Romanticism*, edited by Lisa Low and Anthony John Harding, 84–113. Cambridge: Cambridge University Press, 1994.

Caldwell, Janis McLarren. *Literature and Medicine in Nineteenth-Century Britain: From Mary Shelley to George Eliot*. Cambridge: Cambridge University Press, 2004.

Calvin, John. *Institutes of the Christian Religion*. Vol. 2. London: Thomas Tegg, 1844.

Cameron, Lauren. "Mary Shelley's Malthusian Objections in *The Last Man*." *Nineteenth-Century Literature* 67, no. 2 (2012): 177–203.

———. "Questioning Agency: Dehumanizing Sustainability in Mary Shelley's *The Last Man*." In *Romantic Sustainability: Endurance and the Natural World, 1780–1830*, edited by Ben P. Robertson, 261–73. Lexington: Lexington Books, 2016.

Campbell, Thomas. "The Last Man." In *The Poetical Works of Thomas Campbell*, 130–34. London: Edward Moxon, 1851.

Campbell Orr, Clarissa. "Mary Shelley's *Rambles in Germany and Italy*, the Celebrity Author, and the Undiscovered Country of the Human Heart." *Romanticism on the Net* 11 (1998): n.p. https://doi.org/10.7202/005813ar.

Cantor, Paul. "The Apocalypse of Empire: Mary Shelley's *The Last Man*." In *Iconoclastic Departures: Mary Shelley After Frankenstein*, edited by Syndy M. Conger, Frederick Frank, and Gregory O'Dea, 193–211. Madison: Farleigh Dickinson University Press, 1997.

Carlson, Julie A. *England's First Family of Writers: Mary Wollstonecraft, William Godwin, Mary Shelley*. Baltimore: Johns Hopkins University Press, 2007.

Carroll, Siobhan. *An Empire of Air and Water: Uncolonizable Space in the British Imagination, 1750–1850*. Philadelphia: University of Pennsylvania Press, 2015.

———. "Mary Shelley's Global Atmosphere." *European Romantic Review* 25, no. 1 (2014): 3–17.

Carson, James P. *Populism, Gender, and Sympathy in the Romantic Novel*. New York: Palgrave Macmillan, 2010.

Castellano, Katey. "The Legacy of Gilbert and Gubar's Readings of Mary Shelley's *Frankenstein* and *The Last Man*." In *Gilbert and Gubar's* The Madwoman in the Attic *After Thirty Years*, edited by Annette R. Federico, 76–93. Columbia: University of Missouri Press, 2009.

Chadwick, Owen. *The Victorian Church Part One, 1829–1859*. Eugene: WIPF & Stock Publishers, 1987.

Chatterjee, Ranita. "Our Bodies, Our Catastrophes: Biopolitics in Mary Shelley's *The Last Man*." *European Romantic Review* 25, no. 1 (2014): 35–49.

Cho, Nancy Jiwon, and David Worrall. "William Blake's Meeting with Dorothy Gott: The Female Origins of Blake's Prophetic Mode." *Romanticism* 16, no. 1 (2010): 60–71.

Choudhury, Mita. *The Wanton Jesuit and the Wayward Saint: A Tale of Sex, Religion, and Politics in Eighteenth-Century France*. University Park: Pennsylvania State University Press, 2015. Kindle edition.

Claeys, Gregory. *Citizens and Saints: Politics and Anti-Politics in Early British Socialism*. Cambridge: Cambridge University Press, 1989.

Clapp, Elizabeth J., and Julie Roy Jeffrey. *Women, Dissent, and Anti-Slavery in Britain and America, 1790–1865*. Oxford: Oxford University Press, 2011.

Clark, David Lee. *Shelley's Prose: Or The Trumpet of a Prophecy*. Albuquerque: University of New Mexico Press, 1954.

Clark, J. C. D. *English Society, 1660–1832: Religion, Ideology and Politics During the Ancient Regime*. Cambridge: Cambridge University Press, 2000.

Clery, E. J. *Women's Gothic: From Clara Reeve to Mary Shelley*. Tavistock: Northcote House Publishers, 2000 and 2004.

Colley, Linda. *Britons: Forging the Nation, 1707–1837*. New Haven: Yale University Press, 1992.

Collinson, Patrick, Arnold Hunt, and Alexandra Walsham. "Religious Publishing in England 1557–1640." In *The Cambridge History of the Book, Volume IV, 1557–1695*, edited by John Barnard and D. F. McKenzie, 29–66. Cambridge: Cambridge University Press, 2002.

Conger, Syndy McMillen. "Mary Shelley's Women in Prison." In *Iconoclastic Departures: Mary Shelley After Frankenstein*, edited by Syndy M. Conger, Frederick Frank, and Gregory O'Dea, 81–97. Madison: Farleigh Dickinson University Press, 1997.

———. "Multivocality in Mary Shelley's Unfinished Memoirs of Her Father." *European Romantic Review* 9, no. 3 (1998): 303–22.

Conger, Syndy M., Frederick Frank, and Gregory O'Dea, eds. *Iconoclastic Departures: Mary Shelley After Frankenstein*. Madison: Farleigh Dickinson University Press, 1997.

Conradt, Stacy. "Mary Shelley's Favorite Keepsake: Her Dead Husband's Heart." http://mentalfloss.com/article/65624/mary-shelleys-favorite-keepsake-her-dead-husbands-heart/.

Cooper, Andrew M. "Freedom from Blake's 'Book of Urizen.'" *Studies in Romanticism* 48, no. 2 (2009): 187–218.

Cope, Jonas S. "Passive and Dynamic Sincerity in Mary Shelley's *Falkner*." *Keats-Shelley Journal* 63 (2014): 123–37.

Copeland, Edward. *The Silver Fork Novel: Fashionable Fiction in the Age of Reform*. Cambridge: Cambridge University Press, 2012.

Cox, Jeffrey N. *Romanticism in the Shadow of War: Literary Culture in the Napoleonic War Years*. Cambridge: Cambridge University Press, 2014.

Craciun, Adriana. "Writing the Disaster: Franklin and *Frankenstein*." *Nineteenth-Century Literature* 65, no. 4 (2011): 433–80.

Cragwall, Jasper. *Lake Methodism: Polite Literature and Popular Religion in England, 1780–1830*. Columbus: The Ohio State University Press, 2013.

Crawford, Joseph. "Milton's Heirs: Epic Poetry in the 1790s." *Studies in Romanticism* 49, no. 3 (2010): 427–43.

Crisman, William. "'Now Misery Has Come Home': Sibling Rivalry in Mary Shelley's *Frankenstein*." *Studies in Romanticism* 36, no. 1 (1997): 27–41.

Crook, Nora. "In Defence of the 1831 *Frankenstein*." In *Mary Shelly's Fictions: From Frankenstein to Falkner*, edited by Michael Eberle-Sinatra, 3–21. New York: St. Martin's Press, 2000.

———. "'Meek and Bold': Mary Shelley's Support for the Risorgimento." In *Mary Versus Mary*, edited by Lilla Maria Crisafulli and Giovanna Silvani, 73–88. Napoli: Liguori Editore, 2001.

Curran, Mark. *Atheism, Religion and Enlightenment in Pre-Revolutionary Europe.* Rochester: The Boydell Press, 2012.

Curran, Stuart. Introduction to *Valperga: or, The Life and Adventures of Castruccio, Prince of Lucca*, by Mary Shelley, xii–xxiii. New York: Oxford University Press, 1997.

———. "The Political Prometheus." *Studies in Romanticism* 25, no. 3 (1986): 429–55.

Daly, Gavin. "Plunder on the Peninsula: British Soldiers and Local Civilians During the Peninsular War, 1808–1813." In *Civilians and War in Europe, 1618–1815*, edited by Erica Charters, Eve Rosenhaft, and Hannah Smith, 209–24. Liverpool: Liverpool University Press, 2012.

Darmon, Pierre. "Mystiques chrétiennes ou simulatrices? Les illuminées sous l'ancien régime." *L'histoire* 14 (1979): 74–76.

Darwin, Erasmus. *Zoonomia, or, the Laws of Organic Life.* London: J. Johnson, 1794.

Davidoff, Leonore, and Catherine Hall. *Family Fortunes: Men and Women of the English Middle Class, 1780–1850.* London: Hutchinson, 1987.

Davies, Norman. *Europe: A History.* Oxford: Oxford University Press, 1996.

Davy, Humphrey. *Consolations in Travel, or the Last Days of a Philosopher.* London: John Murray, 1830.

———. *Elements of Chemical Philosophy.* In *The Collected Works of Humphry Davy*, vol. 4, edited by John Davy. London: Smith, Elder, 1839.

Dawson, P. M. S. "Poetry in an Age of Revolution." In *The Cambridge Companion to British Romanticism*, edited by Stuart Curran, 56–81. Cambridge: Cambridge University Press, 1993.

D'Holbach, Baron. *The System of Nature; or, The Laws of the Moral and Physical World, Part the First.* London: G. Kearsley, 1797.

Dickerson, Vanessa D. "The Ghost of a Self: Female Identity in Mary Shelley's *Frankenstein.*" *Journal of Popular Culture* 27, no. 3 (1993): 79–91.

Diderot, Denis. *The Skeptic's Walk.* Translated by Kirk Watson. Amazon Digital Publishing, 2013. Kindle E-book.

Dingley, R. J. "'I Had a Dream': Byron's 'Darkness.'" *Byron Journal* 9 (1981): 20–33.

Dolan, Frances E. *Whores of Babylon: Catholicism, Gender, and Seventeenth-Century Print Culture.* Ithaca: Cornell University Press, 1999.

Domke, Rebecca. "Feminizing the Historical Novel: Mary Shelley's *Perkin Warbeck.*" In *Romantic Explorations: Selected Papers from the Koblenz Conference of the German Society for English Romanticism*, edited by Michael Meyer, 239–47. Trier: Wissenschaftlicher Verlag Trier, 2011.

Duffy, Cian. *Shelley and the Revolutionary Sublime.* Cambridge: Cambridge University Press, 2005.

Dyer, John. "The Ruins of Rome." In *The Poetical Works of John Dyer*, 19–38. Edinburgh: Apollo Press, 1779.

Edwards, Jonathan. *The Works of Jonathan Edwards*. Edited by Anthony Uyl. Woodstock: Devoted Publishing, 2017.

Effinger, Elizabeth. "A Clandestine Catastrophe: Disciplinary Dissolution in Mary Shelley's *The Last Man*." *European Romantic Review* 25, no. 1 (2014): 19–34.

Ellis, Kate. "Monsters in the Garden: Mary Shelley and the Bourgeois Family." In *The Endurance of "Frankenstein": Essays on Mary Shelley's Novel*, edited by George Levine and U. C. Knoepflmacher, 123–42. Berkeley: University of California Press, 1974.

———. "Subversive Surfaces: The Limits of Domestic Affection in Mary Shelley's Later Fiction." In *The Other Mary Shelley: Beyond Frankenstein*, edited by Audrey A. Fisch, Anne K. Mellor, and Esther H. Schor, 220–34. Oxford: Oxford University Press, 1993.

Esdaile, Charles. *The Peninsular War: A New History*. New York: Palgrave Macmillan, 2003.

Faubert, Michelle. Introduction to *Mary, A Fiction and The Wrongs of Woman, or Maria*, by Mary Wollstonecraft, 11–50. Peterborough: Broadview Press, 2012.

Favret, Mary. "Mary Shelley's Sympathy and Irony: The Editor and Her Corpus." In *The Other Mary Shelley: Beyond Frankenstein*, edited by Audrey A. Fisch, Anne K. Mellor, Esther H. Schor, 17–38. New York: Oxford University Press, 1993.

Feder, Helena. "'A Blot upon the Earth': Nature's 'Negative' and the Production of Monstrosity in *Frankenstein*." *Journal of Ecocriticism* 2, no. 1 (2010): 55–66.

Ferriss, Suzanne. "Percy Bysshe Shelley's *The Cenci* and the Rhetoric of Tyranny." In *British Romantic Drama: Historical and Critical Essays*, edited by Terence Allan Hoagwood and Daniel P. Watkins, 208–28. Madison: Associated University Presses, 1998.

Fisch, Audrey A., Anne K. Mellor, and Esther H. Schor, eds. *The Other Mary Shelley: Beyond Frankenstein*. New York: Oxford University Press, 1993.

Foote, Samuel. *A Letter from Mr. Foote*. London, 1760.

Ford, Susan Allen. "'A Name More Dear': Daughters, Fathers, and Desire in *A Simple Story, The False Friend*, and *Mathilda*." In *Re-Visioning Romanticism: British Women Writers, 1776–1837*, edited by Carol Shiner Wilson and Joel Haefner, 51–71. Philadelphia: University of Pennsylvania Press, 1994.

Fordyce, James. *Sermons to Young Women*. Vol. 1. London: T. Cadell, Jun. and W. Davies, 1800.

Franklin, Caroline. *Mary Wollstonecraft: A Literary Life*. Hampshire: Palgrave Macmillan, 2004.

Frank Wake, Ann M. "Women in the Active Voice: Recovering Female History in Mary Shelley's *Valperga* and *Perkin Warbeck*." In *Iconoclastic Departures: Mary Shelley After Frankenstein*, edited by Syndy M. Conger, Frederick Frank, and Gregory O'Dea, 235–59. Madison: Farleigh Dickinson University Press, 1997.

Freeman, John. "Shelley's Early Letters." In *Shelley Revalued: Essays from the Gregynog Conference*, edited by Kelvin Everest, 109–28. Totowa: Barnes and Noble Books, 1983.

Frere, James Hatley. *A Combined View of the Prophecies of Daniel, Esdras, and St. John*. London: J. Hatchard, 1815.

Fruchtman, Jack, Jr. *The Apocalyptic Politics of Richard Price and Joseph Priestley: A Study in Late Eighteenth-Century English Republican Millennialism*. Philadelphia: The American Philosophical Society, 1983.

Frye, Northrop. *Fearful Symmetry: A Study of William Blake*. Princeton: Princeton University Press, 1947.

Fuchs, Rachel G., and Victoria E. Thompson. *Women in Nineteenth-Century Europe*. New York: Palgrave Macmillan, 2005.

Fulford, Tim. "Millenarianism and the Study of Romanticism." In *Romanticism and Millenarianism*, edited by Tim Fulford, 1–22. New York: Palgrave, 2002.

Fuller, J. F. C. *The Conduct of War, 1789–1961*. New Brunswick: Rutgers University Press, 1961.

Garbin, Lidia. "*The Fortunes of Perkin Warbeck*: Walter Scott in the Writings of Mary Shelley." *Romanticism on the Net* 6 (1997): n.p. https://doi.org/10.7202/005752ar.

———. "Mary Shelley and Walter Scott: *The Fortunes of Perkin Warbeck* and the Historical Novel." In *Mary Shelly's Fictions: From Frankenstein to Falkner*, edited by Michael Eberle-Sinatra, 150–63. New York: St. Martin's Press, 2000.

Garcia, Humbert. *Islam and the English Enlightenment, 1670–1840*. Baltimore: Johns Hopkins University Press, 2012.

Gardner, John. *Poetry and Popular Protest: Peterloo, Cato Street and the Queen Caroline Controversy*. Basingstoke: Palgrave Macmillan, 2011.

Garrett, Clarke. *Respectable Folly: Millenarians and the French Revolution in France and England*. Baltimore: Johns Hopkins University Press, 1975.

Garrett, Erin Webster. "White Papers and Black Figures: Mary Shelley Writing America." In *Mary Shelley: Her Circle and Her Contemporaries*, edited by L. Adam Mekler and Lucy Morrison, 185–202. Newcastle upon Tyne: Cambridge Scholars Publishing, 2010.

Garrison, Laurie. "Imperial Vision in the Arctic: Fleeting Looks and Pleasurable Distractions in Barker's Panorama and Shelley's *Frankenstein*." *Romanticism and Victorianism on the Net* 52 (2008): n.p. https://doi.org/10.7202/019804ar.

Gash, Norman. *Aristocracy and the People: Britain, 1815–1865*. Cambridge: Harvard University Press, 1979.

Gay, Peter. *The Enlightenment: An Interpretation*. New York: W. W. Norton, 1969.

Gerson, Noel. *Daughter of Earth and Water: A Biography of Mary Wollstonecraft Shelley*. New York: William Morrow, 1972.

Gibbon, Edward. *The Decline and Fall of the Roman Empire*. Edited by J. B. Bury. 3 vols. New York: Heritage Press, 1946.

———. *A Vindication of Some Passages in the Fifteenth and Sixteenth Chapters of the History of the Decline and Fall of the Roman Empire*. London: W. Strahan, 1779.

Gibson, Edmund. *Observations upon the Conduct and Behaviour of a Certain Sect, Usually Distinguished by the name of Methodists*. London, 1740.

Gilbert, Sandra M. "Horror's Twin: Mary Shelley's Monstrous Eve." In *Critical Essays on Mary Wollstonecraft Shelley*, edited by Mary Lowe-Evans, 39–61. London: Prentice Hall International, 1998.

Gilbert, Sandra M., and Susan Gubar. *The Madwoman in the Attic: The Woman Writer and the Nineteenth-Century Literary Imagination*. New Haven: Yale University Press, 1979.

Gillespie, Gerald. "Prometheus in the Romantic Age." In *European Romanticism: Literary Cross-Currents, Modes, and Models*, edited by Gerhart Hoffmeister, 197–210. Detroit: Wayne State University Press, 1990.

Gillet, Jean. "Du dernier au premier homme: Le Brouillage des signes dans l'époée de Grainville." In *Formes modernes de la poésie épique: Nouvelle approaches*, edited by Judith Labarthe, 113–27. Brussels: Peter Lang, 2004.

Gilmartin, Kevin. *Writing Against Revolution: Literary Conservatism in Britain, 1790–1832*. Cambridge: Cambridge University Press, 2007.

Givens, Terryl L., and Anthony P. Russell. "Romantic Agonies: Human Suffering and the Ethical Sublime." In *Romanticism Across the Disciplines*, edited by Larry H. Peer, 231–54. Lanham: University Press of America, 1998.

Gladden, Samuel Lyndon. "Mary Shelley's Editions of *The Collected Poems of Percy Bysshe Shelley*: The Editor as Subject." *Studies in Romanticism* 44, no. 2 (2005): 181–205.

Glen, Robert. *Urban Workers in the Early Industrial Revolution*. New York: St. Martin's Press, 1984.

Godwin, William. *Autobiographical Fragments and Reflections*. In *Collected Novels and Memoirs of William Godwin*, edited by Mark Philip, 39–66. London: Pickering and Chatto, 1992.

———. *Autobiography*. In *Collected Novels and Memoirs of William Godwin*, edited by Mark Philip, 38. London: Pickering and Chatto, 1992.

———. *An Enquiry Concerning Political Justice*. Oxford: Oxford University Press, 2013.

———. *Memoirs of the Author of "The Rights of Woman."* London: Penguin, 1987.

———. "Of Religion." In *Romantic Period Writings 1798–1832: An Anthology*, edited by Ian Haywood and Zachary Leader, 74–77. London: Routledge, 1998.

———. *St. Leon: A Tale of the Sixteenth Century*. London: Richard Bentley, 1835.

Gonda, Caroline. "*Lodore* and Fanny Derham's Story." *Women's Writing* 6, no. 3 (1999): 329–41.

Goodall, Jane. "*Frankenstein* and the Reprobate's Conscience." *Studies in the Novel* 31, no. 1 (1999): 19–43.

Goodwin, Thomas. *The French Revolution Foreseen, in 1639. Extracts from an Exposition of the Revelation, by an Eminent Divine*. London: J. Johnson, 1796.

Gordon, Charlotte. *Romantic Outlaws: The Extraordinary Lives of Mary Wollstonecraft and Her Daughter Mary Shelley*. New York: Random House, 2015.

Gordon, Eleanor, and Gwyneth Nair. *Public Lives: Women, Family, and Society in Victorian Britain*. New Haven: Yale University Press, 2003.

Gordon, Lyndall. *Mary Wollstonecraft: A New Genus*. London: Little, Brown, 2005.

Gott, Dorothy. *Christ the Standard of Truth*. London, 1798.

Graham, John. "Catholic Emancipation." *Gentleman's Magazine: And Historical Chronicle, Jan. 1736–Dec. 1833* (1826): 356–57.

Grainville, Jean-Baptiste François Xavier Cousin de. *The Last Man*. Translated by I.F. Clarke and M. Clarke. Middletown: Wesleyan University Press, 2002.

Gravitt, Bryn J. "A Feminist Utopia? Revisions of Family in Mary Shelley's *Falkner*." *Parlor* (2016). https://www.ohio.edu/parlour/news-story.cfm?newsItem=05D6019E-5056-A874–1D01618028943F2D/.

Grossman, Jonathan H. *The Art of Alibi: English Law Courts and the Novel*. Baltimore: Johns Hopkins University Press, 2002.

Hadley, Matthew. "Mary Shelley's Literary Laboratory: *Frankenstein* and the Emergence of the Modern Laboratory in Nineteenth-Century Europe." In *Environments in Science Fiction: Essays on Alternative Spaces*, edited by Susan M. Bernardo, 83–100. Jefferson: McFarland, 2014.

Hagemann, Karen. "'Unimaginable Horror and Misery': The Battle of Leipzig in October 1813 in Civilian Experience and Perception." In *Soldiers, Citizens, and Civilians: Experiences and Perceptions of the Revolutionary and Napoleonic Wars, 1790–1820*, edited by Alan Forrest, Karen Hagemann, and Jane Rendall, 157–78. New York: Palgrave Macmillan, 2009.

Hall, Catherine. *White, Male, and Middle-Class: Explorations in Feminism and History*. Cambridge: Polity Press, 1992.

Halmi, Nicholas. "Ruins Without a Past." *Essays in Romanticism* 18, no. 1 (2010): 7–27.

Hamilton, Paul. "Literature and Philosophy." In *The Cambridge Companion to Shelley*, edited by Timothy Morton, 166–85. Cambridge: Cambridge University Press, 2006.

Hammon, William. *Answer to Dr Priestley's Letters to a Philosophical Unbeliever, Part I*. London, 1782.

Hatlen, Burton. "Milton, Mary Shelley, and Patriarchy." *Bucknell Review* 28, no. 2 (1983): 19–47.

Hawes, William. Untitled. London: The Humane Society, 1786. Bodleian Library MS. ADD c. 229. 104b.

Hawley, Erin. "The Bride and Her Afterlife: Female *Frankenstein* Monsters on Page and Screen." *Literature/Film Quarterly* 43, no. 3 (2015): 218–31.

Haykin, Michael A. G., and Kenneth J. Stewart, eds. *The Emergence of Evangelicalism: Exploring Historical Continuities*. Downers Grove, Ill.: InterVarsity Press, 2008.

Hays, Mary. *The Annual Necrology, For 1797–8; Including, Also, Various Articles of Neglected Biography*. In *Memoirs of Women Writers*, edited by Gina Luria Walker, 10:479–534. London: Pickering and Chatto, 2014.

Hazlitt, William. "On the Causes of Methodism." In *The Collected Works of William Hazlitt*, vol. 1, edited by A. R. Waller and Arnold Glover, 57–61. London: J. M. Dent, 1902.

Heber, Reginald. "Review of Marino Faliero, Sardanapalus, The Two Foscari and Cain." In *Lord Byron: The Critical Heritage*, edited by Andrew Rutherford, 236–48. New York: Routledge, 1970.

Hempton, David. *Methodism: Empire of the Spirit*. New Haven: Yale University Press, 2005.

———. *The Religion of the People: Methodism and Popular Religion c. 1750–1900*. London: Routledge, 1996.

Hempton, David, and Myrtle Hill. *Evangelical Protestantism in Ulster Society, 1740–1890*. London: Routledge, 1992.

Herbermann, Charles, et al., eds. *The Catholic Encyclopedia*. Vol. 1. New York: Robert Appleton, 1907.

Hernon, Ian. *Riot! Civil Insurrection from Peterloo to the Present Day*. London: Pluto Press, 2006.

Hill, Jen. *White Horizon: The Arctic in the Nineteenth-Century British Imagination*. Albany: State University of New York Press, 2008.

Hill-Miller, Katherine C. *"My Hideous Progeny": Mary Shelley, William Godwin, and the Father-Daughter Relationship*. Newark: University of Delaware Press, 1995.

Hilton, Boyd. *The Age of Atonement: The Influence of Evangelicalism on Social and Economic Thought, 1785–1865*. Oxford: Clarendon Press, 1988.

———. *A Mad, Bad, and Dangerous People? England 1783–1846*. Oxford: Clarendon Press, 2006.

Hilton, Mary. *Women and the Shaping of the Nation's Young: Education and Public Doctrine in Britain 1750–1850*. Burlington: Ashgate, 2007.

Hinde, Wendy. *Catholic Emancipation: A Shake to Men's Minds*. New Jersey: Blackwell Publishing, 1992.

Hindle, Maurice. Introduction to *Things as They Are; or, The Adventures of Caleb Williams*, by William Godwin, ix–xli. New York: Penguin Books, 1988.

———. "Vital Matters: Mary Shelley's *Frankenstein* and Romantic Science." *Critical Survey* 2, no. 1 (1990): 29–35.

Historicus. "Letter." *Gentleman's Magazine: And Historical Chronicle*, Jan. 1736–Dec. 1833 47 (1777): 421–22.

Hoeveler, Diane Long. "Anti-Catholicism and the Gothic Imaginary: The Historical and Literary Contexts." In *Religion in the Age of Enlightenment*, edited by Brett C. McInelly, 1–31. Brooklyn: AMS Press, 2012.

———. "Screen Memories and Fictionalized Autobiography: Mary Shelley's *Mathilda* and 'The Mourner': Fiction and Autobiographical Theories." In *Romantic Autobiography in England*, edited by Eugene Stelzig, 79–95. Burlington: Ashgate, 2009.

Hogg, Thomas Jefferson. *The Life of Percy Bysshe Shelley*. London: Routledge, 1906.

Hogsette, David S. "Metaphysical Intersections in *Frankenstein*: Mary Shelley's Theistic Investigation of Scientific Materialism and Transgressive Autonomy." *Christianity and Literature* 60, no. 4 (2011): 531–60.

Holmes, Richard. *Shelley: The Pursuit*. New York: E. P. Dutton, 1975.

Homans, Margaret. "Bearing Demons: *Frankenstein*'s Circumvention of the Maternal (1986)." In *Romanticism: A Critical Reader*, edited by Duncan Wu, 379–400. Oxford: Blackwell, 1995.

Hood, Thomas. "The Last Man." In *Whims and Oddities*, 23–32. London: Lupton Relfe, 1826.

Hopkins, James K. *A Woman to Deliver Her People: Joanna Southcott and English Millenarianism in an Age of Revolution*. Austin: University of Texas Press, 1982.

Hopkins, Lisa. *A Hall of Mirrors: Mary Shelley's "Frankenstein."* Sheffield: Sheffield City Polytechnic, 1991.

———. "Memory at the End of History: Mary Shelley's *The Last Man*." *Romanticism on the Net* 6 (1997): n.p. https://doi.org/10.7202/005746ar.

Hopps, Gavin. "Religion and Ethics: The Necessity of Atheism, A Refutation of Deism, On Christianity." In *The Oxford Handbook of Percy Bysshe Shelley*, edited by Michael O'Neill and Anthony Howe, 117–31. Oxford: Oxford University Press, 2013.

Houe, Ulf. "*Frankenstein* Without Electricity: Contextualizing Shelley's Novel." *Studies in Romanticism* 55, no. 1 (2016): 95–117.

Hunt, Leigh. "An Attempt to Shew the Folly and Danger of Methodism." *Examiner* 21 (1808): 334–35.

Hunt, Robert. "Crosse, Andrew (1784–1855)." Rev. J. A. Secord, *Oxford Dictionary of National Biography*. Oxford University Press, 2004. Online ed., May 2009. http://0-www.oxforddnb.com.library.utulsa.edu/view/article/6799/.

Hutchings, Kevin. "'A Dark Image in a Phantasmagoria': Pastoral Idealism, Prophecy, and Materiality in Mary Shelley's *The Last Man*." *Romanticism* 10, no. 2 (2004): 228–44.

Hyman, Gavin. "Atheism in Modern History." In *The Cambridge Companion to Atheism*, edited by Michael Martin, 27–46. Cambridge: Cambridge University Press, 2007.

Irving, Edward. *A Discourse on the Prophecies of Daniel and the Apocalypse*. Philadelphia, 1828.

James, Leighton S. "Invasion and Occupation: Civilian-Military Relations in Central Europe During the Revolutionary and Napoleonic Wars." In *Civilians and War in Europe, 1618–1815*, edited by Erica Charters, Eve Rosenhaft, and Hannah Smith, 225–40. Liverpool: Liverpool University Press, 2012.

Jay, Elisabeth. *The Religion of the Heart: Anglican Evangelicalism and the Nineteenth-Century Novel*. Oxford: Clarendon Press, 1979.

Jeffrey, Lloyd N. "Cuvierian Catastrophism in Shelley's 'Prometheus Unbound' and 'Mont Blanc.'" *South Central Bulletin* 38, no. 4 (1978): 148–52.

Jenkins, Brian. *Era of Emancipation: British Government of Ireland, 1812–1830*. Kingston: McGill-Queen's University Press, 1988.

Joffe, Sharon Lynne. *The Kinship Coterie and the Literary Endeavors of the Women in the Shelley Circle*. New York: Peter Lang, 2007.

Johnson, Barbara. *A Life with Mary Shelley*. Stanford: Stanford University Press, 2012.

Johnson, Samuel. *A Dictionary of the English Language.* 2 vols. London: W. Strahan, 1755.

Jones, Emily. *Edmund Burke and the Invention of Modern Conservatism, 1830–1914: An Intellectual History.* Oxford: Oxford University Press, 2017.

Jones, John H. "'Self-Annihilation' and Dialogue in Blake's Creative Process: Urizen, Milton, Jerusalem." *Modern Language Studies* 24, no. 2 (1994): 3–10.

Jordan, Ellen. *The Women's Movement and Women's Employment in Nineteenth-Century Britain.* London: Routledge, 1999.

Jowell, Sharon L. "Mary Shelley's Mothers: The Weak, The Absent, and The Silent in *Lodore* and *Falkner*." *European Romantic Review* 8, no. 3 (1997): 298–322.

Juster, Susan. *Doomsayers: Anglo-American Prophecy in the Age of Revolution.* Philadelphia: University of Pennsylvania Press, 2003.

Kasmer, Lisa. *Novel Histories: British Women Writing History, 1760–1830.* Madison: Farleigh Dickinson University Press, 2012.

Katz, Beth Dolan. "Spas and Salutary Landscapes: The Geography of Health in Mary Shelley's *Rambles in Germany and Italy*." In *Romantic Geographies: Discourses of Travel, 1775–1844*, edited by Amanda Gilroy, 165–81. Manchester: Manchester University Press, 2000.

Keach, William. "The Ruins of Empire and the Contradictions of Restoration: Barbauld, Byron, Hemans." *Romantic Circles* (2012): n.p. https://www.rc.umd.edu/praxis/disaster/HTML/praxis.2012.keach.html.

Kelley, Theresa M. "Romantic Temporality, Contingency, and Mary Shelley." *English Literary History* 75, no. 3 (2008): 625–52.

Kelly, Gary. "The Subject of Mary Versus Mary: Romantic Versus Revolutionary Feminism." In *Mary Versus Mary*, edited by Lilla Maria Crisafulli and Giovanna Silvani, 9–24. Napoli: Liguori Editore, 2001.

Kilgour, Maggie. "'One Immortality': The Shaping of The Shelleys in *The Last Man*." *European Romantic Review* 16, no. 5 (2005): 563–88.

King-Hele, Desmond. "Shelley and Erasmus Darwin." In *Shelley Revalued: Essays from the Gregynog Conference*, edited by Kelvin Everest, 129–46. Bristol: Leicester University Press, 1983.

Knapp, Andrew, and William Baldwin. *The New Newgate Calendar.* Vol. 4. London: J. and J. Cundee, 1810.

Knight, David. *Humphry Davy: Science and Power.* Oxford: Blackwell, 1992.

Knox, Alexander. "Remarks on the Life and Character of John Wesley." In *The Life of Wesley* and *Rise and Progress of Methodism*, by Robert Southey, edited by Charles Cuthbert Southey. London: Longman, 1864.

Koyanagi, Yasuko. "Mary Shelley's *Mathilda*: 'My Daughter, I Love You!'" In *Centre and Circumference: Essays in English Romanticism*, 593–608. Tokyo: Kirihara Shoten, 1995.

Kozlowski, Lisa. "Resonating Resins: 'Listning to the Voices of the Ground' in William Blake's *Book of Urizen*." *Huntington Library Quarterly* 64, no. 3/4 (2001): 411–27.

Kuznicki, Jason. "Sorcery and Publicity: The Cadière-Girard Scandal of 1730–1731." *French History* 21, no. 3 (2007): 289–312.

Labbe, Jacqueline. "A Family Romance: Mary Wollstonecraft, Mary Godwin, and Travel." *Genre* 25, no. 2–3 (1992): 211–28.

Lackington, James. *Memoirs of the Forty-Five First Years of the Life of James Lackington.* London, 1792.

Lamb, John B. "Mary Shelley's *Frankenstein* and Milton's Monstrous Myth." *Nineteenth-Century Literature* 47, no. 3 (1992): 303–19.

Lamoreaux, Johanne. "*Frankenstein* et *Les ruines* de Volney: L'éducation littéraire de la creature." *Protée: Théories et practiques sémiotiques* 35, no. 2 (2007): 65–73.

Lamotte, Stéphane. "Le P. Girard et la cadière dans la tourmente des pièces satiriques." *Dix-huitième siècle* 39, no. 1 (2007): 431–53.

Lanone, Catherine. "Monsters on the Ice and Global Warming: From Mary Shelley and Sir John Franklin to Margaret Atwood and Dan Simmons." In *EcoGothic*, edited by Andrew Smith and William Hughes, 28–43. Manchester: Manchester University Press, 2013.

Lau, Beth. "*The Rime of the Ancient Mariner* and *Frankenstein*." In *Samuel Taylor Coleridge and the Sciences of Life*, edited by Nicholas Roe, 207–23. Oxford: Oxford University Press, 2001.

Lavington, George. *The Enthusiasm of Methodists and Papists Compared.* Vol. 1. London: J. and P. Knapton, 1754.

Lawrence, William. *An Introduction to Comparative Anatomy and Physiology.* London: J. Callow, 1816.

———. "Mr. Lawrence's Retraction." *Monthly Repository of Theology and General Literature, 1806–1826* 17, no. 199: (1822): 450–51.

LeCussan, Robert James. "*Frankenstein*: The Modern Prometheus." *Keats-Shelley Review* 15, no. 1 (2001): 107–17.

Levine, George. "The Ambiguous Heritage of *Frankenstein*." In *Critical Essays on Mary Wollstonecraft Shelley*, edited by Mary Lowe-Evans, 3–30. London: Prentice Hall International, 1998.

Lew, Joseph W. "God's Sister: History and Ideology in *Valperga*." In *The Other Mary Shelley: Beyond Frankenstein*, edited by Audrey A. Fisch, Anne K. Mellor, Esther H. Schor, 159–81. New York: Oxford University Press, 1993.

———. "The Plague of Imperial Desire: Montesquieu, Gibbon, Brougham, and Mary Shelley's *The Last Man*." In *Romanticism and Colonialism: Writing and Empire, 1780–1830*, edited by Tim Fulford and Peter J. Kitson, 261–78. Cambridge: Cambridge University Press, 1998.

Liggins, Emma. "The Medical Gaze and the Female Corpse: Looking at Bodies in Mary Shelley's *Frankenstein*." *Studies in the Novel* 32, no. 2 (2000): 129–46.

Linley, Margaret. "*Frankenstein* Revisited: Life and Afterlife Around 1831." In *Media, Technology, and Literature in the Nineteenth Century: Image, Sound, Touch*, edited by Colette Colligan and Margaret Linley, 257–85. Burlington: Ashgate, 2011.

Lloyd, Jennifer. *Women and the Shaping of British Methodism: Persistent Preachers, 1807–1907.* Manchester: Manchester University Press, 2009.

Lokke, Kari. "Radical Spirituality and Reason in Mary Wollstonecraft's *A Vindica-tion of the Rights of Woman*." In *Feminist Moments: Reading Feminist Texts*, edited by Susan Bruce and Katherine Smits, 51–58. London: Blooms-bury, 2016.

——. "Sibylline Leaves: Mary Shelley's *Valperga* and the Legacy of Corinne." In *On Cultural Interactions in the Romantic Age: Critical Essays in Comparative Literature*, edited by Gregory Maertz, 157–73. Albany: State University of New York Press, 1998.

London, Bette. "Mary Shelley, *Frankenstein*, and the Spectacle of Masculinity." *Publications of the Modern Language Association* 108, no. 2 (1993): 253–67.

Low, Lisa, and Anthony John Harding, eds. *Milton, the Metaphysicals, and Romanti-cism*. Cambridge: Cambridge University Press, 1994.

Lowe-Evans, Mary. *Frankenstein: Mary Shelley's Wedding Guest*. New York: Twayne Publishers, 1993.

Lutz, Deborah. *Relics of Death in Victorian Literature and Culture*. Cambridge: Cam-bridge University Press, 2015.

MacDonagh, Oliver. *O'Connell: The Life of Daniel O'Connell, 1775–1847*. London: Wiedenfeld and Nicolson, 1991.

Mack, Phyllis. *Heart Religion in the British Enlightenment: Gender and Emotion in Early Methodism*. Cambridge: Cambridge University Press, 2008.

——. "Women as Prophets During the English Civil War." *Feminist Studies* 8, no. 1 (1982): 18–45.

Maison, Margaret. "'Thine, Only Thine!' Women Hymn Writers in Britain, 1760–1835." In *Religion in the Lives of English Women, 1760–1930*, edited by Gail Malmgreen, 11–40. London: Croom Helm, 1986.

Malmgreen, Gail. *Religion in the Lives of English Women, 1760–1930*. London: Croom Helm, 1986.

Malthus, Thomas. *An Essay on the Principle of Population*. Oxford: Oxford University Press, 2008.

Mangion, Carmen M. "Women, Religious Ministry and Female Institution-Building." In *Women, Gender and Religious Cultures in Britain, 1800–1940*, edited by Sue Morgan and Jaqueline de Vries, 72–93. London: Rout-ledge, 2010.

Marino, Elisabetta. "The Italian Risorgimento in Mary Shelley's *Rambles in German and Italy in 1840, 1842, and 1843* (1844)." *British and American Studies* 18 (2012): 55–60.

——. "The Themes of Reanimation and Immortality in Mary Shelley's Short Sto-ries." *British and American Studies* 21 (2015): 25–30.

Markley, A. A. "'Laughing That I May Not Weep': Mary Shelley's Short Fiction and Her Novels." *Keats-Shelley Journal* 46 (1997): 97–124.

Marsden, George M. *Understanding Fundamentalism and Evangelicalism*. Grand Rapids: William B. Eerdmans Publishing, 1991.

Marshall, Bridget M. *The Transatlantic Gothic Novel and the Law, 1790–1860*. Burl-ington: Ashgate, 2011.

Marshall, Peter. *William Godwin: Philosophy, Novelist, Revolutionary*. Oakland: PM Press, 2017.

Marshall, Tim. *Murdering to Dissect: Grave Robbing, "Frankenstein," and the Anatomy Literature*. Manchester: Manchester University Press, 1995.

Mathias, Manon. "Sand, Flaubert, Cuvier: Writing Time and Nature." *French Studies* 70, no. 4 (2016): 519–34.

Maunu, Leanne. "The Connecting Threads of War, Torture, and Pain in Mary Shelley's *Valperga*." *European Romantic Review* 21, no. 4 (2010): 447–68.

McDermott, Lydia. "Birthing Rhetorical Monsters: How Mary Shelley Infuses Mêtis with the Maternal in her 1831 Introduction to *Frankenstein*." *Rhetoric Review* 34, no. 1 (2015): 1–18.

McGrath, Alister. *The Twilight of Modern Atheism: The Rise and Fall of Disbelief in the Modern World*. New York: Doubleday, 2004.

McKeogh, Colm. *Innocent Civilians: The Morality of Killing in War*. Hampshire: Palgrave, 2002.

McKusick, James C. *Green Writing: Romanticism and Ecology*. New York: St. Martin's Press, 2000.

McWhir, Anne. Introduction to *The Last Man*, by Mary Shelley, xiii–xxxvi. Peterborough: Broadview Press, 1996.

———. "Mary Shelley's Anti-Contagionism: *The Last Man* as 'Fatal Narrative.'" *Mosaic* 35, no. 2 (2002): 23–38.

Mee, Jon. *Romanticism, Enthusiasm, and Regulation: Poetics and the Policing of Culture in the Romantic Period*. Oxford: Oxford University Press, 2003.

Mekler, L. Adam. "Broken Mirrors and Multiplied Reflections in Lord Byron and Mary Shelley." *Studies in Romanticism* 46, no. 4 (2007): 461–80.

Mellor, Anne K. "Blake, the Apocalypse and Romantic Women Writers." In *Romanticism and Millenarianism*, edited by Tim Fulford, 139–52. New York: Palgrave Macmillan, 2002.

———. "*Frankenstein*, Racial Science, and the 'Yellow Peril.'" In *Romantic Science: The Literary Forms of Natural History*, edited by Noah Heringman, 173–96. Albany: State University of New York Press, 2003.

———. "The Human Form Divine and the Structure of Blake's *Jerusalem*." *SEL: Studies in English Literature* 11, no. 4 (1971): 595–620.

———. *Mary Shelley: Her Life, Her Fiction, Her Monsters*. New York: Routledge, 1988.

Melville, Peter. "The Problem of Immunity in *The Last Man*." *SEL: Studies in English Literature* 47, no. 4 (2007): 825–46.

Middleton, Conyers. *The History of the Life of Marcus Tullius Cicero, in three volumes*. London: W. Innys, 1742.

Middleton, Victoria. "Exile, Isolation, and Accommodation in *The Last Man*: The Strategies of a Survivor." In *Critical Essays on Mary Wollstonecraft Shelley*, edited by Mary Lowe-Evans, 166–82. London: Prentice Hall International, 1998.

Moers, Ellen. "Female Gothic." In *The Endurance of "Frankenstein": Essays on Mary Shelley's Novel*, edited by George Levine and U. C. Knoepflmacher, 77–87. Berkeley: University of California Press, 1974.

Montagu, Lady Mary Wortley. *Turkish Embassy Letters*. Edited by Malcolm Jack. London: William Pickering, 1993.

Montillo, Roseanne. *The Lady and Her Monsters*. New York: Harper Collins, 2013.

Moore, Jane. Introduction to *Mary Wollstonecraft*, xiii–xxxii. New York: Routledge, 2016.

Moore, Melina. "Mary Shelley's *Mathilda* and the Struggle for Female Narrative Subjectivity." *Rocky Mountain Review* 65, no. 2 (2011): 208–15.

More, Hannah. *Coelebs in Search of a Wife*. Peterborough: Broadview Press, 2007.

———. *Moral Sketches of Prevailing Opinions and Manners, Foreign and Domestic*. London: T. Cardell and W. Davies, 1819.

———. *Remarks on the Speech of M. Dupont, Made in the National Convention of France*. London: T. Cadell, 1793.

———. *Strictures on the Modern System of Female Education*. Dublin: William Porter, 1800.

———. *Thoughts on the Importance of the Manners of the Great to General Society*. London: T. Cadell, 1788.

Morgan, Sue. "Introduction: Women, Religion and Feminism: Past, Present and Future Perspectives." In *Women, Religion and Feminism in Britain, 1750–1900*, edited by Sue Morgan, 1–20. New York: Palgrave Macmillan, 2002.

Morrison, Lucy. "Listen While You Read: The Case of Mary Shelley's *The Last Man*." In *Mary Shelley: Her Circle and Her Contemporaries*, edited by L. Adam Mekler and Lucy Morrison, 151–68. Newcastle upon Tyne: Cambridge Scholars Publishing, 2010.

Moskal, Jeanne. "Gender and Italian Nationalism in Mary Shelley's *Rambles in Germany and Italy*." *Romanticism* 5, no. 2 (1999): 188–201.

Nehemiah. "Observations Occasioned By The Rev. R. W. Hamilton's Letter on Catholic Emancipation." *Imperial Magazine* 11, no. 123 (1829): 219–27.

Nicholls, David. *God and Government in an 'Age of Reason.'* New York: Routledge, 1995.

Nitchie, Elizabeth. Introduction. *Mathilda* by Mary Wollstonecraft Shelley. *Studies in Philology* 3 (1959): vii–xv.

———. *Mary Shelley: Author of Frankenstein*. New Brunswick: Rutgers University Press, 1953.

Noll, Mark A. *The Rise of Evangelicalism: The Age of Edwards, Whitefield and the Wesleys*. Downers Grove, Ill.: InterVarsity Press, 2003.

North, Julian. "Shelley Revitalized: Biography and the Reanimated Body." *European Romantic Review* 21, no. 6 (2010): 751–70.

Nurmi, Martin K. *Blake's "Marriage of Heaven and Hell": A Critical Study*. Kent: Kent State University Press, 1957.

O'Ferrall, Fergus. *Catholic Emancipation: Daniel O'Connell and the Birth of Irish Democracy, 1820–30*. Dublin: Gill & Macmillan, 1987.

Oliver, W. H. *Prophets and Millenialists: The Uses of Biblical Prophecy in England from the 1790s to the 1840s*. Oxford: Oxford University Press, 1978.

O'Neill, Daniel I. *Edmund Burke and the Conservative Logic of Empire*. Oakland: University of California Press, 2016.

O'Neill, Michael. *Percy Bysshe Shelley: A Literary Life*. Basingstoke: The MacMillan Press, 1989.

Oort, Johannes van. "Manichaeism: Its Sources and Influences on Western Christianity." In *Gnosis and Hermeticism from Antiquity to Modern Times*, edited by Roelof van den Broek and Wouter J. Hanegraaff, 37–52. Albany: State University of New York Press, 1998.

O'Rourke, James. "'Nothing More Unnatural': Mary Shelley's Revision of Rousseau." *English Literary History* 56, no. 3 (1989): 543–69.

———. *Sex, Lies, and Autobiography: The Ethics of Confession*. Charlottesville: University of Virginia Press, 2006.

O'Sullivan, Barbara Jane. "Beatrice in *Valperga*: A New Cassandra." In *The Other Mary Shelley: Beyond Frankenstein*, edited by Audrey A. Fisch, Anne K. Mellor, Esther H. Schor, 140–58. New York: Oxford University Press, 1993.

Outram, Dorinda. *Georges Cuvier: Vocation, Science and Authority in Post-Revolutionary France*. Manchester: Manchester University Press, 1984.

Page, Michael R. *The Literary Imagination from Erasmus Darwin to H. G. Wells: Science, Evolution, and Ecology*. Burlington: Ashgate, 2012.

Paine, Thomas. *The Age of Reason*. Paris: Barrois, 1794.

Paley, Morton D. *Apocalypse and Millennium in English Romantic Poetry*. Oxford: Oxford University Press, 1999.

———. "Le dernier homme: The French Revolution as the Failure of Typology." *Mosaic* 24, no. 1 (1991): 67–76.

———. "Envisioning Lastness: Byron's 'Darkness,' Campbell's 'The Last Man,' and the Critical Aftermath." *Romanticism* 1, no. 1 (1995): 1–14.

———. "*The Last Man*: Apocalypse Without Millennium." In *The Other Mary Shelley: Beyond Frankenstein*, edited by Audrey A. Fisch, Anne K. Mellor, and Esther H. Schor, 107–23. New York: Oxford University Press, 1993.

P.A.N. "On Catholic Emancipation." *Gentleman's Magazine: And Historical Chronicle, Jan. 1736–Dec. 1833* (1825): 210–13.

Pappin, Joseph L., III. *The Metaphysics of Edmund Burke*. New York: Fordham University Press, 1993.

Paterson-Morgan, Emily. "The Bloodless Church: Dualist Asceticism and Romantic Vegetarianism." In *Romantic Sustainability: Endurance and the Natural World, 1780–1830*, edited by Ben P. Robertson, 95–114. Lanham: Lexington Books, 2016.

Paul, Charles Kagan. *William Godwin: His Friends and Contemporaries*. Vol. 2. Boston: Roberts Brothers, 1876.

Penelhum, Terence. *Themes in Hume: The Self, the Will, Religion*. Oxford: Clarendon Press, 2000.

Perkins, William. *A Treatise tending unto a declaration, whether a man bee in the state of damnation, or in the estate of grace*. London: Thomas Orwin, 1591.

Phillips, Bill. "*Frankenstein* and Mary Shelley's 'Wet Ungenial Summer.'" *Atlantis* 28, no. 2 (2006): 59–68.

Pickering, Paul A., and Alex Tyrrell. *The People's Bread: A History of the Anti-Corn Law League*. London: Leicester University Press, 2000.

Pionke, Albert D. *Plots of Opportunity: Representing Conspiracy in Victorian England*. Columbus: The Ohio State University Press, 2004.

Pirie, Alexander. *French Revolution Exhibited, in the Light of the Sacred Oracles*. Perth: R. Morison Junior, 1795.

Polhemus, Robert M. *Lot's Daughters: Sex, Redemption, and Women's Quest for Authority*. Stanford: Stanford University Press, 2005.

Poole, Robert. "'By the Law or the Sword': Peterloo Revisited." *History* 91, no. 302 (2006): 254–76.

———. "French Revolution or Peasants' Revolt? Petitioners and Rebels in England from the Blanketeers to the Chartists." *Labour History Review* 74, no. 1 (2009): 6–26.

Poovey, Mary. *The Proper Lady and the Woman Writer: Ideology as Style in the Works of Mary Wollstonecraft, Mary Shelley, and Jane Austen*. Chicago: The University of Chicago Press, 1984.

Price, Richard. *Additional Observations on the Nature and Value of Civil Liberty*. London: T. Cadell, 1777.

———. *A Discourse on the Love of our Country*. London: George Stafford, 1789.

Priestley, Joseph. *A History of the Corruptions of Christianity*. London: The British and Foreign Unitarian Association, 1871.

———. *Memoirs of Dr. Joseph Priestley to the Year 1795*. Northumberland, 1806.

———. *The Present State of Europe compared with Antient Prophecies*. London: K. Johnson, 1794.

———. *Reflections on Death*. Birmingham: J. Belcher, 1790.

Priestman, Martin. *Romantic Atheism: Poetry and Freethought, 1780–1830*. Cambridge: Cambridge University Press, 1999.

Prochaska, F. K. *Women and Philanthropy in Nineteenth-Century England*. Oxford: Clarendon Press, 1980.

Punter, David. "Mary Shelley (1797–1851): The Gothic Novel." In *The Cambridge Companion to European Novelists*, edited by Michael Bell, 176–91. Cambridge: Cambridge University Press, 2012.

Rack, Henry D. *Reasonable Enthusiast: John Wesley and the Rise of Methodism*. London: Epworth Press, 2014.

Rajan, Tilottama. Introduction to *Valperga*, by Mary Shelley, 7–45. Peterborough: Ontario, 1998.

———. "The Poetry of Philology: Burckhardt's *Civilization of the Renaissance in Italy* and Mary Shelley's *Valperga*." In *Dante and Italy in British Romanticism*, edited by Frederick Burwick and Paul Douglass, 105–16. New York: Palgrave Macmillan, 2011.

Randel, Fred V. "The Political Geography of Horror in Mary Shelley's *Frankenstein*." *English Literary History* 70, no. 2 (2003): 465–91.

Ransom, Amy J. "The First Last Man: Cousin de Grainville's *Le Dernier homme*." *Science Fiction Studies* 41, no. 2 (July 2014): 314–40.

Reese, Diana K. *Reproducing Enlightenment: Paradoxes in the Life of the Body Politic*. Berlin: Walter de Gruyter, 2009.

Reynolds, James. *The Catholic Emancipation Crisis in Ireland, 1823–1829*. New Haven: Yale University Press, 1954.

Rieger, James. *The Mutiny Within: The Heresies of Percy Bysshe Shelley*. New York: George Braziller, 1967.

Riggs, David. *The World of Christopher Marlowe*. New York: Henry Holt, 2004.

Robinson, Charles E. "Mathilda as Dramatic Actress." In *Mary Shelley in Her Times*, edited by Betty T. Bennett and Stuart Curran, 76–87. Baltimore: Johns Hopkins University Press, 2000.

———. "Percy Bysshe Shelley's Text(s) in Mary Wollstonecraft Shelley's *Franken-stein*." In *The Neglected Shelley*, edited by Alan M. Weinburg and Timothy Webb, 117–36. New York: Routledge, 2015.

———. "Shelley and the Roger Dodsworth Hoax." *Keats-Shelley Journal* 24 (1975): 20–28.

Rousseau, Jean-Jaques. *Emile*. Translated by Barbara Foxley. London: Everyman, 1992.

Rovee, Christopher. "Monsters, Marbles, and Miniatures: Mary Shelley's Reform Aesthetic." *Studies in the Novel* 36, no. 2 (2004): 147–69.

Rubenstein, Marc A. "'My Accursed Origin': The Search for the Mother in *Fran-kenstein*." *Studies in Romanticism* 15, no. 2 (1976): 165–94.

Rudwick, Martin J. S. *The Meaning of Fossils: Episodes in the History of Paleontology*. New York: Science History Publications USA, 1976.

Russell, Paul. *The Riddle of Hume's Treatise: Scepticism, Naturalism and Irreligion*. Oxford: Oxford University Press, 2008.

Ruston, Sharon. "Resurrecting *Frankenstein*." *Keats-Shelley Review* 19, no. 1 (2005): 97–116.

Ryan, Robert M. "Mary Shelley's Christian Monster." *Wordsworth Circle* 19, no. 3 (1988): 150–55.

———. *The Romantic Reformation: Religious Politics in English Literature, 1789–1824*. Cambridge: Cambridge University Press, 1997.

Sandy, Mark. "'The Colossal Fabric's Form': Remodelling Memory, History, and Forgetting in Byron's Poetic Recollections of Ruins." *Romanticism and Victorianism on the Net* 51 (2008): n.p. https://doi.org/10.7202/019258ar.

Saunders, Julia. "Rehabilitating the Family in Mary Shelley's *Falkner*." In *Mary Shelley's Fictions: From Frankenstein to Falkner*, edited by Michael Eberle-Sinatra, 211–23. New York: St. Martin's Press, 2000.

Schildgen, Brenda Deen. "Cardinal Paleotti and the *Discorso Intorno Alle Imagini Sacre E Profane*." In *Sacred Possessions: Collecting Italian Religious Art, 1500–1900*, edited by Gail Feigenbaum and Sybille Ebert-Schifferer, 8–16. Los Angeles: Getty Research Institute, 2011.

Schlereth, Eric R. *An Age of Infidels: The Politics of Religious Controversy in the Early United States*. Philadelphia: University of Pennsylvania Press, 2013.

Schoene-Harwood, Berthold. *Writing Men: Literary Masculinities from "Franken-stein" to the New Man*. Edinburgh: Edinburgh University Press, 2000.

Schoina, Maria. *Romantic 'Anglo-Italians': Configurations of Identity in Byron, the Shelleys, and the Pisan Circle*. Burlington: Ashgate, 2009.

Schönfelder, Christa. *Wounds and Words: Childhood and Family Trauma in Romantic and Postmodern Fiction*. Verlag: Bielefeld, 2013.

Schroeder, Ronald A. "Byron's 'Darkness' and the Romantic Dis-Spiriting of
Nature." In *Approaches to Teaching Byron's Poetry*, edited by Frederick
W. Shilstone, 113–19. New York: The Modern Language Association of
America, 1991.

Seymour, Miranda. *Mary Shelley*. New York: Grove Press, 2000.

Sha, Richard C. "Volta's Battery, Animal Electricity, and *Frankenstein*." *European
Romantic Review* 23, no. 1 (2012): 21–41.

Shakespeare, William. *The Sonnets*. London: Collector's Library, 2009.

Sheehan, Jonathan. "Enlightenment, Religion, and the Enigma of Secularization:
A Review Essay." *American Historical Review* 108, no. 4 (2003): 1061–80.

Shelley, Mary. "The Convent of Chaillot." In *The Keepsake for MDCCCXXVIII*, edited
by Frederic Mansel Reynolds, 267–84. London: Hurst, Chance, 1828.

———. *Falkner*. Vol. 7 of *The Novels and Selected Works of Mary Shelley*. Edited by
Pamela Clemit. London: Pickering and Chatto, 1996.

———. *The Fortunes of Perkin Warbeck*. Vol. 5 of *The Novels and Selected Works of Mary
Shelley*. Edited by Doucet Devin Fischer. London: Pickering and Chatto,
1996.

———. *Frankenstein* (1818). Vol. 1 of *The Novels and Selected Works of Mary Shelley*.
Edited by Nora Crook. London: Pickering and Chatto, 1996.

———. *Frankenstein* (1831). New York: Signet Books, 2013.

———. *History of a Six Weeks' Tour*. Vol. 8 of *The Novels and Selected Works of Mary
Shelley*. Edited by Jeanne Moskal. London: Pickering and Chatto, 1996.

———. *The Journals of Mary Shelley, 1814–1844*. Edited by Paula R. Feldman and
Diana Scott-Kilvert. Baltimore: Johns Hopkins University Press, 1987.

———. *The Last Man*. Vol. 4 of *The Novels and Selected Works of Mary Shelley*. Edited by
Jane Blumberg and Nora Crook. London: Pickering and Chatto, 1996.

———. *The Letters of Mary Shelley*. Edited by Betty T. Bennett. 3 vols. Baltimore:
Johns Hopkins University Press, 1988.

———. *Lives of the Most Eminent Literary and Scientific Men of France*. Vol. 2. London:
Longman, 1839.

———. *Lodore*. Vol. 6 of *The Novels and Selected Works of Mary Shelley*. Edited by Fiona
Stafford. London: Pickering and Chatto, 1996.

———. *Mary Shelley: Collected Tales and Stories*. Edited by Charles E. Robinson.
Baltimore: Johns Hopkins University Press, 1976.

———. *Mathilda*. Vol. 2 of *The Novels and Selected Works of Mary Shelley*. Edited by
Pamela Clemit. London: Pickering and Chatto, 1996.

———. "The Mourner." In *Mary Shelley: Collected Tales and Stories*, 81–99.

———. *Rambles in Germany and Italy*. Vol. 8 of *The Novels and Selected Works of Mary
Shelley*. Edited by Jeanne Moskal. London: Pickering and Chatto, 1996.

———. "Roger Dodsworth: The Reanimated Englishman." In *Mary Shelley: Collected
Tales and Stories*, 43–50.

———. *Selected Letters of Mary Wollstonecraft Shelley*. Edited by Betty T. Bennett.
Baltimore: Johns Hopkins University Press, 1995.

———. "The Trial of Love." In *Mary Shelley: Collected Tales and Stories*, 231–44.

———. "Valerius: The Reanimated Roman." In *Mary Shelley: Collected Tales and
Stories*, 332–44.

———. *Valperga; or, The Life and Adventures of Castruccio*. Vol. 3 of *The Novels and Selected Works of Mary Shelley*. Edited by Nora Crook. London: Pickering and Chatto, 1996.

Shelley, Percy. "A Defence of Poetry." In *Shelley: Selected Poetry, Prose and Letters*, edited by A. S. B. Glover, 1023–55. London: The Nonesuch Press, 1951.

———. "Epipsychidion." In *Shelley's Poetry and Prose*, edited by Donald H. Reiman and Sharon B. Powers, 373–88. New York: W. W. Norton, 1977.

———. "Essay on Christianity." In *The Complete Works of Percy Bysshe Shelley*, edited by Roger Ingpen and Walter E. Peck, 6:227–54. New York: Gordian Press, 1965.

———. "Essay on the Devil and Devils." In *Shelley's Prose: The Trumpet of a Prophecy*, edited by David Lee Clark, 264–74. Albuquerque: University of New Mexico Press, 1954.

———. *The Letters of Percy Bysshe Shelley*. Edited by Frederick L. Jones. Oxford: Clarendon Press, 1964.

———. *The Necessity of Atheism and Other Essays*. New York: Prometheus Books, 1993.

———. "Ozymandias." In *Shelley's Poetry and Prose*, edited by Donald H. Reiman and Sharon B. Powers, 103. New York: W. W. Norton, 1977.

———. *The Prose Works of Percy Bysshe Shelley*. Edited by E. B. Murray. Oxford: Clarendon Press, 1993.

———. "Queen Mab." In *Shelley's Poetry and Prose*, edited by Donald H. Reiman and Sharon B. Powers, 14–68. New York: W. W. Norton, 1977.

———. *A Refutation of Deism*. In *The Complete Works of Percy Bysshe Shelley*, edited by Roger Ingpen and Walter E. Peck, 6:23–60. New York: Gordian Press, 1965.

Sheps, Arthur. "Sedition, Vice, and Atheism: The Limits of Toleration and the Orthodox Attack on Rational Religion in Late Eighteenth-Century England." In *Orthodoxy and Heresy in Eighteenth-Century Society: Essays from the DeBartolo Conference*, edited by Regina Hewitt and Pat Rogers, 51–69. Lewisburg: Bucknell University Press, 2002.

Sheridan, Claire. "A Tragedy Called 'The Last Man:' Hazlitt's Joke on Francis Place." *Hazlitt Review* 7 (2014): 47–56.

Simpson, Antony E. "The 'Blackmail Myth' and the Prosecution of Rape and Its Attempt in 18th Century London: The Creation of a Legal Tradition." *Journal of Criminal Law and Criminology* 77, no. 1 (1986): 101–50.

Simpson, George Gaylord. "Extinction." *Proceedings of the American Philosophical Society* 129, no. 4 (1985): 407–16.

Sites, Melissa. "Chivalry and Utopian Domesticity in Mary Shelley's *The Fortunes of Perkin Warbeck*." *European Romantic Review* 16, no. 5 (2005): 525–43.

———. "Utopian Domesticity as Social Reform in Mary Shelley's *Falkner*." *Keats-Shelley Journal* 54 (2005): 148–72.

Sleigh, Charlotte. "The Judgments of Regency Literature." *Literature and History* 19, no. 2 (2010): 1–17.

Small, Christopher. *Mary Shelley's "Frankenstein": Tracing the Myth*. Pittsburgh: University of Pittsburgh Press, 1972.

Smith, Allan Lloyd. "'This Thing of Darkness': Racial Discourse in Mary Shelley's *Frankenstein*." *Gothic Studies* 6, no. 2 (2004): 208–22.

Smith, Orianne. *Romantic Women Writers, Revolution, and Prophecy: Rebellious Daughters, 1786–1826*. Cambridge: Cambridge University Press, 2013.

Snodgrass, John. *A Commentary, With Notes, on the Part of the Book of the Revelation of John*. Paisley: Neilson and Weir, 1799.

Snyder, Robert Lance. "Apocalypse and Indeterminacy in Mary Shelley's *The Last Man*." *Studies in Romanticism* 17, no. 4 (1978): 435–52.

Somerset, Richard. "Transformism, Evolution, and Romanticism." *Nineteenth-Century French Studies* 29, no. 1–2 (2000–2001): 1–20.

Southcott, Joanna. *The Long-Wished for Revolution*. London: S. Rousseau, 1806.

———. *A Warning to the World: Joanna Southcott's Prophecies*. London: S. Rousseau, 1804.

Southey, Robert. *The Book of the Church*. Boston: Wells and Lilly, 1825.

———. *Vindiciae Ecclesiae Anglicanae: Letter to Charles Butler, Esq*. London: John Murray, 1826.

Soyka, David. "*Frankenstein* and the Miltonic Creation of Evil." *Extrapolation* 33, no. 2 (1992): 166–77.

Spark, Muriel. *The Informed Air: Essays by Muriel Spark*. Edited by Penelope Jardine. New York: New Directions Books, 2014.

Spring, David. "The Clapham Sect: Some Social and Political Aspects." *Victorian Studies* 5, no. 1 (1961): 35–48.

Springer, Carolyn. *The Marble Wilderness: Ruins and Representation in Italian Romanticism, 1775–1850*. Cambridge: Cambridge University Press, 1987.

Staniforth, Sampson. "Sampson Staniforth." In *Wesley's Veterans: Lives of Early Methodist Preachers Told by Themselves*, edited by John Telford, 60–106. London: Hazell, Watson, and Viney, 1912.

St. Clair, William. *The Godwins and the Shelleys: The Biography of a Family*. New York: W. W. Norton, 1989.

Sterrenburg, Lee. "*The Last Man*: Anatomy of Failed Revolutions." *Nineteenth-Century Fiction* 33, no. 3 (1978): 324–47.

———. "Mary Shelley's Monster: Politics and Psyche in *Frankenstein*." In *The Endurance of "Frankenstein": Essays on Mary Shelley's Novel*, edited by George Levine and U. C. Knoepflmacher, 143–71. Berkeley: University of California Press, 1974.

Stott, Anne. "'A Singular Injustice Towards Women': Hannah More, Evangelicalism and Female Education." In *Women, Religion and Feminism in Britain, 1750–1900*, edited by Sue Morgan, 23–38. New York: Palgrave Macmillan, 2002.

Sunstein, Emily. *Mary Shelley: Romance and Reality*. Baltimore: Johns Hopkins University Press, 1989.

Suzuki, Rieko. "'A Romantic Truth of History': Gender in Mary Shelley's *Valperga* and Robert Browning's *Sordello*." *La questione romantica* 1, no. 1 (2009): 55–67.

Tannenbaum, Leslie. "From Filthy Type to Truth: Miltonic Myth in *Frankenstein*." *Keats-Shelley Journal* 26 (1977): 101–13.

Tapper, Alan. "Priestley on Politics, Progress and Moral Theology." In *Enlightenment and Religion: Rational Dissent in Eighteenth-Century Britain*, edited by Knud Haakonssen, 272–86. Cambridge: Cambridge University Press, 1996.

Taylor, Barbara. "The Religious Foundations of Mary Wollstonecraft's Feminism." In *The Cambridge Companion to Mary Wollstonecraft*, edited by Claudia L. Johnson, 99–118. Cambridge: Cambridge University Press, 2002.

Taylor, David. "'A Vacant Space, An Empty Stage': *Prometheus Unbound, The Last Man*, and the Problem of Dramatic (Re)form." *Keats-Shelley Review* 20, no. 1 (2006): 18–31.

Thomas, Helen. *Romanticism and Slave Narratives: Transatlantic Testimonies*. Cambridge: Cambridge University Press, 2000.

Thompson, E. P. *The Making of the English Working Class*. New York: Vintage Books, 1966.

Thorslev, Peter L., Jr. "The Romantic Mind Is Its Own Place." *Comparative Literature* 15, no. 3 (1963): 250–68.

Tichelaar, Tyler R. *The Gothic Wanderer: From Transgression to Redemption*. Ann Arbor: Modern History Press, 2012.

Todd, Janet. Introduction to *Mary and Maria by Mary Wollstonecraft and Matilda by Mary Shelley*, vii–xxviii. London: Pickering and Chatto, 1991.

———. *Mary Wollstonecraft: A Revolutionary Life*. London: Weidenfeld & Nicolson, 2000.

Tomkins, Stephen. *The Clapham Sect: How Wilberforce's Circle Transformed Britain*. Oxford: Lion, 2010.

Tomko, Michael. *British Romanticism and the Catholic Question: Religion, History, and National Identity, 1778–1829*. New York: Palgrave Macmillan, 2011.

Towers, J. L. *Illustrations of Prophecy*. London, 1796.

Trelawny, Edward John. *Recollections of the Last Days of Shelley and Byron*. London: Edward Moxon, 1858.

Trott, Nicola. "The Coleridge Circle and the 'Answer to Godwin.'" *Review of English Studies* 41, no. 162 (1990): 212–29.

Tuite, Clara. "Frankenstein's Monster and Malthus' 'Jaundiced Eye': Population, Body Politics, and the Monstrous Sublime." *Eighteenth-Century Life* 22, no. 1 (1998): 141–55.

Tweedy, Roderick. *The God of the Left Hemisphere: Blake, Bolte Taylor, and the Myth of Creation*. London: Karnac Books, 2012.

Tyerman, L. *The Life and Times of the Rev. John Wesley*. 2 vols. London: Hodder and Stoughton, 1876.

Valenze, Deborah M. *Prophetic Sons and Daughters: Female Preaching and Popular Religion in Industrial England*. Princeton: Princeton University Press, 1985.

Vargo, Lisa. "The Aikins and the Godwins: Notions of Conflict and Stoicism in Anna Barbauld and Mary Shelley." *Romanticism* 11, no. 1 (2005): 84–98.

———. "*Lodore* and the 'Novel of Society.'" *Women's Writing* 6, no. 3 (1999): 425–40.

———. "(Re)placing a Site of Friendship: Frances Wright and Mary Wollstonecraft Shelley." *La questione romantica* 1, no. 1 (2009): 83–93.

Vatican. "History of the Vatican Museum." http://www.museivaticani.va/content/museivaticani/en/musei-del-papa/storia.html#giulio-ii/.

Vattel, Emmerich de. *The Law of Nations.* London: G. G. and J. Robinson, 1797.

Veil, Jeffrey. "'The Bright Sun Was Extinguish'd': The Bologna Prophecy and Byron's 'Darkness.'" *Wordsworth Circle* 28, no. 3 (1997): 183–92.

Venn, Henry. *The Complete Duty of Man; or, A System of Doctrinal and Practical Christianity.* London: J. Newbery, 1763.

Vernon, Peter. "*Frankenstein*: Science and Electricity." *Études Anglaises* 50, no. 3 (1997): 270–83.

Vickery, Amanda. "Golden Age to Separate Spheres? A Review of the Categories and Chronology of English Women's History." *Historical Journal* 36, no. 2 (1993): 383–414.

Vincent, Patrick. "'This Wretched Mockery of Justice': Mary Shelley's *Frankenstein* and Geneva." *European Romantic Review* 18, no. 5 (2007): 645–61.

Volney, M. *The Ruins, Or A Survey of the Revolutions of Empires.* London: A. Seale, 1792.

Wade, Philip. "Shelley and the Miltonic Element in Mary Shelley's *Frankenstein.*" *Milton and the Romantics* 2 (1976): 23–25.

Wagner, Peter. "The Pornographer in the Courtroom: Trial Reports About Cases of Sexual Crimes and Delinquencies as a Genre of Eighteenth-Century Erotica." In *Sexuality in Eighteenth-Century Britain*, edited by Paul-Gabriel Boucé, 120–40. Manchester: Manchester University Press, 1982.

Wagner-Lawlor, Jennifer A. "Performing History, Performing Humanity in Mary Shelley's *The Last Man.*" *SEL: Studies in English Literature* 42, no. 4 (2002): 753–80.

Walker, Gina Luria, ed. *Memoirs of Women Writers.* Vol. 10. London: Pickering and Chatto, 2014.

Wallace, Jennifer. "'Copying Shelley's Letters': Mary Shelley and the Uncanny Erotics of Greek." *Women's Studies* 40, no. 4 (2011): 404–28.

Walling, William. *Mary Shelley.* New York: Twayne Publishers, 1972.

Walpole, Horace. *The Yale Edition of Horace Walpole's Correspondence.* Edited by W. S. Lewis. 48 vols. New Haven: Yale University Press, 1937–83.

Warburton, William. *The Doctrine of Grace: or, the Office and Operations of the Holy Spirit Vindicated from the Insults of Infidelity, and the Abuses of Fantaticism.* London: A. Millar and J. and R. Tonson, 1763.

Ward, W. R. *Early Evangelicalism: A Global Intellectual History, 1670–1789.* Cambridge: Cambridge University Press, 2006.

Warner, William B. *Licensing Entertainment: The Elevation of Novel Reading in Britain, 1684–1750.* Berkeley: University of California Press, 1998.

Wasserman, Earl R. *Shelley: A Critical Reading.* Baltimore: Johns Hopkins University Press, 1971.

Watson, Richard. *An Apology for Christianity in a Series of Letters, Addressed to Edward Gibbon, Esq.* Cambridge: T. & J. Merrill, 1776.

Watts, Michael R. *The Dissenters.* Vol. 1, *From the Reformation to the French Revolution.* Oxford: Clarendon Press, 1978.

Watts, Ruth. *Gender, Power and the Unitarians in England, 1760–1860*. London: Routledge, 1998.

———. "Rational Religion and Feminism: The Challenge of Unitarianism in the Nineteenth Century." In *Women, Religion and Feminism in Britain, 1750–1900*, edited by Sue Morgan, 39–52. New York: Palgrave Macmillan, 2002.

Webb, R. K. "The Emergence of Rational Dissent." In *Enlightenment and Religion: Rational Dissent in Eighteenth-Century Britain*, edited by Knud Haakonssen, 12–41. Cambridge: Cambridge University Press, 1996.

Webb, Samantha. "Reading the End of the World: The Last Man, History, and the Agency of Romantic Authorship." In *Mary Shelley in Her Times*, edited by Betty T. Bennett and Stuart Curran, 119–33. Baltimore: Johns Hopkins University Press, 2000.

Webb, Timothy. "Reading Aloud in the Shelley Circle." In *Publishing, Editing, and Reception: Essays in Honor of Donald H. Reiman*, edited by Michael Edson, 97–131. Lanham: Rowman and Littlefield, 2015.

Wesley, John. *The Journal of the Rev. John Wesley, A.M.* Edited by N. Curnock. 8 vols. London: Charles H. Kelly, 1911.

———. *The Letters of the Rev. John Wesley*. Edited by John Telford. 8 vols. London: The Epworth Press, 1931.

Weston, Rowland. "Politics, Passion, and the 'Puritan Temper': Godwin's Critique of Enlightened Modernity." *Studies in Romanticism* 41, no. 3 (2002): 445–70.

White, Daniel E. *Early Romanticism and Religious Dissent*. Cambridge: Cambridge University Press, 2006.

———. "Mary Shelley's *Valperga*: Italy and the Revision of Romantic Aesthetics." In *Mary Shelley's Fictions: From Frankenstein to Falkner*, edited by Michael Eberle-Sinatra, 75–94. New York: St. Martin's Press, 2000.

Wilberforce, William. *A Practical View of the Prevailing Religious System of Professed Christians in the Higher and Middle Classes in this Country Contrasted with Real Christianity*. London: T. Cadell Jun., 1797.

Williams, Carolyn. "'Inhumanly Brought Back to Life and Misery': Mary Wollstonecraft, *Frankenstein*, and the Royal Humane Society." *Women's Writing* 8, no. 2 (2001): 213–34.

Williams, Gwyn A. "Romanticism in Wales." In *Romanticism in National Context*, edited by Roy Porter and Mikuláš Teich, 9–36. Cambridge: Cambridge University Press, 1988.

Williams, Nicholas M. "Angelic Realism: Domestic Idealization in Mary Shelley's *Lodore*." *Studies in the Novel* 39, no. 4 (2007): 397–415.

Williams, Sarah C. "Is There a Bible in the House? Gender, Religion, and Family Culture." In *Women, Religion and Feminism in Britain, 1750–1900*, edited by Sue Morgan, 11–31. New York: Palgrave Macmillan, 2002).

Wilson-Bareau, Juliet. "Goya: *The Disasters of War*." In *Disasters of War: Callot, Goya, Dix*, edited by Alexander Boxill, 27–56. Manchester: Cornerhouse Publications, 1998. Exhibition Catalogue.

Winn, James. *"When Beauty Fires the Blood": Love and the Arts in the Age of Dryden.* Ann Arbor: University of Michigan Press, 1992.

Wolfson, Susan J. *"'This Is My Lightning'; Or, Sparks in the Air." SEL: Studies in English Literature* 55, no. 4 (2015): 751–86.

Wollstonecraft, Mary. *Collected Letters of Mary Wollstonecraft.* Edited by Ralph M. Wardle. Ithaca: Cornell University Press, 1979.

——. *Mary.* In *Mary and Maria by Mary Wollstonecraft and Matilda by Mary Shelley,* edited by Janet Todd. London: Penguin Books, 1991.

——. *A Short Residence in Norway, Sweden, and Denmark.* London: Penguin Books, 1987.

——. *A Vindication of the Rights of Woman and a Vindication of the Rights of Men.* Oxford: Oxford University Press, 2009.

Wordsworth, William. "The Tables Turned." In *The Major Works,* edited by Stephen Gill, 131. Oxford: Oxford University Press, 1984.

Wright, Eamon. *British Women Writers and Race, 1788–1818: Narrations of Modernity.* New York: Palgrave Macmillan, 2005.

Wroe, Ann. *Being Shelley: The Poet's Search for Himself.* New York: Pantheon Books, 2007.

Yu, Jie-Ae. "Byron's Reworking of Thomas Campbell: Unfolding Gloom in Darkness." *Journal of English Language and Literature* 58, no. 3 (2012): 379–94.

# INDEX

# RELIGION AROUND

**BOOKS IN THE SERIES:**